# DICTIONARY OF AGRICULTURE

# DICTIONARY OF AGRICULTURE

SANDEEP BAJPAI

**CYBER TECH PUBLICATIONS**
4264/3, Ansari Road, Daryaganj, New Delhi-110002 (India)
Ph.: 011-23244078. Fax: 011-23280028
E-Mail: cyberpublicationsdelhi@yahoo.com

*Dictionary of Agriculture*



First Edition 2009

Published by G.S. Rawat

**For Cyber Tech Publications**

4264/3, Ansari Road, Daryaganj, New Delhi - 110 002

E-mail : cyberpublicationsdelhi@yahoo.com

Phone : 011-23244078,

Fax : 011-23280028



Printed at

**Asian Offset Printers**

# PREFACE

Dictionary of Agriculture vocabulary terms used in agriculture, horticulture and other related areas. The vocabulary ranges from the equipment used on a farm to breeds of livestock, varieties of crops, types of pesticide and herbicide, and farm building construction. It covers not only agriculture in temperature regions, but also makes particular reference to the agricuture.

Simple English in a way which makes them easily accessible to the student; examples of usage are given. Dictionary of Agriculture for helpful comments and suggestions for improvement which they made in the course.

*—Editor*

# A

**Abattoir.** Place where animals are slaughtered and prepared for sale to the public as meat.

**Abdomen.** The space in an animal's body containing the stomach, intestines, liver and other vital organs.

**Aberdeen Angus.** An early maturing breed of beef cattle, naturally hornless and usually black all over. Angus cattle can be rather small-headed with a long deep body. They are highly valued for quality beef.

**Abomasum.** The fourth stomach of a ruminant.

**Abort.** (a) To miscarry; to produce an embryo or foetus and so end a pregnancy before the foetus is fully developed (b) (in plants and animals) to remain underdeveloped; to wither away.

**Abreast.** Side by side; abreast parlour = one of the four basic designs of milking parlour: the cows stand side by side with their backs to the milker.

**Abscess.** Collection of pus formed in the body, which may be acute or chronic.

**Absinthe.** Perennial aromatic herb used as medicine and in making alcoholic drinks; also called "wormwood".

**Absolute.** (i) complete; (ii) terminal point (not compared with anything else); absolute humidity = vapour concentration or ratio of the mass of water vapour in a given quantity of air to the amount of air.

**Absorb.** To take in any substance; (of a solid) to take in a liquid

**Absorption.** Removal; abstraction licence = a licence issued by a Water Board to allow abstraction of water from a river or lake for domestic or commercial use. The licence is needed for irrigation.

**Acacia.** Species of tree, including the wattle, often grown as ornamental trees.

**Acarid.** Mite or tick, a small insect which feeds on plants or animals by piercing the outer skin and sucking juices.

**Acaridicide.** Poison used to kill mites and ticks.

**Acarina.** Scientific name for the order of animals including mites and ticks.

**Access.** Right of access = (i) right of someone to be ale to get to land by passing over someone else's property; (ii) right of the public to walk in areas of the countryside, providing they do not harm crops or farm animals; access order = court order which gives the public the right to go on private land.

**Acclimatize.** (i) to make something become used to a different sort of environment, usually a change in climate; (ii) to become used to a different sort of environment plants take some time to become acclimatized to tropical conditions; acclimatized sheep = sheep which have become used to their local environment and as a result are less likely to stray.

**Accommodation Land.** Land available for short-term tenancy.

**Accredit.** To recognize officially; accredited herd = herd of cattle registered under a scheme as being free from Brucellosis;

accredited milk = milk from a herd accredited as being free from Brucellosis.

**Accetonaemia.** Disease affecting cows, caused by ketone bodies accumulating. The animal loses appetite and the smell of acetone affects the breath, the urine and milk.

**Achene.** Small dry one-seeded fruit, which does not split open to release its seed.

**Acid.** Chemical compound containgin hydrogen, which dissolves in water and forms hydrogen, or reacts with an alkali to form a salt and water, and turns litmus paper red hydrochloric acid is secreted in the stomach and forms part of the gastric juices; inorganic acids = acids which are derived from minerals, such as hydrochloric acid and sulphuric acid; organic acids = weak acids which contain carbon, some of which are pesticides.

**Acidic.** Referring to acids soil and vegetation in high altitude forests are directly exposed to an extremely acidic could base; acidic properties = properties associated with acids.

**Acidosis.** Disease of cattle caused by excess concentrate feed.

**Acid Soil.** Soil which as a pH value of 6 or less.

**Acre.** Unit of measurement of land area, equal to 4,840 square yards or 0.4047 hectares.

**Actinobacillosis.** Disease of cattle affecting the tongue and throat; it also occurs in sheep as swellings on the lips, cheeks and jaws. It is also known as "cruels".

**Activate.** To make a chemical reaction take place.

**Actuals.** Stocks of commodities, such as cotton or rice, which are available for shipping (as opposed to "futures", commodities for delivery in the future, which have not yet been produced)

**Acute.** Which comes on suddenly and can be very serious; acute toxicity = level of concentration of a toxic substance, which makes animals seriously ill, or can even cause death.

**Additive.** Substance which is added, especially one which is added to animal feeding stuffs, which may include antibiotics, mineral supplements, vitamins and hormones, or one added to human food to improve the taste, smell, appearance or keeping.

**Added Egg.** Rotten egg, an egg which produces no chick.

**Adlay.** Tropical millet with very large seeds grown in the Philippines and some other areas of South-East Asia; also known as "Job's tears"

**Admixture.** The proportion of a seed crop which is made up of weed seeds or other crop species.

**Advanced Register.** Book which records breeding performance of outstanding livestock.

**Adventitious.** Which develops from a plant's stem and not from another root.

**Adzuki Bans.** Tropical legume grown in Japan and China.

**Aerate.** To put air into a substance, especially to replace stagnant air in soil with fresh air worms are useful because they aerate the soil.

**Aerial.** Which exists in the air; aerial roots = roots of certain plants, which hang in the air or wrap around other plants, and take up moisture from he air; aerial spraying = spraying of crops by lane or helicopter. This spraying mainly involves pesticides and fertilizers. Spraying is subject to various safety precautions and care must be taken to avoid drifting of harmful chemicals.

**Aerobic.** Needing oxygen for its existence.

**Affect.** To have a result on the restrictions cover a twenty mile radius, affecting thirty farms and smallholdings; the disease affects mainly young animals.

**Afforestation.** Growing trees as a crop; (ii) planning of trees on land previously in another use there is likely to be an increase in afforestation of upland areas if the scheme is introduced.

**Aflatozin.** Toxicsubstance formed by a fungus Aspergillus flavus, which grows on seeds and nuts, and is found in stored grain or in groundnut meal; it is harmful to cattle and pigs.

**African Buffalo.** Undemsticated buffao indigenous to Africa, including the Black Cae Buffalo and the Congo Buffalo; these buffalo can carry in their blood parasites that cause sleeping sickness.

**Africander.** Breed of cattle found in parts of Southern Africa; originally used as draught animals. They are now use for beef production. The animals are red, with curved horns; they are resistant to heat and to disease.

**African Swine Fever.** A virus disease which is highly contagious among pigs. Animals suffer fever and high temperature followed by death; in Europe, it occurs in parts of Spain.

**Afrormosia.** Hardwood from West Africa, now becoming scarce.

**Afferbirth.** The remains of the placenta pushed out of the uterus of the dam at the birth of a young animal.

**Aftermath.** Grass which grows quickly after cutting for hay, and which will provide a second cut.

**Agar.** Culture medium, the gelatin in which bacteria or tissue can be grown.

**Agave.** Succulent tropical plant which gives sisal.

**Age.** To treat flour to make the dought more elastic and whiter

**Agglutination.** Action of grouping cells together (as of bacteria cells in the presence of serum or blood cells when blood of different types is mixed); agglutination tests = (i) tests to identify bacteria; (ii) tests used to detect Brucellosis in cattle.

**Agistment.** Money paid for Grazing stock on land owned by another person. The owner of the land is responsible for the feeding and care of the livestock.

**Agitator.** Part of a machine for harvesting root crops, such as potatoes, which shakes the earth off the crop after it has been lifted.

**Agrarian.** Referring to matter of land tenure and problems arising from land ownership.

**Agregado.** Brzilian term for a tenant farmer.

**Agribusiness.** The business of forming and making products and equipment used by farmers.

**Agriculture.** Cultivation of the land, including horticulture, fruit growing, crop and seed growing, dairy farming and livestock breeding.

**Agriculture Act.** Acts of Parliament, introduced to update legislation affecting agricultural policy.

**Agriculture Service.** A service provided by a branch of ADAS, which have specialist advice to farmers, and ran several experimental stations in parts of England and Wales; now replaced by the Farm and countryside Service and the Research and Development Service.

**Agricultural.** Referring to farming; agricultural holding = a basic unit for agricultural production.

**Agricultural Waste.** Waste matter produced on a farm such as manure from animals or excess fertilizers and pesticides which run off the fields.

**Agricultural Chemicals Approval Scheme (ACAS).** Scheme which gave advice to farmers on the use and efficiency of chemicals and which tested chemicals before use by farmers (operated by the Agricultural Chemicals Approved Organisaiton). It was a voluntary scheme which has now been replaced by the FEPA legislation.

**Agricultural Development and Advisory Service (ADAS).** A branch of the MAFF, providing scientific, professional and technical advice to farmers. It has three divisions; farm and Countryside Service Veterinary Service, and the Research and Development Service.

**Agricultural holdings Act 1984.** An Act of Parliament which gives protection to tenants in questions of the fixing of rent and security of tenure. It makes provision for tenancies for a life time and for short-term littings.

**Agricultural Improvement Scheme.** A scheme introduction in 1985 to provide capital grants to farmers.

**Agricultural Land Tribunal.** A court established in 1947 to hear appeals against decision affecting owners or tenants of agricultural land.

**Agricultural Mortgage Corporation.** A corporation which makes loans available to borrowers on the security of agricultural land and buildings in England and Wales.

**Agricultural and Food Research council (AFRAC).** A council established to organize and provide funds for agricultural and food research.

**Agricultural Stabilization and Conservation Service (ASCS).** US service of the federal Department of Agriculture which operates the department's various schemes throughout the USA.

**Agricultural Training Board.** A body established under the

Industrial Training Act of 1966 to provide training for agricultural workers and farmers.

**Agricultural Wages Board.** A board which fixes minimum wages and holiday entitlements for agricultural workers, and deals with terms and conditions of their employment.

**Agricultural Revolution.** The changes in agriculture which transformed Britain's countrywide in the 18th and 19th centuries. The changes were in techniques such as crop rotation, selective breeding, new implements, and also in land tenure, with removal of the open field system wit common right, and the gradual enclosure of land, and farm consolidation.

**Agrochemicals.** Pesticides and fertilizers developed artificially for agricultural use; the agrochemical industry – the branch of industry which produces pesticides and fertilizers used on farms.

**Agroclimatology.** Study of climate and its effect on agriculture.

**Agroforestry.** Growing farm crops and tress together as a farming unit.

**Agronomy.** Scientific study of the cultivation of crops.

**Agronomist.** Person who studies crop cultivation; pasture agronomist = person who specializes in the study of types of grass grown in pastures.

**Akee.** Evergreen tree found in the West Indies; the fruit can be eaten raw, but is more usually cooked.

**Alar.** Chemical used by apple growers to make more buds set and grow into mature fruit.

**Albino.** Animal, with little or no pigmentation in skin, hair or eyes.

**Albinism.** Complete absence of pigmentation.

**Alder.** Fine European hardwood (Alnus glutinosa) which is waterproof.

**Aldosterone.** Hormone which regulates the sodium balance in the body.

**Aldrin.** One of the organochlorine insecticides, used to control cabbage root fly, wireworms and leatherjackets. There is an agreement to restrict the use of this insecticide.

**Aleurone.** Protein found in the outer skin of seeds.

**Alfalfa.** Arabic name for Lucerne, a plant of the Leguminosae family, grown to use as fodder.

**Alimentary Canal.** The digestive tract, the passage from the mouth to the rectum along which food passes and is digested.

**Alkall.** One of many substances which neutralize acids and form salts.

**Alkaline.** Containing more alkali than acid.

**Alkallnity.** Amount of alkali in something such as soil or water.

**Alkaloid.** (1) Similar to an alkali (2) one of many poisonous substances (such as atropine or morphine or quinine) found in plants which use them as defence against herbivores; they are also useful as medicines.

**Allele.** One of two or more alternative forms of a gene.

**Allergy.** Being sensitive to certain substances, which cause a physical reaction.

**Allergen.** Substance which produces a sensitive physical reaction.

**Allogamy.** Fertilization by pollen from different flowers or from flowers of genetically different plants of the same species.

**Allopatric.** (Plants of the same species) which grow in different parts of the world and so do not crossbreed.

**Allotment.** Small are of land which islet on an annual basis by the municipality which owns it to an allotment-holder for the cultivation and production of vegetables and fruit for the consumption of the holder and his family. Under the 1947 Agriculture Act an allotment should not be larger than 0.25 acre, or 01 hectare.

**Allspice.** Tropical tree grown in Jamaica; its dried berries are used as a flavouring.

**Alluvium.** Silt deposited by rivers when they flood, or by lakes; usually very fertile.

**Alluvial.** Referring to alluvium; alluvial deposits or alluvial soils =deposits of silt on the bed of a river or lake.

**Almond.** Small tree (Prunus dulcis) grown for its edible nuts; it grows in most Mediterranean countries, and also in California, South Australia and South Africa.

**Alp.** A high mountain pasture, above the treeline.

**Alphine.** Rerring to the Alps or to other high mountains; alpine Alpaca. Animal which is similar to the Ilama; a native of the Andes, it is domesticated and reared for its very soft and elastic wool.

**Alpha Acids.** A number of related compounds found in hops, and which give them their bitter taste; the ability of hope to give beer a bitter taste is assessed by their alpha acid content.

**Alpha Amylase.** An enzyme present in wheat seed, which changes some starch to sugar. Excessive amounts can result in loaves of bread with sticky texture. Alpha amylase activity can be measured by the Hagberg test or the Farrand test.

**Alternate Husbandry.** Husbandry in which arable and grassland cultivation are alternated every few years.

**Altiplano.** High plateau land of Bolivia.

**American Bison.** North American animal of the cattle family, of which large numbers were slaughtered during the nineteenth century; it is now protected, and small numbers can be seen in some National Parks. The bison will breed with ordinary cattle.

**Amino Acid.** Chemical compound which is broken down from proteins in the digestive system and then used by the body to form its own protein proteins are first broken down into amino acids; essential amino acids = amino acids which are essential for growth, but which cannot be synthesized and so must be obtained from food or medicinal substances.

**Ammonia.** Gas with a strong smell, a compound of nitrogen and hydrogen, which is a normal product of organic metabolism, and is used in compounds to make artificial fertilizers; ammonia treatment = method of treating straw, using ammonia to make it more palatable and nutritious.

**Ammoniacal.** Referring to ammonia; ammoniacal nitrogen = nitrogen derived from ammonia.

**Ammonium Fixation.** The absorption of ammonium ions by the soil; ammonium nitrate = a popular fertilizer used as top dressing. It is available in a special prilled or granular form, and can be used both as a straight fertilizer and in compounds; ammonium phosphate = fertilizer which can be used straight, but is more often used in compounds. A certain amount of care is needed in its use, as applications may increase the acidity of the soil; ammonium sulphate = fertilizer which can be used straight, but is more often used in compounds. A certain amount of care is needed in its use, as applications may increase the acidity of the soil; ammonium sulphate.

**Amniotic Fluid.** Fluid which surrounds the foetus in the uterus

**Amoeba.** Form of animal life made up of a single cell.

**Amoebic.** Caused by amoebae; amoebic dysentery = mainly

tropical form of dysentery which is caused by *Entamoeba histolytica* a parasite which enters the body through contaminated water.

**Amylase.** Enzyme which converts starch into maltose; see also ALPHA AMYASE.

**Anaemia.** Deficienc of red blood corpuscles. In young pigs it is caused by a shortage of iron in the sow's milk. Anaemia results in lack of condition and may cause death.

**Anaerobically.** Without using eoxygen slurry is digested anaerobically by bacteria.

**Anaerobism.** Lack of oxygen (as in gley soils).

**Analyse.** To examine something in detail; to separate something into its component parts the laboratory is analyzing the soil samples; when the water sample was analysed it was found to contain traces of bacteria.

**Analyst.** Person who examines samples of substances or tissue, to find out what they are made of. (Chemical and electrical methods are used in soil analysis to determine the pH and lime requirements of a soil. Portable testing equipment, using colour charts, is sometimes used to test for pH.

**Ancona.** A laying breed for chicken, with white tips on black feathers.

**Andalusian.** (a) a dark red breed of cattle, used both as draught animals and for beef. (b) a lying breed of chicken with blue features.

**Angelica.** Plant with dark green stems, which are crystallized with sugar and used in confectionery.

**Angora.** Breed of rabbit, bred mainly for its fur; (ii) breed of goat, important as a source of mohair; Texan angora goat = breed of goat with very fine hair, imported from America.

(The original colour was white, but there are now grey, pale brown and other shades. The wool is extremely fine).

**Anoestrus.** Situation where a female animal does not come on heat at the usual time.

**Antheimintic.** Substance (such as thiabendazole) which is used as a treatment against parasites, as in worming livestock.

**Anther.** Par of a stamen which produces pollen.

**Anthrax.** A notifiable disease of animals, commonest among cattle and sheep. Pigs and horses can also be affected. Anthrax is caused by the bacterium Barillus anthracis, which is difficult to destroy and can stay in the soil and infect animals. Anthrax can be transmitted to humans by touching infected skin, meat, or other parts of an animal (including bone meal used at fertilizer). It causes pustules on the skin, or in the lungs.

**Anti-caking Additive.** Substance added to processed food to prevent it becoming solid when dam.

**Antigen.** Substance such as a virus which makes the body produce antibodies to attack it.

**Antioxidant.** Substance which prevents oxidation, added to processed, food to prevent it going bad.

**Antiseptic.** Which prevents germs spreading. Substance which prevents germs growing or spreading and is applied as a disinfectant to wounds the wound was painted with antiseptic.

**Antiserum.** Serum taken from an animal which has developed antibodies to bacteria, used to give temporary immunity to a disease.

**Aphid.** Small insect (called blackfly or greenfly) which sucks sap from plants and can multiply very rapidly analysis of the effects on the aphid population showed a 19 per cent increase in the rate of production. Cereal aphids are various species of greenfly. Winged females are found feeding on cereal crops in May and June. The grain aphid causes empty or small grain by puncturing the grain in the milk ripe stage, letting the grain contents seep out. Aphids can carry virus diseases from infected plants to clean ones.

**Apiarist.** Beekeeer, person who keeps bees.

**Appropriate Technology.** Technology that is suited to the local environment, usually involving skills or materials that are easily available locally biomethanation seems a very appropriate technology for use in rural areas. In many parts of world, devices to help the local population cultivate the land can be made out of simple pipes or pieces of metal, Expensive tractors may not only be unsuitable for the terrain involved, but also use fuel which costs more than the crops produced.

**Arviretyn.** Collection of trees from different parts of the world, grown for scientific study.

**Arboriculture.** Cultivation of trees and shrubs.

**Artichoke.** Vegetable grown as a specialized crop. There are two types of artichoke: the globe artichoke, a tall thistle-like plant (the eaves of the head are cooked and eaten), and the Jerusalem artichoke, a tall plant which develops tubers like a potato.

**Artificial Insemination.** Way of breeding livestock by fertilizing females with sperm from specially selected males; AI is important in cattle breeding. The Milk Marketing Board operates a number of AI centres.

**Asparagus Pea.** Plant (Lotus tetagonolobus) grown in southern Europe; the pods are edible.

**Aspect.** The direction in which land faces. It can affect the amount of sunshine (and heat) absorbed by the soil. In the UK, the temperature of north-facing slopes may be 1°C lower than on similar slopes facing sought.

**Assortive Mating.** Mating animals that have a similar appearance.

**Atrazine.** A residual herbicide which acts on the soil.

**Atrium.** One of the two upper cambers of the heart.

**Atropine.** The alkaloid contained in the leaves and root of the deadly nightshade; it can cause atropine poisoning in animals which feed on the plant.

**Attestation.** Action of attesting; certificate of attestation = certificate given to an attested herd. In 1960, the whole of the UK was declared an attested area, since bovine tuberculosis had by then been almost completely eradicated from all herds of cattle.

**Aubrac.** Rare breed of cattle from southern France; the animals are light yellow or brown in colour and are used for draught, milk and meat.

**Auctoneer.** Person who conducts an auction.

**Aujesky's Disease.** A virus disease of animals, characterized by intense itching. The disease is most serious in young pigs, and often leads to death. A notifiable disease.

**Auricle.** Small protection at the base of a leaf blade.

**Automatic Cluster Removal (ACR).** Automatic removal of the cluster of the milking machine from the udder at the end of milking.

**Automatic Pick-up Hitch.** Mechanism on a tractor, operated by the hydraulic system, which allows the driver to hitch up to a trailer without leaving his seat.

**Average All Pigs Price (AAPP).** The average price for pigs, calculated each week and used in contracts for payment.

**Aviary System.** A poultry housing system using a deep litter house with extra raised area inside it for the birds to feed, roost and exercise in.

**Away-going Crop.** Crop sown by a tenant farmer before leaving the farm at the end of his tenancy; he is permitted to return and harvest the crop and remove it.

**Axillary Bud.** Bud in the angle between a leaf and the main stem, producing a side shoot, as in the case of tomatoes.

# B

**Baara Irrigator.** A flexible hose with sixteen folding sprinklers, used for irrigating.

**Baby Beef.** Meat from cattle slaughtered around 12 months of age.

**Bacillus.** Bacterium shaped lie a rod.

Bacillary. Referring to bacillus; bacillary dysentery = dysentery caused by the bacillus Shigella in contaminated food; bacillary white diarrhoea = acute, infectious and highly fatal disease of chicks, caused by *Salmonlla pullorum*.

**Backboard.** Board at the back of a cart.

**Backcrossing.** Breeding a crossbred offspring back to one of its parents, usually a purebred.

**Bacon.** Cured back and sides of a pig; bacon may be green or smoked.

**Baconer.** Pig bred and reared for bacon. Bacon is cured in brine for several days; some bacon is also smoked by hanging in smoke, which improves its taste; unsmoked bacon is also known as "green" bacon.

**Bacterial.** Referring to bacteria or caused by bacteria.

**Bacteriophage.** Virus which affects bacteria. Bacteria can be shaped like rods (bacilli), like balls (cocci) or have a spiral form (such as spirochaetes). Bacteria, especially bacilli and spirochaetes, can move and reproduce very rapidly.

**Bactrian Camel.** Asian camel, found in the dry deserts of Mongolia and Turkestan; it has two humps.

**Badiands.** Intensely dissected are of land which is unsuitable for agriculture.

**Bag.** 1 (a) Unit of measurement used in the coffee trade (one bag contains 60 kilos) (b) udder of a cow 2 verb to cut wheat with a sickle.

**Bagot.** Rare breed of goat; the preferred colouring is black head, neck and shoulders, with the rest of the body white. The hair is long. Both sexes have horns.

**Bakers.** Large potatoes, graded by size, and used to cook as baked potatoes.

**Balanced Diet.** Diet which provides the animal with all the nutrients it needs in the correct proportions.

**Baler.** Machine that picks up loose hay or straw and compresses it into bales of even size and weight, and then ties them with twine. The completed bale is dropped onto the ground at the back of the baler; baler twine = cord used to tie bales, now often made of rot-proof polypropylene. There are two types of big bale, the round and the rectangular. The baling is slower with the round bale, but the completed bale is more weatherproof and can be safely left out in the field for longer periods of time. One of the main advantages of the big bales is that the number of bales per hectare is very low.

**Balling.** Dosing of larger animals, by rolling the drug into a ball which is then swallowed; baling gun = instrument used to force balls of drugs down the throats of animals.

**Bamarra Groundnut.** An exotic legume (Vaandzieia subterranean).

The seeds have a low oil content and are grown for their protein and starch. Found mainly in West Africa, and also in Zambia.

**Bamboo.** Plant (*Bambusa vulgaris*) growing mainly in temperate and subtropical regions of China, Japan and Korea; bamboo produces very long straight seems which are cut and dried and used in construction work; in horticulture, thin bamboo stems are widely used as supports for plants.

**Banana.** Fruit of a large tropical plant (*Musa sapientum*) and its varieties. The banana is grown on plantations, especially in South and Central America the West Indies, the Canary is lands and the Philippines. All varieties of banana need high temperatures, a great deal of moisture and deep soil. The bananas row in "hands" of 12 to 16 fingers along a main stem. Together forming a bunch. Another species of Musa yields the plantain, which is grown in the tropics for food.

**Band Sprayer.** Crop sprayer that applies chemicals in narrow strips, mostly used with precision seeders.

**Bapedi.** Breed of black and white dairy cattle found in Eastern Transvaal.

**Barking.** Removing the bark of a tree (as in harvesting cork from cork oaks); of bark from a tree as a means of making the tree more productive; I restricts growth and encourages fruiting.

**Barley.** Common cereal crop (Hordeum sativum) grown in temperate areas; barley yellow dwarf virus (BYDV) =virus spread by aphids, which causes poor root development in plants. Red and yellow colour changes occur in leaves and yields are much reduced. Also affects wheat and grass. Barley has six spielets at each node. If each of these develops it forms a six-rowed barley: in other varieties the lateral spikelets are much smaller than the central one, and these form four rowed or two-rowed barley. Barley is widely growing in northern temperate countries, with the largest production in Germany and France;

it is a very important arable crop in the UK. The grain is mainly used for livestock feeding (six-rowed barley) and for malting (two-rowed barley) for use in producing alcoholic drinks. It is rarely used for making flour. Barley straw is used mainly for litter, but some is fed to cattle.

**Barnyard.** Farmyard, the area round a barn.

**Barnevelder.** Breed of fowl.

**Bar Pig.** Castrated male pig.

**Basidiomycetes.** Large group of fungi, including mushrooms and toadstools.

**Basil.** Aromatic herb (Ocimum Basilicum), used in cooking, particularly with fish. Although probably native to India, basil is widely grown in Europe, especially in Italy. It is frost-tender, and usually grown as an annual in northern areas.

**Bain Irrigation.** Form of irrigation where the water is trapped in basins surrounded by low mud walls (as in rice paddies).

**Bastard Fallow.** Land left fallow for the time between harvesting and sowing, usually ploughed to control weeds.

**Batch Drying.** A process for drying bales of hay in batches; bales are placed on a platform and heated air is blown up between the bales.

**Batt.** Long wooden handle of a scythe.

**Battery.** System of raising chickens for egg production, where thousands of birds are kept in small cages.

**Battery Hens.** Laying birds reared and kept in multi-bird cages arranged in rows one above the other. A method of egg production which is very energy-efficient. It is criticized, however, because of the quality of the eggs, the possibility of disease and the polluting substances produced, and also on grounds of cruelty because of the stress caused to the birds.

**Beans.** Various varieties of legumes with edible seeds *French bean* = *Phaseolus vulgaris*, a common green vegetable grown for sale fresh of for canning and freezing (its dried ripe seeds are known as haricot beans); *runner bean* = *Phaseolus coccineus*, a common vegetable crop grown almost only for the fresh trade; *bean aphid* = black fly (*Aphis fabae*). Very small, oval-bodied, black or dark greenfly; on summer host plants, colonies of aphids make the plants wilt.

**Beaumont Period.** Period of 48 hours during which temperatures do not fall below 10°C and relative humidity remains above 75 percent potato blight is likely to occur within 21 das of this though spraying may prevent the blight from appearing.

**Bedding.** (a) Materials such as straw, shavings or sand, used as litter for animals o lie on (b) plating out small flower plants into a flowerbed; bedding plants = small annual flower plants which are used for bedding out.

**Bee.** Four –winged stinging insect; honey bees are kept in hives for commercial production of honey.

**Beehive.** Housing for a colony of bees, containing the frames in which bees store honey.

**Beekeeper.** Person who keeps bees for honey.

**Beef.** Meat of bull or cow.

**Beef Bull.** Bull reared to produce beef.

**Beef Cow.** Cow kept for rearing calves for beef production.

**Beefalo.** American breed of cattle, brown in colour; it is derived from crossing bison, Charolais and Hereford breeds.

**Beer.** Alcoholic drink made by fermenting malted barley with large quantities of water.

**Beet.** Plant with a succulent root, a source of sugar; weed beet = wild beet which can be self-sown in beet crops.

**Beetroot.** Salad vegetable with a bright red root.

**Belgian Blue.** Dual-purpose breed of cattle, the result of crossing Friesians and Shorthorns with naïve Belgian stock. The animals are coloured blue and white; there is a British breed, derived from this, called British Belgian Blue.

**Belgian Hare.** Reed of rabbit.

**Belted Galloway.** Breed of beef cattle, coloured black with a white belt round the body. The animals are longhaired with a dense undercoat. It is a medium-sized polled breed used for cross-breeding with White Shorthorn bulls to produce blue-grey suckler cows.

**Beneder.** African breed of large goat, found in Somalia; the animals are red or black-spotted.

**Benomyl.** Fungicide used against eyespot in cereals.

**Bent.** (i) Stiff-stemmed grasses of the genus Agrostis, found in hill pastures and tolerant of poor conditions; (ii) old dry stalls of dead grass.

**Benzene Hexachloride (BHC).** Insecticide used as a dust or spray against pea and bean weevil, and as a seed dressing against wireworm.

**Berkankamp Scale.** Scale used o describe the growth stages in oilseed rape crop.

**Berkshire.** Breed of small pig, dark coloured with a compact body, short head and prick ears; the snout, feet and tail are white.

**Berkshire Knot.** Local breed of sheep crossed with Southdown to develop the Hampshire Down breed.

**Betel Nut.** Seed of the betel palm (*Areca catechu*) small pieces of which are chewed alone or mixed with other ingredients.

**Beulah Speckle Face.** Breed of sheep, with a black and white speckled face; it is native to the hills of Wales.

**Blennial.** (1) Happening every two years; (plant which takes two years to complete its life cycle. (2) Plant which completes its life cycle over a period of two years. Binnial plants spend the first year producing roots, stem and leaves. In the following year he flowering stem and seeds are produced, after which the plant dies. Sugar beet and Swedes are typical biennial, although they are grown as annuals, and are harvested at the end of their first year when the roots are fully developed.

**Big Bud.** Swelling of black currant buds caused by gall mites.

**Bilharziasis.** Disease of man and domestic animals, caused by parasites in the blood stream.

**Binder.** Machine formerly used to cut and bind corn, drawn by tractor; now replaced by the combine harvester.

**Bindweed.** Perennial weed with creeping roots, which climbs by twisting round other plant.

**Binomial Classification.** Way of naming living organisms, devised by Linnaeus, using two Latin names.

**Biocide.** Substance which kills living organism biocides used in agriculture run off into lakes and rivers.

**Biocontrol.** Biological control.

**Biodegradable.** Which can easily be decomposed by organisms.

**Biogas.** Gas (partly methane and partly carbon dioxide) which is produced from fermenting waste, such as animal refuse farm biogas systems may be uneconomic unless here is a constant demand for heat; the use of biogas systems in rural areas of developing countries is increasing.

**Biological Control.** Control of pests by using predators to eat them. Biological control of insects involves using bacteria, viruses, parasites ad predators to destroy the insects. Plants can be controlled by herbivorous animals such as cattle.

**Biomass.** All Living Organisms in a given area. About 2500 million people, half the world's population, rely on biomass for virtually their cooking, heating and lighting. Mot of these people live in rural areas of developing countries, Concern over the global environment could provide the impetus for determined research and development of biomass.

**Biotechnology.** The use of technology to manipulate and combine different genetic materials to produce living organisms with particular characteristics artificial insemination of cattle was one of the first examples of biotechnology. Biotechnology offers great potential to increase farm production and food processing efficiency, to lower food costs, to enhance food quality and safety and to increase international competitiveness.

**Birds Foot Trefoll.** Plant with small yellow flowers, grown for fodder. All birds are members of the class Aves. They have feathers, and the front limbs have developed into wings, though not all birds are now able to fly. Birds are closely related to reptiles, and have scales on their legs. Birds (rooks, pigeons, pheasants) can cause very serious damage to crops; various controls can be used such as shooting, bird-scarers and destruction of nests. Birds also destroy many pests, such s wireworms, leatherjackets and caterpillars. In general birds are more helpful than harmful. Though this will depend on the type of farming undertaken.

**Blackberry.** Soft black fruit of the bramble.

**Black Bindweed.** Common weed (Bilderdykia convolvulus) which is widespread in spring arable crops.

**Blackcurrent.** Soft Fruit grown for its small black berries, used also in making soft drinks.

**Blackhead.** Common and fatal disease of young turkeys.

**Blackgrass.** Whchis widespread among winter cereals, especially on heavy soils; also known as slender foxtail.

**Blackhead.** Common and fatal disease of young turkeys.

**Blackleg.** (a) Bacterial disease of potatoes, affecting the base of the stem which turns black and rots. (b) bacterial disease of sheep and cattle; it causes swellings containing gas on the shoulders, neck and thigh, and can cause death within 24 hours of the appearance of the symptoms.

**Black Leghorn.** One of the several varieties of leghorn chicken; the breed is black all over, with a large red single comb; it has yellow legs and flesh ad lays white eggs.

**Black Mustard.** Variety of rape sown in spring and harvested by combine in August. The oil and powder from the seeds is an important ingredient of table mustard.

**Blackwood.** Australian hardwood tree.

**Bleach.** To remove all colour from a substance (as in the preparation of white flour).

**Bloat.** Swelling of a cow's rumen due to gas from lucerne and clovers which is unable to escape; the gas presses on the diaphram and the animal may die of asphyxiation.

**Bloodstream.** Blood as it passes round the body.

**Blood Sucker.** Insect or parasite which sucks blood from an animal.

**Blossom.** Flower or flowers which come before an edible fruit (such as apple blossom or cherry blossom).

**Blower.** Machine which blows; *snow blower* = machine which picks up snow from the ground and blows it away to clear a path; *blower unit* = part of an agricultural machine which blows out waste.

**Blue-faced Leicester.** Middle-sized long wool breed o sheep, with dense curly flee. The ram is excellent for crossing with smaller types of ewe; it is the sire of the "mule" and the so-called "Welsh mule"

**Boarding.** Titling a plough towards he ploughed land so as to increase the pressure on the mould boards.

**Boer.** South African breed of goat, white with red head markings. The animals are raised both for meat and for their skins.

**Boil.** To cook in water at 100°C.

**Boll.** Seed pod of the cotton or flax plant; boll number = number of bolls per cotton plant; boll weevil = American beetle (*Anthonomus grandis*) which attacks cotton plants.

**Bolter.** Plant which grows too fast, producing a low seed yield. Bolting occurs as a response to low temperatures and results in the plant failing to build up food reserves in the root, so producing seed in its first year; bolting is highly undesirable in many plants, especially in the sugar beet, where the roots become woody and have a low sugar content.

**Bordeaux mixture.** Mixture of copper sulphate, lime and water, used as a fungicide.

**Border Disease.** Disease affecting sheep, caused by a virus. Ewes may abort, or lamp may be born weak and may show muscle tremors. Infection enters the flock hen diseased sheep are brought in and an infected ewe excretes the virus.

**Border Leicester.** Breed of long wool sheep, derived from the English Leicester; its head is bare of wool and has a pronounced "Roman" nose; the breed is used o produce ram lambs for breeding.

**Boreray.** Rare breed of horned sheep, with grey or cream coloured fleece.

***Botany.*** Scientific study of plants.

**Botanical.** Referring to botany; botanical insecticide = insecticide made from a substance extracted from plants (the best-known botanical insecticides are pyrethrum, derived from the chrysanthemum, and nicotine, derived from the tobacco plant).

**Botanist.** Scientist who studies plants.

**Bottle.** 1. Glass container for liquids or preserves; *bottle feeding* = feeding young animals with liquids form a bottle with a teat 2. To keep in a bottle; to preserve (food) by heating it inside a glass jar with a suction cap.

**Bovidae.** Larges class of even-toed unulates, including cattle, sheep and goats.

**Bovine.** Referring to cattle; bovine leucosis = cancerous disease in cattle.

**Bovine Tuberculosis.** Bacterial disease of cattle which has been almost completely eliminated for the UK by the attested herds scheme.

**Bovine Somatotropin.** Natural hormone found in cows, which has been produced artificially by genetic engineering; it is used to increase milk yields and is said to increase them by up to 40%. It is not licensed for use in the UK, but is being used in trial.

**Bramble.** Wild blackberry bush with edible black fruits.

**Bramley's Seedling.** A common variety of cooking apple.

**Bran.** (a) Outside covering of the wheat seed, removed when making white flour, but an important source of roughage and some vitamin B.

**Brangus.** Crossbreed of cattle obtained by crossing a Brahman with an Aberdeen Angus. It is a black polled breed, and is found in Central and South America, the USA, Canada, Australia and Zimbabwe.

**Brassica.** Generic term for members of the cabbage family, such as broccoli, Brussels sprouts, cauliflowers, kales, savoys, Swedes and turnips.

**Brawn.** (a) meat dish prepared from cut, boiled and pickled pig's head (b) obsolete term for a stag boar.

**Break Crop.** Crop grown between periods of continuous cultivation of a main crop; on a cereal growing farm, crops such as sugar beet or potatoes may be introduced to give a "Break" from continuous cereal growing.

**Break Feeding.** Method of rationing animal feed by moving animals from one grazing area to another.

**Break Rolls.** Heavy rollers with grooves in them, through which the grain passes when being milled; as the grain goes through it is broken into pieces and finally reduced to flour.

**Breeching.** A leather strap round the hindquarters of a shaft horse, which allows the horse to push backwards and so make the cart go backwards.

**Breed in.** To introduce a characteristic into an animal breed or plant variety, by breeding until it is a permanent characteristic of the breed.

**Breeder.** Person who breeds new forms of animals or plants a cat breeder; a rose breeder.

**Breeding.** The action of raising a certain type of animal or plant.

**Breeding Crate.** Box construction designed to take the weight of a bull, when mating with a heifer or cow.

**Breeding Stock.** Prime animals kept for breeding purposes to maintain and improve quality of stock.

**Breeze Fly.** Large two-winged blood-sucking fly, similar to a gadfly.

**Brew.** To make beer by fermenting water and malted barley.

**Brickearth.** Common name for loess; soils developed in brick earth are fertile and well drained; they are used for intensive crop production.

**Brewers' Grain.** By-product of brewing; the residue of barley after malting. It is a valuable cattle food, fed wet or dried, and is a source of fibre and protein.

**Brickearth.** Common name for loess; soils developed in brick earth are fertile and well drained; they are used for intensive crop production.

**British Sugar Corporation.** A corporation which buys sugar beet each year from farmers; the corporation is responsible for processing and marketing the sugar.

**Broadcast Fertilizer Distributor.** Machine which scatters fertilizer; the most common makes have a hopper for fertilizer and a horizontal spinning disc below it. Another type has a horizontal spout which moves from side to side. Most broadcasters are mounted with hopper capacities of up to 600kg; trailed hoppers may have capacities of up to five tones.

**Broadleaf or Broadleaved Trees.** Deciduous trees (such as beech, Oak, etc.) which have wide leaves, as opposed to the needles on confers the plant is to plant 12,000 hectares of agricultural land a year, one third of which will be broadleaves.

**Brome Grass.** Weed grass found in arable fields and short leys; there are many species (Bromus) and none are of any value.

**Brown Swiss.** Medium-sized Swiss dual-purpose breed of grey-brown cattle, now found in many parts of the world including Canada, Mexico and Angola.

**Browser.** Animal which browses goats are useful browsers.

**Brucella.** Type o rod-shaped bacterium.

**Brucellosis.** Infectious disease, also known as contagious abortion, which is usually associated with cattle where it results in reduced milk yields, infertility and abortion; the UK is now a Brucellosis-free takes the form of Brucellosis often takes the form of undulant fever. Agglutination tests are used to detect Brucellosis.

**Bruise.** To harm the flesh under the skin, usually by hitting ripe pears have to be handled carefully to avoid bruising.

**Brushwood.** Low undergrowth or thicket.

**Brussels Sprouts.** Variety of cabbage with a tall min stem, which develops buds which are picked and eastern as fresh vegetables or may be kept frozen.

**BSE.** Bovine Spongiform Encephalopathy a fatal brain disease of cattle.

**BST.** Bovine Somatotropin natural hormone foudn in cows, which has been produed artificially by genetic engineering; it is used ot increase milk yields and is said to increase them by between 12 percent and 20 percent.

**Bucket Feeding.** Feeding a young animal with milk from a bucket.

**Buckrake.** Machine for collecting green crops cut for silage; the machine has a number of steel tines, usually rear-mounted in a tractor linkage system. A buckrake is used by going backwards along a swath with the tines pointing downwards.

**Buckwheat.** Grain crop which is not a member of the grass family; it can be grown on the poorest of soils. In the USA, when buckwheat is ground into flour, it is used to make grits.

**Bud.** 1. Young shoot on a plant, which will later become a leaf or flower; *tree in bud* = tree which has buds which are swelling and about to produce leaves or flowers 2 To propagate plants by grafting a bud from one in place of a bud on the stock.

**Budding.** Way of propagating plants, where a bud from one plant is grafted in place of a bud on the stock (used, for example, to propagate roses)

**Buffalo.** (a) Animal of the cow family, a common domestic animal in tropical countries, where it is used both for milk and also as a draught animal; dairy buffaloes contribute substantially to income and employment in India.

**Buffer Stock.** Stock of a commodity (such as coffee) held by an international organisation and used to control movements of the price on international commodity markets.

**Buff Orpington.** Dual-purpose breed of chicken, brown in colour.

**Bug.** Any small insect.

**Bulb.** Fleshy stem like an onion, formed of layers of tissue, which can be planted and which will produce leaves, flowers and seed.

**Bulk Milk Collection.** Collection of large quantities of milk by tankers from farms.

**Bulk Storage.** Storing of fertilizer or grain in dry covered barns, rather than in bags.

**Bull.** Uncastrated adult male ox.

**Burnt Lime.** Form of lime produced by burning lumps of limestone or chalk. It is usually ground up ready for spreading; also called "quicklime", "lump lime", and "shell lime"

**Bullock.** (a) Young male ox (b) castrated bull also called a "steer"; bullocks are more docile than bulls and "finish" quicker than entire animals. They are used a draught animals in many parts of the world.

**Butter.** Fatty substance made from cream by churning; butter is high in saturated fat; butter beans = leguminous plant (phaseolus lnatus) with large white seeds; also called "*lima bean*".

**Buttercup.** Ranunculus, a common weed wit yellow flowers.

**Butterfat.** Fatty substance contained in milk; butter at content = the amount of butterfat in milk; this will vary with the breed of cow. Jersey cow milk contains 5.14% butterfat, and is much used for butter-making; the Gerber test is used to measure butterfat content.

**Buttermilk.** The liquid which remains after the churning of cream, when making butter.

# C

**$C_3$** Metabolic pathway in plants, which uses three-carbon compounds to fix $CO_2$ from the atmosphere.

**$C_4$** Metabolic pathway for $CO_2$ fixation, which uses four-carbon mechanism, called $C_4$ plants, such as maize, are adapted to high sunlight and arid conditions; they have low photorespiration.

**Cabbage.** Cultivated vegetable (*Brassica oleracea*) with a round heart or head, a useful food for stock; other suitable varieties are grown for human consumption.

**Cabbage Root Fly.** (*Erioschia brassiae*) a fly whose larvae attack the roots of Brassica seedlings, the plants turn bluish in colour and wilt and die.

**Cabbage White Butterfly.** Common white butterfly (*Pieris brassicae*) which lays eggs on the leaves of plants of the cabbage family; the caterpillars cause much damage to the plants.

**Caboclo.** Subsistence farmer in South America.

**Cacao.** Term used instead of cocoa, when referring to the growing cocoa tree (Theobroma cacao) or its products.

**Cadmium.** Metallic element which is naturally present in soil and rock in association with zinc. Cadmium is used for making rods for nuclear reactors. It is also present in tobacco smoke, and is found in fish and shellfish such as oysters. It is often found in sewage sludge from industrial sources.

**Caesium.** Metallic element which is one of the main radioactive pollutants taken up by fish.

**Cafezal.** A coffee plantation in Brazil.

**Cage.** Housing made of wood or metal, used for battery hen; *laying cage* = specially built cage for laying hens; the cages are arranged in tiers and each cage should allow the birds to sand comfortably, allow the eggs roll forward and permit access to food and water, easy cleaning and easy handling of the birds; *cage rearing* = method of rearing poultry in which birds are taken right through from day-old chicks to placement in laying cages. Chicks are started in the top their and then spread through al the tiers of cages within a few weeks. Cases are designed so that chicks can be brooded in them and yet they may also be used as laying cages.

**Cage Wheel.** Metal wheel fitted to the outside of a normal tractor wheel in order to reduce ground pressure.

**Calabrese.** Variety of sprouting broccoli, grown as a vegetable for human consumption; it produces a large central head, and after this is cut, sprouts are produced for several months. Large produced for several months. Large quantities are grown for quick-freezing or canning.

**Calcifuge.** Plant which prefers acid soils and cannot exist on chalky or alkali soils.

**Calcimorphic Soil.** Soil which is rich in lime.

**Calcium.** Metallic chemical element which is naturally present in limestone, chalk and is essential to biological life (it is a major component of bones and teeth); *calcium borogluconate* = Chemical which is given in the form of injections to cows suffering from milk fevers, as a result of calcium deficiency; *calcium carbonate* = chalk, white mineral found widely in many parts of the world, formed from animal organism; *calcium cycle* = cycle of events by which calcium in the soil is taken up into plants, passed to animals which eat the plants, and the n passed back to the soil again when the animals die and decompose; *calcium deficiency* = lack of calcium in an animals' bloodstream; *calcium hydroxide* = slaked lime, mixture of calcium oxide and water, used on soils to improve their quality; *calcium oxide* = quicklime or chemical used in many industrial processes and also spread on soil to reduce acidity; *Calcium sulphate* = gypsum, sometimes used to improve salt-affected soils; *calcium supplement* = addition of calcium to the diet, or as injections, to improve the level of calcium in the bloodstream; *calcium uptake* = the taking of calcium into an animal's bloodstream as it eats.

Calcium is essential for various body processes such as blood clotting, and is an important element in a correct diet. Milk, cheese, eggs and certain for human consumption. In birds, calcium is responsible for the formation of strong egg shells. Lack of calcium in the bloodstream of cattle may lead to a disorder known as milk fever.

**Calver.** Cow which has had calves; first calver = cow which has produced her first calf. Freshly calved cows should not enter the milking herd until 3-5 days after calving. If the cow is eating well and has orally expelled the placenta, she should then be moved from the calving pen to the milking herd.

**Calyx.** Part of a flower shaped like a cup, made up of the green sepals which cover the flower when it is in bund.

**Cambridge Roller.** Heavy roller with a ribbed surface, consisting of a number of heavy iron wheels or rings, each of which has a ridge about 4cm high; the ribbed soil surface left b the roller provides an excellent seedbed for grass and clover seeds.

**Cannula.** Tube through which a trocar is inserted, used to puncture an animal's rumen to allow an escape of gas.

**Canterbury Hoe.** Hoe which does not have a blade, but is like a three –pronged fork, with the prongs set a right angles to the handle.

**Canterbury Lamb.** Lamb reared in New Zealand, mainly for export.

**Capacity.** Amount which something can contain; *field capacity* = the amount of water which is retained by soil after free drainage has taken place; *moisture-holding capacity* (MHC) = the amount of water held between field capacity and permanent wilting point.

**Capillary.** (a) tiny tube carrying a liquid in an organism such as a very small blood vessel (b) capillary flow = movement of a liquid upwards inside a narrow tube or upwards through the soil

**Capillarity.** Capillary flow. Capillary flow is important in water in soil, as it does not drain away. It moves through the soil by capillary action, i.e., by the surface tension between the water and the walls of the fine tubes or capillaries. It is a very slow movement, and may not be fast enough to supply plant roots in a soil which is drying out.

**Capping.** Hard crust which sometimes forms on the surface of soil, often only abut 2-3cm thick. It can be caused by heavy rain on dry soil; also by tractors and other heavy farm machinery.

**Capsicum.** Group of plants (also called "peppers") grown for their pod-like fruit, some of which are extremely pungent, such as the chilli and Cayenne peppers. Others, including the red, green or sweet peppers are less pungent and are used as vegetables.

**Capsid Bug.** Tiny insect which sucks the sap of plants, one of a large family of sucking insects that chiefly attack fruit trees.

**Capsule.** (a) Membrane round an organ or egg, etc. (b) dry seed case which bursts open to allow the seeds to shoot out (the seed cases of poppies are capsules).

**Captan.** Fungicide, used to fight apple and pear scab; it is also used in seed dressings for peas and other vegetables.

**Carambola.** Yellow fruit of a tropical tree (*Averrhoa carambola*) found in Indonesia; the fruit are used in preserves and drinks.

**Caraway.** Seeds of a herb (*Carum, carvi*) used as a flavouring in bread and cakes.

**Carbohydrates.** Organic compounds which derive from sugar and which are the main ingredients of many types of food. Carbohydrates are compounds of carbon, hydrogen and oxygen. They are found in particular in sugar and starch from plants, and provide the body with energy. Plants build up valuable organic substances from simple materials. The most important part of this process, which is called photosynthesis, is the production of carbohydrates such as sugars, starches an cellulose. They form the largest part of food of animals.

**Carbonate.** Compound formed from a base and carbonic acid; calcium carbonate = chalk, a white mineral found widely in many parts of the world, formed from animal organisms.

**Carbon Dioxide ($CO_2$).** Colourless gas produced when carbon is burnt with oxygen. Carbon dioxide exists naturally in air and is produced by burning or rotting organic matter. In animals, the body's metabolism makes the tissues burn carbon, which is then breathed out by the lungs as waste carbon dioxide. Carbon dioxide is removed from the atmosphere by plants when it is split by chlorophyll in photosynthesis to form carbon and oxygen. It is also dissolved from the atmosphere is sea water The increasing release of carbon dioxide into the atmosphere, especially from burning fossil fuels, adds to the greenhouse effect. Carbon dioxide is used in solid form as a means of keeping food cold.

**Carcass.** Dead body of an animal; especially in the meat trade, the body of an animal after removing head, limbs and offal; carcass classification scheme = system of judging the thickness of flesh on a carcass, and the fat cover over a carcass. The fat classes in the Beef Carcass Classification scheme range from Class I with the least fat cover through Class 3, which is average, to 5H which has the highest fat cover.

**Cardamoms.** Elettaria cardamomum, a crop grown in India and Sri Lanka for its seeds, which are used in the preparation of curry powder.

**Carboon.** Vegetable (Cynara cardunculus) grown in Mediterranean areas, similar to the globe artichoke.

**Carnivore.** Animal (such as the cat or dog) which lives on flesh of other animals.

**Carotene.** Orange or red pigment in carrots, egg yolk and some natural oils, which is converted by an animal's liver into vitamin A.

**Carpel.** Female part of a plant, formed of an ovary and stigma.

**Carrier.** Animal which has recovered from disease or in which the disease is latent, and which is capable of passing on the infection to another animal.

**Carrot.** Vegetable root crop (Daucus carota) grown for human consumption; most are grown for fresh sale, some for canning and freezing. Damaged roots which cannot be sold can be fed to cattle.

**Carrot Fly.** A small fly (Psila rosae) with a reddish brown head and yellowish wings; it lays its eggs in the soil surface near plants and the larvae burrow into the root. The foliage wilts and dies, and in cases of severe infestation, the whole crop is lost.

**Carry.** To keep (cattle) on farmland; *carrying capacity* = maximum number of productive livestock that can be supported by a given area of land, so that the vegetation eaten by the grazing animals does not exceed the rate at which it grows again.

**Carthorse.** Farm work horse.

**Carter.** Person in charge of a cart being used to move produce.

**Cartilage.** Thick connective tissue which lines the joints and acts as a cushion, and which forms part of the structure of an organ. The chief diseases which affect cartilage in animals are necrosis, resulting in the death o cells of the cartilage, and caused by injury, and ossification of the cartilage (also caused by injury), where the cartilage turns into bone.

**Case.** (a) Hard outer cover; *seed case* = hard outside cover which protects the seeds in certain plants; *case hardening* = formation of a hard surface on a piece of food, by deposition of sugar or self (b) quantity of produce (one or salt (b) quantity of produce (one dozen bottles of wine, thirty dozen eggs).

**Casein.** Protein found in milk. Casein is precipitated when milk comes into contact with an acid, and so makes milk form cheese.

**Cash Crops.** Crops which are grown to be sold rather than eaten by the person who grows them, or for feeding to livestock on the farm.

**Cashew Nut.** Nut from a tropical tree (*Anarcardium Occidentale)* popular when roasted as dessert nuts; grown extensively in India and East Africa.

**Cashmere.** Very fine down undercoat on a goat, less than 18 microns.

**Cassava.** Starchy root crop; there are two varieties, the sweet cassava (*Mnihot dulcis*) and the bitter cassava or manioc plant (*Manihot utilissima*) Cassava is an important world crop. The root of the bitter cassava is poisonous, and has to be washed before being made into flour for human consumption. The flour is called tapioca in Asia, in Brazil it is mandioc, and in Spanish Latin America it is yucca; cassava is also used in animal feedingstuffs. Brazil is the largest producer, followed by Zaire and Nigeria.

**Cast.** (1) Worm cast = waste matter rejected by an earthworm (2) (a) to bear an offspring prematurely a cast calf (b) to place an animal on its side on the ground; cast seep = sheep lying on its back and unable to get up again.

**Casting.** Method of ploughing, in which the area is ploughed in a circle, going in an anticlockwise direction.

**Castor Oil.** Oil derived from the seeds of the castor oil plant (*Ricinus communism*), used as a common purgative for fowls and calves.

**Castration.** Removal of the essential sex organs, testes and ovaries, from male or female animals; this allows bullocks and heifers to be housed together, as castrated animals are more docile.
Castration may be by cutting the scrotum, as in pigs, or by atrophication which follows ringing, as in sheep and cattle. In fowls, a sex-inhibiting hormone is used.

**Catch Crop.** (a) Fast-growing crop grown in the time interval between two main crops (b) fast-growing crop planted between the rows of a main crop.

**Catch Drain or Catch-water Drain.** Type of drain designed to take rainwater from sloping ground.

**Catchment (area).** Area of land which collects and drains the water which falls on it (such as the area round a lake or the basin of a river)

**Caterpillars.** Soft-bodied larvae of many species of butterflies and moths; caterpillars feed mainly on foliage, but can also attack roots, seeds and bark of crops.

**Cation.** Ion with a positive electric charge; cation exchange = exchange which takes place when the ions of calcium, magnesium and other metals found in soil replace the hydrogen ions in acid.

**Cattle.** Domestic farm animals of the class Bovidae, raised for their milk and meat.

**Cattle Grid.** Type of grill made of parallel bars, covering a hole dug in the road; it prevents stock from crossing the grid and leaving their pasture, but allows vehicles and humans to pass.

**Cattle Plague.** Disease of cattle, eradicated from the UK in 1877, but still found in parts of Asia and Africa.

**Cattle Rustler.** Person who steals cattle.

**Cattle Rustling.** Stealing of cattle.

**Cattleman.** Person who looks after cattle. Domesticated cattle belong o the genus Bos, of the family Bovidae, and within the genus there are a number of different species. The European domesticated cattle are *Bos Taurus*; the Indian and African domesticated cattle are Bos indivcus; the buffalo is *Bos bubalus*. The main breeds of European dairy cattle are; Ayrshire, Dairy Shorthorn, Friesian, Guernsey, Holstein, and Jersey. The dairy cow is now of the most valuable domesticated animals, providing high quality human foods. Milk is the main product, although cull cows are an important source of meat. The main breeds of beef cattle are: Aberdeen Angus, Galloway, Hereford. The main dual purpose breeds (i.e. Breeds which provide both beef and dairy products) are Dexter, South Devon and Welsh Black.

**Cauliflower.** Plant of the cabbage family, with a large white head made up of mass of curds; it may be eaten raw, but more often is cooked.

**Cavings.** Broken pieces of straw from a threshing machine.

**Cayenne Pepper.** Plant (Capsicum frutescens) producing a pungent red pepper from ground dried pods; it is grown in a the tropics and in warm temperate areas.

**Cedar.** Apium graveolens, a variety of celery with a thick edible root; the root is used as a vegetable in soups and salads.

**Celery.** Vegetable Plant. (Graveolens), with thick edible leaf stalls; the plant is grown in tenches to help growth and to blanch the stems; some varieties are self-blanching.

**Cell.** Tiny unit of matter surrounded by membrane, which is the base of all plant and animal tissue.

**Cell Division.** Way in which a cell reproduces itself by mitosis.

**Cell Membrane.** Outside wall of all cells, both plants and animals.

**Cell Wall.** Outside wall of a plant cell, formed of cellulose (does not exist in animal cells).

**Cellular.** (a) Referring to cells or formed of cells (b) Made of many similar parts connected together.

**Cellular Tissue.** Form of connective tissue with large spaces. The cell is a unit which can reproduce itself. It is made up of a jelly-like substance (cytoplasm) which surrounds a nucleus, and contains many other small organisms or organelles which vary according to the type of cell. Cells reproduce by division (mitosis). Some microorganisms are formed of a single cell, but most organisms are formed by the divisions and reproduction of many millions of cells.

**Census.** See *Agricultural Census*.

**Centigrade.** Scale of temperature where the freezing and boiling points of water are 0° and 100°; see note at Celsius.

**Centrifugation.** Separation of solids from a liquid by spinning.

**Cereal.** Specialized types of grasses that are cultivated for their large seeds or grains, especially to make flour for bread making or for animal feed the common Market grows large quantities of cereals. Cereal plants are all members of the Graminales family or grasses. The commonest are oats, wheat, barley, maize and rye in colder temperate areas, and rice and sorghum in warmer regions. Other cereals of local importance are millet, teff in Ethiopia and adlay in India. Cereal production has considerably expanded and improved with the introduction of better methods of sowing. Combine harvesters, driers, bulk handling.

**Cerrado.** Tropical savanna grassland of Brazil.

**Cesspool or cesspit.** Septic tank or tank in the ground which collects sewage from a house, and fro which the sewage gradually seeps away, not connected to a mains drainage system.

**Chaff.** Husks of corn which separate from the grain during threshing; short lengths of cut straw, used as feed for ruminants and as a component of manures.

**Challenge Feeding.** Feeding of dairy cows with concentrates to provide extra nourishment.

**Channel.** Bed of a river or the ground across which a river or stream flows.

**Channel Island Breeds.** To make straight a stream which has many bends, so as to make the water flow faster.

**Chapati.** Flat unleavened bread made from cereal flour and water, eaten as a staple food throughout the Indian subcontinent.

**Chaptalization.** Addition of sugar to wine which has not reached the standard level of alcohol, in order to increase the level of alcohol (the additive can be ordinary white sugar or some form of alcohol).

**Charlock.** A widespread weed (*Sinapsis arvensis*) mainly affecting spring cereals and other spring crops; also commonly called brasics or wild mustard.

**Charolais.** Breed of beef cattle originating in central France; creamy whit in colour, valued for their fast growth and lean meat. They tend to have large hindquarters which, when passed on to an unborn calf, can lead to difficulties at birth. They are large heavy cattle, and have been exported all over the world in recent years.

**Charollais.** Breed of sheep originating in France and having a characteristic "red' face; used as an alternative to Suffolk and Texel rams on lowland crossbred or mule flocks.

**Chats.** Small potatoes, separated from larger (or ware) potatoes during the grading process. Chayote. Pear-shaped vegetable (*Sechium edule*) grown in the West Indies.

**Cheddar.** Hard yellow cheese, originally made in the West Country.

**Cheese.** Food made from cow's milk curds. Cheese is also made from goat's milk, and more rarely from ewe's milk. The curd is pressed and left to mature for a period of time (longer in the case of hard cheese). There are may varieties of both hard and soft cheese: the British Caerphilly, Gloucester, Cheddar and Cheshire are all hard cheeses; the French Brie and Camembert are soft.

**Chernozem.** Dark fertile soil, full of organic matter containing abundant calcium carbonate in its lower horizons. Chernozem is found in the temperate grass-covered plains of the Soviet Union and North and South America.

**Cheviot.** Medium-sized hardly breed of sheep; white-faced and usually hornless. The wool is of good quality, of middle length and fairly dense.

**Chewings Fescue.** Common variety of grass used for pastures in New Zealand.

**Chianina.** Breed of beef cattle, originating in Tuscany in Italy: one of the largest breeds of cattle, it is white in colour with black hoves, muzzle and horn tips. It is a dual-purpose breed, used both for beef production and as draught animals.

**Chick.** Newly hatched bird, up to the time when it is weaned from the hen or brooder.

**Chicken.** (a) A young bird of a domestic fowl (b) the meat of domestic poultry.

**Chickpea.** One of the pulses (*Cicer arietinum*) important in India and Pakistan as a source of protein; also called gram, ad in South America garbanzos.

**Chickweed.** A widespread choking weed (*Stellaria media*) found in cereals and grass; it germinates and flowers all the year round. Also called "white bird's-eye."

**Chicory.** Blue-flowered plant (*Cichorium intybus*) cultivated for its salad leaves and roots; dried chicory root is used as a substitute for coffee.

**Chill.** (1) Coldness; wind chill factor = way of calculating the risk of exposure in cold weather by adding the speed of the wind to the number of degrees of temperature below zero. (2) To preserve by cooling to a temperature just above freezing. (See also *Cook Chill.*

**Chilli.** Very pungent spice (*Capsicum frutescens*), with bright red seed pods.

**Chinese Goose.** Breed of goose with a lighter carcass, raised for meat production.

**Chnook.** Warm wind which blows from the Rocky Mountan down onto the Canadian plains in winter; similar to FOEHN.

**Chip Basket.** Basket woven from thin strips of wood.

**Chlorinated.** Treated with chlorine; chlorinated Hydrocarbon Insecticide = organochlorine, a type of insecticide make synthetically as a compound of chlorine. Chlorinated hydroccaron insecticides include DDT, aldrin and lindane. Thee types of insecticide are very persistent, with a long half-life of up to 15 years, while organophosphorous insecticides have a much shorter life. Chlorinated hydrocarbon insecticides not only kill insects, but also enter the food chain and kill small animals and birds which feed on the insects.

**Chlorine.** An element, a powerful greenish gas occurring in nature as various sales or chlorides. It is a nutrient of major importance both in the animal diet and in the growth of plants.

**Chlorosis.** Reduction of chlorophyll in plants, making the leaves turn yellow. Chlorophyll absorbs light energy from the sun and supplies plants with the energy to fix CO2 from the atmosphere. It is also used as a colouring (E140) in processed food.

**Chocolate.** Popular sweet food made from the cocoa bean (the beans are roasted, and then mixed with oils and sugar); Chocolate spot = fungal disease of winter beans, occurring in two forms, Botrytis cinerea or the more severe Botrytis fabae. The disease appears as a small round brown spots on leaves and stems. In bad attacks, the symptoms move to flowers and pods.

**Chopper.** Machine for chopping; straw chopper = device attached to a combine harvester, which chops the straw into small pieces.

**Chorleywood Breed Process.** Method of making bread, developed by the British Baking Industries Research Association, in which the long fermentation period is eliminated by mixing the dough vigorously by mechanical means.

**Chrmosome.** Rod-shaped structure in the nucleus of a cell, formed of DNA which carries the genes.

**Chromosomal.** Referring to chromosomes. Each species has its own chromosomal make-up. The human cell has 46 chromosomes, 23 inherited from each parent. Cattle have 60 chromosomes, horses 64, and chickens 78. Plants have fewer chromosomes than animals; carrots have 18, maize 20, rice 24 etc. See also *the comment at SEX.*

**Chrysanthemum.** Genus of composite plants, many of which are cultivated for their flowers; the insecticide pyrethrum is derived from *Chrysanthemum roseum.*

**Cinnamon.** Aromatic inner bark from a tropical tree, used as a spice.

**Citrus Fruit.** Edible fruits of evergreen citrus trees, grown throughout the tropics and subtropics; the most important are oranges, lemons, grapefruit and limes; citrus fruit have thick skin and are very acidic.

**City Farm.** Community project that utilizes wasteland in inner cities, or the urban fringe areas, to farm and garden with an ecological approach to the conservation management of land and resources.

**Claypan.** Not dirty; clean air = air which does not contain impurities or air which is free from pollution; clean cattle = cattle which have not been used for breeding.

**Clean Crop.** Measure of wheat or other cereal, not mixed with seeds of other plants..

**Clean Land.** Land which is free of weeds

**Clean Pasture.** Pasture that has been left ungrazed for four to six weeks after contamination with parasitic worm larvae, and is considered free of the parasites.

**Clearfell.** To clear an area of forest by felling all the trees the greatest threat to wildlife is the destruction of habitats by clearfelling the forest for paper pulp.

**Cleavers.** A widespread weed (Galium aparine) affecting winter cereals, oilseed and early-sown spring crops (it has seed pods (burs) with tiny hooks which catch onto the coats of poassing animals).

**Clevis.** U-shaped iron attachment, used to couple an implement to a tractor towbar.

**Clingstone.** Varieties of peach, where the flesh is attached to the stone, as opposed to the fresthone varieties.

**Clippers.** Shears, used for clipping sheep.

**Cloning.** Method of making an exact copy of a living organism by asexual reproduction, or possibly by genetic engineering.

**Clun Forest.** Hardy grass hill breed of sheep; it has fine dense fleece, a dark brown face and a permanent topknot which extends out over the forehead.

**Cluster.** The four cup attachments of a milking machine, attached to the teats of the cow's udder.

**Coat.** The hair on he body of an animal some breeds of goat have very thick coats. Most animals have a thicker topcoat of coarse hair, which gives protection against the weather and a softer undercoat of fine wool which keeps the animal's body warm.

**Cobalt.** Metallic element, which forms the centre piece in the molecular structure of vitamin $B_{12}$. Sheep grazing on land whose soil is deficient in cobalt may suffer from a wasting disease know as "pining".

**Cochin.** Breed of domesti꜀ fowl originating in China.

**Coconut.** Tropical palm tree (Cocosnucifera) with a large hard fruit containing a white edible pulp; the outer husk is used to made a rough fibre called coir; coconut oil = oil extracted from dried coconut flesh or copra. The dried flesh of the coconut is called "copra"; it is the a in form in which coconuts are traded on the world markets; it is used for the extraction of coconut oil, which is used in making margarine, soap and other products. The Philippines. Malaysia and Mexico are also important producers.

**Coffee.** Shurb (*Coffea*) which bears fruit (coffee cherries) each of which contains two beans, which are roasted and ground to make the drink.

**Coffee Rust.** Fungus disease which attacks coffee plants; green coffee = fresh coffee beans, before they are roasted. The two main varieties of coffee are arabica and Robusta. The Arabica shurb, (*Coffea arabica*) was originally grown in the southern parts of the highlands of Ethiopia, and was later introduced into south-western Arabia. The Arabica plant only grows well on altitudes of 1000m and above. It represents 75% of the world's total coffee production. Arabica coffee beans are generally considered to produce a higher quality drink than those obtained from the Robusta coffee plant (*Coffea canephora*) which originated in west Africa. Robusta coffee ha a stronger and more bitter taste than Arabica. The most important area for growing coffee is South America, especially Bolivia. Brazil and Colombia though it is also grown in Kenya and Indonesia.

**Coir.** Rough fibre from the outer husk of coconuts, used as a material for stuffing chairs and mattresses, and also to make floor matting.

**Collective Farming.** Farm organisation which originated in the USSR. All land is owned by the State, and amalgamated into large collective farms which are either leased permanently to shareholder farm workers who run the holding as a single unit (kolkhoz), or run by a manager, who directs the work of laborers.

**Coolie.** Scottish breed of sheepdog.

**Colonial.** Referring to a colony; Colonial Animals = animals (such as ants) which usually live in colonies.

**Colonizer.** Animal or plant which colonizes an area.

**Combine Harvester.** Machine used to harvest a vast range of crops: cereals, grass, clover, peas, oilseed rape, and other arable crops. The combine cuts the crop, passes it to the threshing mechanism, then sorts the grain or seed from the straw or chaff. The straw is leaf in a swath behind the combine, and the chaff is blown out of the back. The grain is lifted to a hopper form which is it unloaded into trailers. Most combine harvesters are self-propelled, with cab for the driver, power-steering and monitoring systems for the key components. Special attachments used with combines include straw spreaders, straw choppers, pick-up attachments for grass and clover crops, and maize pickers.

**Commodity.** Substance sold in very large quantities, such as raw materials or foodstuffs such as corn, rice, butter; primary or basic commodities = farm produce grown and sold in large quantities; commodity exchange = place where commodities are bought and sold; Commodity futures = trading in commodities for delivery at a later date (often, the produce will not yet have been grown or harvested); commodity mountain = surplus of a certain agricultural product produced in the EC, for example the 'butter mountain".

**Common Agricultural Policy (CAP).** Agreement between members of the EC to protect farmers by paying subsidies to fix prices of farm produce.

The European Community has set up a common system of

agricultural price supports and grants. The system attempts to encourage stable market conditions for agricultural produce, to ensure a fair return for farmers and reasonable market prices for the consumer, and finally to increase yields and productivity on farms in the Community. The EC has established a system of common prices for the main farm products with intervention buying as the main means of market support.

**Companion Plants.** (i) Plants which grow best with other plants; (ii) Plants which are grown with others by horticulturists because they encourage growth or because they reduce pest infestation. Some plants grow better when planted near other. Beans and peas help roots plants such as carrots and beetroot. Most herbs (except fennel) are helpful to other plants. Marigolds help reduce aphids if they are planted near plants such as broad beans or roes which are subject to aphid infestation. The strong all of onions is disliked by the carrot fly, so planting onions near carrots makes sense. On the other hand, most other plants (and especially peas and beans) dislike onions and will not grow well near them.

**Complementary Feeders.** Animals which feed in areas which complement other animals (i.e. they do not compete with them); so goats, which browse, complement sheep which graze.

**Complete Diet.** Winter feed for livestock involving mixing of concentrates with forage and allowing the animals free feeding of the mix.

**Composition.** Milk composition = the percentages of protein, lactose, fat, minerals and water which make up milk; the composition varies according to the breed of cow, but average percentages are; protein (2.4%), milk sugar (4.75%), fat (3.75%), minerals (0.75%). Water (87.35%); milk compositional quality scheme = a scheme organized by the Milk Marketing Board, which categorizes milk and pays farmers according to the quality of milk produced.

**Compost.** (a) Vegetation decomposed under aerobic conditions. (b) Prepared soil or peat mixture in which plants are grown in horticulture.

**Compost Activator.** Chemical added to a compost heap to speed up the decomposition of decaying plant matter.

**Compost Heap.** Pile of rotting vegetation in a garden, which, when fully rooted, can be spread on the soil as a fertilizer or mulch.

**Compound Feed.** Animal feed made up of several different ingredients, including vitamins and minerals, providing a balanced diet; usually fed to animals in the form of compressed pellets.

**Compound Fertilizer.** Fertilizer that supplies two or more of the nutrients N, P and K, available in the form of granules which are easy to store and handle. Trace elements, such as boron and iron, my be added.

**Conifer.** Evergreen tree with long thin leaves (called needles), which produces fruit in the form of cones afforestation with conifers has had a noticeable effect on the landscape of the upland region.

**Connective Tissue.** Tissue which forms the main part of bones, cartilage, tendon and ligaments in which a large proportion of fibrous material surrounds the tissue cells.

**Conservation.** (a) Keeping or not wasting; Conservation of Energy = making consumption of energy more efficient; preventing loss or waste of energy (such as the loss of heat from buildings); conservation of soil or soil conservation = preventing soil from being eroded or over cultivated (by irrigation, mulching, etc.) (b) maintenance of environmental quality or resources by the use of ecological knowledge and principles; *nature conservation* = preserving nature as it is at present, and taking steps to make sure that it is not polluted or disturbed.

**Convenience Foods.** Food which has been prepared so that it I ready to be served, after simply reheating it.

**Cook Chill or Cook Freeze.** Methods of preparing food for preserving, where the food is cooked to a certain temperature and then chilled or frozen.

**Copper Deficiency.** Lack of copper in an animal's diet, sometimes caused by poisoning with molybdenum. Symptoms of copper deficiency vary, but can include lack of growth and change of colour, where black animals turned or grey. In severe cases, bones can fracture, particularly the shoulder blade. Diarrhoea can also occur, as ell a anaemia. Copper deficiency in ewes can cause swayback in lambs. The condition is treated with injections of copper sulphate.

**Corm.** Bottom part of the stem of a plant which, like a bulb, can be preserved and from which the plant sprouts again in the spring.

**Corn.** (i) Any cereal crop, but especially wheat in England; (ii) in Scotland, also used to refer to oats; corn cockle = poisonous weed (*Agrostema githago*) with a tall tem and purple flowers.

**Corn Marigold.** Common weed (*chrysanthemum segetum*). Corn poppy = common weed (*Papaver rhoeas*) affecting cereals.

**Corn Spurrey.** Common weed (*Spergula arvensis*) with matted growth which makes it difficult to eradicate in row crops. (mainly US) maize.

**Corn Cob.** Seed head of maize; corn-on-the-cob–head of maize, cooked and eaten as a vegetable; corn gluten – high protein animals feed obtained after corn starch has been extracted from maize.

**Corn Oil.** Vegetable oil obtained from maize grand, used for cooing and as a salad oil; *corn starch* = corn flour; *Four corn*

= variety of maize with large soft grains and friable endosperm, making it easy to grind to flour.

**Corn Belt.** Region of the mid-western United States, covering the states of Illinois, Indiana, Iowa, Minnesota, Nebraska and Ohio, where maize is grown on a vast scale.

**Corned Beef.** Beef which has been cured in brine and is preserved in cans.

**Cornflour or US Corn Starch.** Flour extracted from maize grain, used in cooking ((it contains a high proportion of starch, and is used for thickening sauces).

**Cornflower.** Common weed (Centaurea cyanus) which tall stems and bright blue flowers.

**Cotton.** White downy fibrous substance surrounding the seeds of the cotton plant, a substropical plant (gossypium sp.). Cotton is the world's most important textile fibre; cotton gin = machine which separates the seeds from the cotton fibres; cotton grasses = types of grass found in boggy areas, only of limited value for grazing.

**Cottonseed.** Seed of the cotton plant, one of the world's most important sources of oil; cottonseed cake or *cottonseed meal* = residue of cottonseed after the extraction of oil; it is used as a feeding stuff. Cotton is widely grown in tropical and sub-tropical areas, including China, India, Pakistan, Paraguay and the southern states of the USA: it is the main crop of Egypt. It is sold in standard bales.

**Cottonwood.** North American hardwood tree.

**Cotyledon.** First leaf of a plant as a seed sprouts. Cotyledons are thicker than normal leaves, and contain food for the growing plant. Plants are divided into two groups: those which produce a single cotyledon (monocotyledons) and those which produce two cotyledons (dictotyledons).

**Couch Grass.** Kind of grass (*Agropyron repens*) with long creeping rhizomes, which is difficult to eradicate from cultivate crops; also called "scotch" or "twitch".

**Coupling.** Attachment which couples an implement to a tractor.

**Cover Crop.** (a) Crop which is sown to cover the soil and prevent it from drying out and being eroded; when the cover crop has served its purpose, it is usually ploughed in, hence leguminous plants which are able to enrich the soil are often used as cover crops (b) Crop which is grown to give protection to another crop which is sown with it; see also Nurse Crop (c) crop which is sown to give cover for game birds.

**Cow.** Female bovine animal; *cow beef* = beef from dairy cows no longer needed for milk production

**Cowman.** Person in charge of a dairy herd.

**Cratch.** Rack used for feeding livestock out of doors.

**Crawler Tractor.** Large powerful caterpillar tractor, used for heavy work.

**Crazy Chick Disease.** Disease of chicks associated with a diet which is too rich in fats or deficiency of vitamin E; the symptoms include falling over and paralysis.

**Creamery.** Factory where butter and other products are made from milk.

**Creep.** Small entrance through which young animals can pass; *creep feed* = fee given to small animals during creep feeding; *creep feeding* = allowing a young animal (such as a calf) access to concentrates through a small entrance, while the adult cow is unable to reach the feed; *creep grazing* = type of rotational grazing using creep gates, which allow the lambs access to the pasture before the ewes.

**Crofting.** System of farming in Scotland where the arable land of small farms, which was previously held in common, was divided among the joint tenants into separate crofts, while the pasture remains in common.

**Crop.** (a) Plants grown for food crop breeders depend on wild plants to develop new and stronger strains; *crop husbandry* = practice of growing and harvesting crops; rotation of crops or crop rotation = system of cultivation where two or more crops are grown in a field in a fixed sequence, covering three consecutive growing seasons; this is done to prevent the nutrients in the soil being totally used up (each plant uses different nutrients, and the land is allowed to lie fallow for the fourth year). Rotation also helps to limit damage to crops from pests and diseases; *crop year* = period of twelve months calculated as the time from the sowing and harvesting of one crop until the next sowing season. (b) amount of produce from a plant or from a field the tree has produced a heavy crop of applies; the first crop was a failure; the potato crop was bad this year (c) bag-shaped part of a bird's throat where food is stored before digestion.

**Cropland.** Agricultural land which is used for growing crops.

**Cropper.** *Heavy cropper* = tree or plant which produces a large crop of fruit.

**Crossbred.** Which is the result of breeding from two breeds a herd of crossbred sheep or a herd of crossbreds.

**Cross-breed.** Animal which is bred from two different pure breeds.

**Cross-Breeding.** Mating of animals of different breeds, both being purebred, in order to combine the best characteristics of the two reeds.

**Cross-Fertilization.** Fertilizing one individual plant from another of the same species.

**Cross-infection.** Infection of other animals in a herd or flock from an infected animal.

**Cross-Pollination.** Pollinating a plant with pollen from another plant of the same species (the pollen goes from the anther of one plant to the stigma of another.)

**CRP.** Conservation Reserve Programme.

**Crude Protein.** An approximate measure of the protein content of foods.

**Cryophilous.** Which needs a spell of cold weather to grow properly. Cryophilous crops need a certain amount of cold weather in order to proide flowers later in the growing period. If such crops do not undergo this cold period, their growth remains vegetative, or they only form abortive flowers with no seeds. Cereal crops, such as whet, barley and oats; peas; root crops like sugar beet and potatoes, are all cryophilous.

**Cryophyte.** Plant which lives in cold conditions (as for example in snow).

**Cubed.** In small blocks; cubed concentrates = concentrates for livestock in the form a of small cubes.

**Cuber.** Machine used for making cubes or pellets from meal; meal mixed with molasses is forced through small holes and cut into various lengths.

**Cucumber.** Creeping plant (*Cucumis sativus*) with long green fleshy fruit, used as a salad vegetable. Cucumbers are native to India, and are used as a cooked vegetable in oriental cooking: they are a major glasshouse crop.

**Cultivate.** (a) To dig and manure the soil ready for growing crops. The fields are cultivated in the spring, ready for sowing corn; cultivated land = land which has been dug or manured for growing crops (b) to grow (a crop) they cultivate rice in paddy fields.

**Cultivar.** Variety of a plant which has been developed under cultivation and which does not occur naturally in the wild, but which is a distinct subspecies.

**Cultivation.** Action of cultivating land; land under cultivation = land which is being cultivated or which has crops growing on it the area under rice cultivation has grown steadily in the past 40-50 years; *shifting cultivation* = form of cultivation practicised in some tropical countries, where land is cultivated until it is exhausted and then left as the farmers move onto another area.

**Cultivator.** (a) Person who cultivates land (b) Implement used for seedbed preparation, especially after ploughing.

A cultivator has a frame with a number of tines which break up and stir the soil as the implement is pulled across the surface. There are several types of tine, both rigid and spring-loaded. Cultivators can also be used for cleaning stubble and general weed control: the tines can be grouped together so that they pass easily between the rows of growing plants.

# D

**DAFS.** Department of Agriculture and Fisheries, Scotland.

**Dairy.** (a) Building used for cooling milk at the farm, before it is taken to a commercial factory. (b) company which receives milk from farms and bottles it and distributes it to the consumer; company which produces cream, butter, cheese and other milk products.

**Dairy Cows.** Cows and heifers kept for milk production and for rearing calves to replace older cows in a dairy herd.

**Dairy Farm.** Farm which is principally engaged in milk production.

**Dairy Farming.** Rearing cows for milk production.

**Dairy Fax.** Viewdata service operated by the Milk Marketing Board in England and Wales; it gives information on TV about milk quality results and other general information of interest to dairy farmers.

**Dairy Products.** Foods prepared from milk, such as butter, cream, cheese, yoghurt, etc.

**Dairying.** Agricultural system which involves the production of milk and other dairy products from cows kept on special farms.

**Dairyman.** Person who works with dairy cattle; person employed in a commercial dairy.

**Dairy Shorthorn.** Dual-purpose breed of cattle; the colour may be red, white of red and white.

**Dal or Dhal.** Indian term for pulses, such as lentils; also used for curries and soups prepared from these pulses.

**Dalesbred.** Local sheep of the Swaledale type; it has a white spot on either side of a black face, with a grey muzzle; it provides a long coarse fleece.

**Dam.** (a) Female parent of an animal (b) construction built to block a river. Dams are constructed either to channel the flow of water into hydroelectric power stations or to regulate the water supply to irrigation schemes. In tropical areas, dams encourage the spread of bacteria, insects and parasites, leading to an increase in diseases such as bilharziasis; they may increase salinity in watercourses. A dam also holds back silt which would normally be carried down the river and be deposited as fertile soil in the plain below.

**Damascus.** Breed of dairy goat found in Syria, Lebanon and Cyprus; it has a red and white coat with long lop ears.

**Damietta.** Type of Egyptian cattle.

**Damson.** Small dark purple plum (*Prunus damascena*).

**Dandelion.** Yellow weed (*Taraxacum officinale*) found in grassland; also sometimes eaten as salad.

**Dartmoor.** Breed of large moorland sheep, white-faced with black spots, and a long curly fleece.

**Date.** Rut of the date palm, a staple food of many people in the Middle East.

**Date Palm.** A tall subtropical tree (*Phoenix dactlifera*) with very large frond leaves; its fruit are dates. The biggest producers of dates are Saudi Arabia, Iraq and Algeria, though most Middle Eastern countries produce small quantities.

**Daucus.** Latin name the family of plants which includes the carrot.

**Day-nettle.** Another name for the common hemp nettle.

**Day-old Chick.** Chick up to 24 hours old, sent from a breeder or hatchery to a buyer.

**DDT.** Dichlorodiphenyl-Trichloroethane. DDT-resistant insect = Insect which has build up a resistance to DDT.
DDT is an organochlorine insecticide, which remains for a long time as a deposit in animal organisms. It accumulates as a breakdown product in fatty material and gradually builds up in the food chain as smaller animals are eaten by larger ones with the result that raptors (such as eagles and hawks) can be killed by the DDT which builds up in their systems from the bodies of smaller animals which they have eaten.

**Dead Heading.** Cutting the dead flower heads from a plant, so as to prevent the formation of seeds.

**Dead-in-shell.** Referring to chicks which die in the egg, because they cannot break out, or can only break part of the way out of the shell.

**Deadly Nightshade.** Poisonous plant (*Atropa belladonna*) sometimes eaten by animals.

**Deadnettle.** See Red Deadnettle.

**Dead Stock.** A comprehensive term for all implements, tools, appliances and machines used on a farm; it can also be used to include seed, fertilizer and feeding stuffs.

**Deadweight.** Weight of a dressed carcass.

**Deadweight Certification Centre.** Slaughterhouse which has been given approval by the Meat and Livestock Commission, where cattle and sheep carcasses are presented for certification as being eligible for premium payment.

**Decay.** Rotting of dead organic matter wood is treated to resist decay.

**Deciduous.** (a) (Woody Plant) which loses its leaves in the autumn and produces new leaves from buds the following spring (b) deciduous teeth = the first teeth of an animal, in humans called milk teeth, which are gradually replaced by permanent teeth.

**Decompose.** (Of organic material) to break down into simpler chemical compounds.

**Decomposer.** Organism (such as a fungus) which obtains its energy from decomposing matter in the ecosystem; animal (such as the earthworm) which helps the decomposition of organic matter.

**Decomposition.** Action of decomposing organic matter.

**Decortication.** Removing husks from seeds.

**Decumbent.** Used to describe plants stems, which lie on the surface of the soil for part of their length, but turn upwards at the end.

**Deep Freezing.** Storing of produce in temperatures below freezing point; many crops, such as peas and beans, are grown specifically for the freezer market.

**Deep Litter.** System of using straw, wood shavings, pet moss of sawdust for bedding cattle or poultry.

For poultry an inch of well-composted horse manure is laid down first; on this wood shavings, peat moss, or cut straw are placed. The litter is changed after each crop of birds. Deep litter also has value as a manure. For cattle, straw, shavings and sawdust form a deep litter; warmth is given off as faces in the litter ferment, and additions of fresh litter can be made on top of the old.

**Deep Ploughing.** Ploughing very deep into the soil (used when reclaiming previously virgin land for agricultural purposes).

**Deep-rooting.** With long roots which go deep into the soil (as opposed to a surface-rooting plant).

**Deer.** Ruminant animal; the males have distinctive antlers; the meat of deer is venison; dear farming = commercial farming of deer to be sold as venison.

**Dear Forest.** Extensive tract of upland, usually treeless, but managed by keepers to provide deer-staling.

**Deer-stalking.** Hunting of deer in the wild. There are three wild species in the UK: the fallow deer (*Dama dama*) the roe deer (*Capreolus*) and the red deer (*Cervus elaphus*), which is also raised commercially. Deer are hardly animals, and are well adapted to severe winters; they can suffer from tuberculosis, and the British government has introduced a compulsory slaughter scheme for animals suffering from the disease. Since 1970, more than 200 deer farms have been established in Britain. 13,000 hinds are estimated to be farmed, with a projected increase to 65,000 by 1993. The west of Scotland is the most important area for deer in the UK; there are over 140 deer farms in the Highlands and Islands of Scotland.

**Deficiency.** Lack of something essential; deficiency disease = disease of plants or animals caused by the lack of an essential nutrient, such as a vitamin, protein mineral element or amino acid; heart front and stem rot are two common plant diseases of this type; deficiency payment = payment made to a producer, where the price for a commodity at the market does not reach a preset guaranteed price.

**Definite Inflorescence.** Inflorescence here the main stem ends in a flower and stops growing when the flower is produced.

**Definitive Host.** Host on which a parasite settles permanently, lives and produces its eggs.

**Deflector Plate.** Attachment in a slurry spreader which spreads the slurry over a wide area.

**Deflocculation.** State where clay particles repel each other instead of sticking together deflocculation may occur, when clays are worked in a wet condition or if the soil becomes saline.

**Defollant.** Type of herbicide which makes the leaves falloff plants.

**Deforest.** To cut down forest trees for commercial purposes or to make arable land timber companies have helped to deforest the tropical regions; abut 40,000 square miles are deforested each year.

**Deforestation.** Cutting down forest trees to make arable land.

**Degrade.** (i) To reduce the quality of something; (ii) to make a chemical compound decompose into its elements the land has been degraded through overgrazing; ozone may make nutrient leaching worse by degrading the water resistance coating on pine needles.

**Degradable.** Which can be degraded; compare Biodegradable.

**Degradation.** (i) Making worse; becoming worse; (ii) decomposition of a compound into its elements chemical degradation of the land can be caused by over-use of fertilizers and by pollutants from industrial processes; degradation of air = making clean air become polluted.

**Dehiscent.** Which bursts open to allow the seeds to scatter.

**Dehorn.** To remove the horns of an animal, down by disbudding when the animal is young (note that by selective breeding, many breeds are now hornless).

**Dehusk.** To remove the husk from seeds such as corn.

**Dehydrate.** To remove water from something, to preserve it; dehydrated milk = milk which has been dried and reduced to a powder.

**Dehydration.** Removing water from something to preserve it. Food can be dehydrated by drying in the sun (as in the case of dried fruit), or by passing through various industrial processes, such as freeze-drying.

**Deintensified Farming.** Farming which was formerly intensive, using chemical fertilizers to increase production, but has now become extensive; overproduction of cereals has led to less intensive farming; see also *Set-Aside*.

**Denature.** (i) To make something change its nature; (ii) To convert a protein into an amino acid; denatured wheat = wheat which has been stained to make it unusable for human consumption.

**Denaturing.** Process of staining wheat grain with a dye, so as to make it unusable for human consumption; such grain may be used as animal feed.

**Dendrochronology.** Finding the age of wood byte study of tree rings.

**Denitrification.** Conversion by bacteria of nitrates into gaseous nitrogen products which are then lost into the atmosphere.

**Dental.** Referring to teeth; *dental formula* = a formula indicting the number of each type of teeth for a certain animal species.

**Dentition.** Arrangement of teeth in an animal's mouth; an examination of an animal's teeth may help in estimating its age.

**Denude.** To make bare the timber companies have denuded the mountains.

**Denudation.** Making land or rock bare by cutting down trees, so contributing to erosion.

**Department of Agriculture.** Department of the US federal government, which deals with agricultural matters.

**Deposition.** Action of depositing; dry deposition = falling of dry particles from polluted air (they form a harmful deposit on surfaces such as buildings or leaves of trees).

**Derbyshire Gritstone.** Blackfaced, hornless hardy breed of sheep, which produces a soft fleece of high quality.

**Derelict.** (Land) which is not used for anything.

**Derris.** Powdered insecticide extracted from the root of a tropical plant, used against fleas, lice and aphids.

**Desalinate.** To remove salt from water.

**Desalination.** Removing salt from a substance such as sea water.

**Desalination Plant.** Factory which takes sea water and removes the salt to produce fresh drinking water.
Desalination can refer simply to the removal of salts from soil by the action of rain. It is most commonly used to mean the process of removing salt from sea water to make it fit to drink. Desalination plants work by distillation, dialysis or by freeze drying. The process is very expensive, and is only cost-effective in desert countries where the supply of freshwater is minimal.

**Desert.** Area of land with very little rainfall, arid soil and little or no vegetation; the soil is unproductive in terms of food production, being unable to support plant life with the exception of sparse vegetation; desert soil = the soil in a desert (it is normally sandy with little organic matter).

**Desertify.** To make land into a desert it is predicted that half the country will be desertified by the end of the century. A desert will be formed in areas where rainfall is very low (less than 25 centimeters per annum) whether the region is hot or not. About 30 percent of all the land surface of the earth is desert o in the process of becoming desert. The spread of desert-type conditions in arid and semi-arid regions is caused not only by climatic condition, but also by human pressures. So overgrazing of pasture and the clearing of forest for fuel and for cultivation, both lead to the loss of organic material, a reduction in rainfall by evaporation and to soil erosion. Reclaiming desert is a very expensive operation and usually not very successful.

**Desiccate.** To dry out cattle travel across the desiccated pastures in search of fodder.

**Desiccant.** (i) substance which dries; (ii) type of herbicide which makes leaves wither and die before harvesting.

**Dessert Fruit.** Fruit which are sweet and can be eaten raw, as opposed to being cooked a variety of *dessert gooseberry.*

**Determination.** Identifying what something it; sex determination = was in which the sex of an individual organism is determined by the number of chromosomes which make up its cell structure.

**Devon.** Breed of fine-boned dual-purpose cattle; worth and South Devons are dark red, and belong to a type of red cattle bred for centuries in England; they thrive on pasture which would not be sufficient for larger breeds, and provide both meat and milk.

**Devon and Cornwall Longwool.** Breed of sheep with long curly, high-quality fleece; the lambs have a fine soft white wool.

**Dew.** Water which condenses on surfaces in the open air as humid air cools at night; dew point = temperature at which dew forms on grass or leaves, etc.

**Dew Claw.** Rudimentary fifth digit found on the heels of fogs, pigs and cattle.

**Dewpond.** Small pond which forms on high chalky soil (it is formed from rainwater not dew); small pond made to maintain a supply of drinking water for livestock.
Dewponds are found in areas of chalk or limestone country. To make a dewpond, a hollow is scooped out and lined with clay. The pond is kept full by rainwater.

**Dewatering.** Extraction of water from a crop by pressing (this reduces the cost of artificial drying)

**Dewlap.** Fold of loose skin hanging from the throat of cattle.

**Deter.** Rare breed of cattle, originating from the west of Ireland; the animals are small in size, coloured black or red.

**Dextrose.** Simple sugar found in fruit; also extracted from corn starch.

**Diamonds Disease.** See *Erysipelas*.

**Diarrhoea.** Condition where an animal frequently passes liquid faeces.

**Dibber.** Hand tool for making holes in soil to plant small plants.

**Dicotyledon.** Plant of which the cotyledon ha two leaves dicotyledons form the largest group of plants compare Cotyledon, Monocotyledon.

**Die Back.** (a) fungus disease of certain trees which kills shoots or branches (b) gradual dying of trees caused by acid ran (starting at the ends of branches) half the trees in the forest are showing signs of dieback.
There are many theories to try to explain the cause of dieback; sulphur dioxide, nitrogen oxides, ozone, are all possible causes; also acidification of the soil or aid rain on leaves.

**Dieldrin.** Organochlorine insecticide which kills on contact. It is very persistent and can kill fish, birds and small mammals when it enters the food chain.

**Diet.** Amount and type of food eaten; balanced diet = diet which contains the right quantities of basic nutrients.

**Dietary.** Referring to diet; dietary fibre = fibrous material in feeding stuff, which cannot be digested.

**Digger.** Type of plough body with a short, sharply curved mould board; used for deep ploughing, especially to prepare for root crops of for land reclamation.

**Digging Stick.** One of the earliest agricultural implements, still used in areas where shifting cultivation is practiced; the stick has a sharpened end, sometimes with a metal tip, and is used to dig holes to plant crops.

**Digest.** (a) To break down food in the alimentary tract and convert it into elements which are absorbed by the body (b) to process waste, especially organic waste such as manure, to produce biogas 55 percent of UK sewage sludge is digested; wastes from food processing plants can be anaerobically digested.

**Digester.** Machine which takes refuse and produces gas such as methane from it anaerobic digesters can be used to covert cattle manure into gas.

**Digestible.** Which can be digested glucose is an easily digestible form of sugar.

**Digestibility.** The proportion of food which is digested and is therefore of value to the animal which eats it.

**Digestibility Coefficient.** The proportion of food digested and not excreted, shown as a percentage of the total food eaten; digestibility coefficients can be calculated for individual nutrients in foods; digestibility trial = test to measure the digestibility of a know food by recording the weight of food eaten, and then excreted; digestibility value (D value) = amount of digestible organic matter in the dry matter of plants.

**Digestion.** (i) Process by which food is broken down in the alimentary tract into elements which can be absorbed by the body; (ii) process which produces biogas from refuse; salivary digestion = the first part of the digestive processes, which is activated by the saliva in an animal's mouth; stomach digestion = the part of the digestive processes which takes place in the animal's stomach.

**Digestive.** Referring to digestion; digestive juices = juices in an animal's digestive tract, which convert food into a form which is absorbed into the body.

**Digestive System.** All the organs in the body (such as the liver and pancreas) which are associated with the digestion of food.

**Dioecious.** With male and female flowers on different plants (such as hops or cucumbers).

**Dip.** (1) Chemical which is dissolved in water, used for dipping animals, mainly sheep, to remove lice and ticks; dips usually contain organophosphorous chemicals (2) To plunge an animal in a dip (for about thirty seconds).

**Dipper.** Deep trench into which sheep are guided to be dipped.

**Dipping.** The process of plunging an animal in a chemical solution to remove ticks etc.

**Dipping Batch.** Dipper, a trench in which animals are dipped.

**Compulsory Dipping Period.** Period of time (usually some weeks) during which all sheep in the country must be dipped. Sheep are dipped to eradicate parasites such as lice and ticks, and to prevent sheep scab. Dipping varies from region to region according to custom, breed and climate. Dipping may be ordered by the MAFF to control outbreaks of disease, and in certain cases it has to be witnessed by a local authority inspector.

**Diphtheria.** Serious infectious disease where a membrane forms in the throat passages of an animal (as in calf diphtheria).

**Diploid.** Organism with twice the usual number of chromosomes diploid grasses are less palatable than tetraploids.

**Dipterous.** Insect (such as a fly) with two wings.

**Direct Drilling.** Form of minimal cultivation, where the seed is sown directly into the field without previous cultivation; several types of drill are used, with heavy discs for cutting narrow drills, or strong cultivator tines.

**Direct Proportional Application (DPA).** System of making sure that the output from a sprayer is proportional to the speed at which it moves forward.

**Direct Reseeding.** Sowing grass seed without a cover crop; Direct sowing = sowing grass seed on a prepared seed bed; grass and clover seeds are small, and therefore must be sow shallow and a fine firm seedbed is necessary.

**Directive.** Order from the Council of Ministers or Commission of the European Community, referring to a particular problem.

**Dirt Tares.** Tares which grow among sugar beet plants.

**Disadvantaged Area.** Name for land in mountainous and hilly areas, which is capable of improvement and use as breeding and rearing land for sheep and cattle; divided into Disadvantaged or Severely Disadvantaged Areas; the EC recognizes such areas and gives financial help to farmers in them.

**Disbud.** (a) To remove the horn buds from calves, soon after birth (b) to remove small flower buds from a plant, to allow the main flower to develop more strongly (s when growing chrysanthemums or paeonies).

**Disc Plough.** Type of plough with large rotating discs in place of the mouldboard; used for deep cultivation, but not common in Great Britain.

**Discolour.** To change the colour of something fruit can be discoloured by the use of sprays.

**Disease.** Illness (of people or animals or plants, etc.) where the body functions abnormally the herd caught the disease from infected feedingstuff; the rice crop has been affected by a virus disease.

**Diseases of Animals Act (1950).** Act of Parliament covering he diseases listed under notifiable diseases

**Disorder.** (i) Illness or sickness; (ii) State where part of the body is not functioning correctly; congenital disorder = disorder which is present at birth.
An animal may be abnormal at birth because of a genetic defect (a congenital disorder); such disorders may be misshapen heads of calves; other congenital disorders such as swayback in lamb, may be caused by deficiencies in the mother (in the case of swayback, material copper deficiency).

**Dispersion.** Pattern in which animals or plants are found over a wide area.

**Distill.** To produce an alcohol or essential oil by heating and condensing the vapour.

**Distillation.** Process of producing a pure liquid by heating and then condensing the vapour, used in the production of alcohol and essential oils.

**Distiller.** Person who distils alcohol from grain; *distillers' grains* = by-product of whisky production, which consists of the remains of malted barley, used as a valuable cattle food which may b fed wet or dry.

**Distort.** To change the shape of something, so that it does not look normal, as when brassica roots are distorted by club root disease.

**Ditch** (1) Channel dug to take away rainwater (2) to dig channels for land drainage.

**Ditcher.** Mechanical excavator used in ditching. Ditches may be enough to drain an area by themselves, but usually they serve as outlets for underground drains. Ditches can deal with large quantities of water in very wet periods. They should be kept cleaned to their original depth, a process carried out usually once a year. Many type s of machine are now available for making new ditches or cleaning neglected ones.

**Diversify.** To do a number of different things farmers are being encouraged to diversify land use by using it for woodlands or for recreational facilities.

**Diversification.** Changing to a different way of working. The main alternative enterprises undertaken by farmers are: farm holidays and bed-and-breakfast; farm shops, selling produce from the farm; camping and caravan sites; country sports, such as horse riding pony-trekking and fishing.

**DNOC.** Dinitro-Ortho-Cresol chemical used in a compound with petroleum oil to destroy the eggs of fruit tree pests; DNOC is a poisonous yellow dye, and can also be used as a weed killer.

**Dock.** (1) Broadleaved or curled weed (Rumex) with a long tap root, making it difficult to remove (2) To cut off the tail of an animal; lowland breeds of sheep are often docked to prevent dirt and faeces accumulating on the tail; docking disorder = disorder of sugar beet, caused by eelworms, found on sandy soils in East Anglia, causing irregularly stunted plants with split root growth.

**Dockage.** Waste material which is removed from grain a it is being processed before milling.

**Dolly.** *Corn Dolly* = ornament woven from straw, used formerly as decoration on farms at harvest time.

**Domestic.** Referring to the home; domestic animal = animal (such as a dog or cat) which lives with human begins; domestic livestock = farm animals which live near the farmhouse.

**Domesticate.** (i) To breed wild animals so that they become tame and can fill human needs; (ii) To breed wild plants, selecting the best strains so that they become useful for food or decoration.

**Domesticated.** (i) (Wild animal, such as a dog or cat) which has been trained to live near a house and not be frightened of humans; (ii) (species of animal or plant) which was formerly wild, but has been bred to fill human needs.

**Domestication.** Breeding wild animals or plants for use by humans the domestication of wheat, barley and other grains took place in the Middle East about 10,000 years ago.

**Dominance.** State where one group in society rules other groups.

**Dominant.** (1) The plant or species which has most influence on the composition and distribution of other species of plants; the plant which is most prevalent in a vegetation community (2) which is more powerful than other recessive genes.

Since each physical trait is governed by two genes, if one is recessive and the other dominant, the resulting trait will be that of the dominant gene, and only if two recessive genes are present will the recessive trait be shown.

**Dorking.** Breed of fowl, with dark and silver-grey plumage; also a silver-grey breed of bantam.

**Dormancy.** State of an animal or plant, where metapolism is slowed during the winter months; *seed dormancy* = period when a seed is not active.

**Dormant.** Not actively growing; dormant plant = plant which is not actively growing (as during the winter).

**Dorset Down.** Medium-sized down breed of sheep; with a brown face, and wool growing over the forehead; providing a good-quality fine stringy fleece.

**Dorset Horn.** Breed of sheep in the south-west of England; both rams and ewes have long curly horns; it produces a fine white clear wool, and is unique among British breeds in that it can lamb at any time of the year.

**Dorset Wedge Silage.** Method of storing silage in wedge-shaped layers, usually covered with polythene sheeting. The first loads are tipped against the end wall and further loads are built up with a buckrake to form a wedge.

**Dose.** (1) Amount of medicine given to an animal to cure it of a disorder (2) Give an animal medicine; dosing gun = device used to give an animal medicine in the form of pellets; the pellet is forced into the back of animal' throat.

**Double Chop Harvester.** Type of forage harvester, which chops the crop into short lengths rather than just lacerating it; the chopping unit is a vertical rotating disc, usually with three knives and three fan blades.

**Double Cropping.** Multi-cropping, taking more than one crop off a piece of land in one year.

**Double Suckling.** Method of raising beef calves, where a second calf is placed with the cow's own calf and allowed to suckle.

**Dough.** Mixture of flour and water prepared to make bread; it can have salt and yeast added. Bread (such as chapattis) made from dough without yeast is "unleavened"

**Dove.** White domesticated pigeon.

**Dove Cote.** Special building for keeping doves.

**Down.** (a) Soft first plumage of young birds; an adult bird's under plumage, used to make pillows (b) undercoat of very soft hair on a goat.

**Down Breeds.** Breeds of short-wooled sheep, giving wool of a creamy colour, the sheep have dark faces and legs, and are hornless. They are found in hilly areas, and include the Southdown, Hampshire Down, Dorset Down and Suffolk.

**Down-calver.** Cow or heifer about to calve.

**Downland.** Area of downs.

**Drag Harrow.** Heavy type of harrow, used in the preparation of seedbeds.

**Drain.** (1) Open channel for taking away surplus water from farmland; *mole drain* = underground drain formed by a mole plough as it is pulled across a field; mole drains are normal drawn 3 to 4 metres apart, and are used infields with a clay subsoil; *pipe drain* = underground drain made of lengths of clay tiles linked together; they may also be made of concrete or plastic pipes. The spacing of the pipes will depend on the nature of the soil; *storm drain* = specially wide channel for taking away large amounts of rainwater which fall during tropical storms (2) (a) To remove liquid silage liquor drains into a slurry tank (b) to remove water from farmland; on most types of farmland, except free-draining soils some sort of artificial drainage is necessary to carry away surplus water and so keep the water table at a reasonable level; *draining pen* = pen for sheep to go in after dipping, where surplus liquid can drain off the wet fleece and go back into the sheep dip.

**Drainage.** Removing of water by laying drains in or under fields.

**Drainage Basin.** Catchment area or area of land which collects and drains away the rainwater which falls on it.

The main methods of drainage are open channels (ditches) and underground pipe drains and mole drains. Underground pipe drains and mole drains. Signs of bad drainage may be; machinery getting bogged down in mud; poaching by stock in grazing pastures; water lying in pools after heavy rain; weeds such as rushes, sedges and horsetail common in grassland; young plants being pale green or yellow; subsoil is various shades of blue or grey.

**Draught.** The effort needed to pull an implement through the soil.

**Draught Control System.** System of preventing damage to an implement such as a harrow, as it is being pulled through the soil (when the draught reaches a set level, the implement is automatically raised out of the soil).

**Draught Animals.** Animals which are used to pull vehicles or carry heavy loads.
Considerable use is made of draught animals in many areas of the world. Oxen, buffaloces, yaks, camels, elephants, donkeys, horses are all used as draught animals. The advantages of using animals are many: they produce young so do not always have to be bought: they are cheaper to buy than machines: they do not use expensive fuel, even though they cat large quantities of food: they may be slower than machines but they can work in difficult terrains. Their most important advantage is that they are appropriate to the local conditions.

**Drawbar.** Metal bar at the back of a tractor, used to pull trailed implements; some tractors have a drawbar which can be attached to the hydraulic linkage; swinging drawbar = moveable drawbar which is used to pull heavy trailed equipment.

**Drawbar Power.** Power available to pull an implement, as opposed to the brake horsepower of a tractor. Under field conditions, not all brake horsepower will be available to pull implements, because some of it is needed to make the tractor itself more forwards and overcome the resistance of the bearing and the soil on the wheels.

**Draw Hoe.** Hoe whose blade is at right angles to the handle and is pulled backwards towards the worker.

**Dredge Corn.** Mixture of cereals grown together and used for livestock feeding; the commonest type is a mixture of barley and oats; sometimes cereals and pulses are mixed.

**Dried Blood.** Organic fertilizer with a nitrogen content of 10% - 13%; a soluble quick-acting fertilizer, used mainly by horticulturists.

**Dried Fruit.** Fruit that has been dehydrated to preserve it for late ruse (currants and raisins are dried grapes).

**Dried Gras.** Grass which has been artificially dried; used as an animal feed of high nutritional value (dried grass has a high carotene content and a crude protein content of 10% - 20%).

**Dried Milk.** Milk powder produced by removing water from liquid milk; the techniques involved include roller-drying and spray-drying.

**Drill.** (1) (a) Implement used to sow seed; a drill consists of a hopper carried on wheels, with a feed mechanism which feeds the seed into seed tubes.

**Combine Drill.** Drill which sows grain and fertilizer at the same time; some drills have separate tubes for the seed and fertilizer, others have one tube for both (b) little furrow for sowing seed.
Most seed drills are designed to plant seed in prepared seed beds; drills for cereals and grasses sow the seed at random while precisions drills, used mainly for sugar beet and vegetable crops, place seed at present intervals in the rows; these are also called "seeder units". Grain drill feed mechanisms

maybe internal force feed, external force feed or studded roller. Some drills have hopper divided into two parts; one contains the seed, the other fertilizer; this is the combine drill which drills grain and fertilizer at the same time.

**Drip Irrigation.** Irrigation system where water is brought to the base of each plant and drips slowly into the soil, also called 'trickle system".

**Drop.** (1) Small quantity of liquid a drop of acid burned through the material; drops of rain soon began to fall. (b) Fall (of fruit); *June drop* = fall of small fruit in early summer, which allows the remaining fruit to grow larger (2) to give birth to a lamb.

**Drought.** Long period without rain at a time when rain normally falls.

**Droughtmaster.** Australian breed of beef cattle derived from the Indian Brahman and the British. Shorthorn. The animals are red, with a characteristic small hump.

**Dry.** Dry adiabatic lapse rate = rate of temperature change in rising dry air.

**Dry Cow.** Cow not giving milk; between lactations.

**Dry Curing.** Curing meat in salt, as opposed to brine.

**Dry Farming.** System of extensive agriculture, producing crops in areas of limited rainfall, without using irrigation; soil moisture is retained by mulching, frequent fallowing and removing the weeds that would take up some of the moisture.

**Dry Feeding.** Feeding of meal to animals without the addition of water; this my cause problems with pigs and poultry.

**Dry Deposition.** Falling of dry particles from polluted air (they form a harmful deposit on surfaces such as buildings or leaves of trees).

**Dry Matter (DM).** Components of a feed left after drying.

**Dry Period.** In cattle, a period of six to eight weeds between lactations, when a cow is rested form giving milk.

**Drystone Wall.** Wall made of stones carefully placed one on top of the other without using any mortar; these are features of much of Britain's hill country. Most walls are wider at the base than at the top.

**Dumping.** Selling of agricultural products at a price below the true cost, to get rid of excess produce cheaply, usually in a oversea market.

**Dunes.** Area of sand blown by the wind into rides which have very little soil for vegetation; dunes can be stabilized by planting with marram grass.

**Dung.** Solid waste excreta from animals (especially horses and cattle), often used as fertilizer (2) (a) to spread dung on the land as a fertilizer, (b) To clear away animals' dung; Dunging passage = passage at the back of a cow shed, into which dung can be washed with water.

**Dust Storm.** Storm of wind which blows dust and sand with it, common in North Africa.

**Dutch Harrow.** Implement with metal or wooden frame, with heavy tine bars almost at right angles to the direction of travel; the tines loosen the soil and the heavy bars level the surface.

**D Value.** Digestibility value of organic matter in the dry matter of plants.

**Dwarf Beans.** Term used for French or kidney beans, which make a bushy plant, as opposed to runner beans which climb.

**Dwarfling Rootstock.** Rootstock used for grafting fruit trees;

it produces a tree which does not grow very tall, and so makes fruit-picking easier.

**Dyke.** (a) Long wall of earth built to keep water out, (b) ditch for drainage. To build walls of earth to help prevent water from flooding land.

Dyke pond farming is a system of organic agriculture combining crop growing on the dykes which surround ponds in which fish are bred; it is common in China.

# E

**E number.** Classification of additives to food, according to the European Community.

**Ear.** Head or spike of a cereal, containing the flowers or seeds.

**Ear Emergence.** The main date for heading; in the case of a sward, this is the date at which 50 percent of the inflorescences have appeared.

**Earmarking.** Identifying an animal by attaching a tag to its ear; also sometimes done by cutting a notch in the edge of the ear.

**Earlies.** Potatoes grown for harvesting early in the season, as opposed to "main crop potatoes"

**Early Bite.** Grazing in the spring, provided by new growths of grass which sprout when the weather gets warmer.

**Early Weaning.** Removing young from the dam earlier than is usual.

**Earth.** Soil, a soft substance formed of mineral particles, decayed organic matter, chemicals and water in which plants can grow.

**Earth Up.** To move soil to make a ridge, in which a crop such as potatoes or celery can grow. Plants are earthed up to protect the tender stems from frost, or to make them white. Potatoes are earthed upto prevent the tubers from turning green and lasting bitter.

**Earthworm.** Kind of invertebrate animal (*Lumbricidae*), with a long thin body, living in large numbers in the soil. Earthworms provide a useful service by aerating the soil as they tunnel. They also eat organic matter and help stabilize the soil structure by compressing material and mixing it with organic matter and calcium. It is believed that they also secrete a hormone which encourages rooting by plants.

**Easy Feed.** Means of feeding livestock which allows easy access to feed by means of hopers or feeding passages.

**Ecology.** Stud of the relationships among organisms and the relationship between them and their physical environment.

**Human Ecology.** Study of man and communities, the place which they occupy in the natural world, and the ways in which they adapt to or change the environment.

**Ecological.** Referring to ecology; ecological balance = situation where relative numbers of organisms remain more or less static (by polluting the environment, destroying habitats, and increasing their own numbers, people can cause major changes in populations which may be irreversible).

**Ecological Disaster.** Disaster which seriously disturbs the balance of the environment.

**Ecological Factors.** Factors which influence the distribution of a plant species in a habitat.

**Ecological Succession.** Series of communities of organisms which follow on one after the other, until a climax community is established.

**Ecologist.** (a) Scientist who studies ecology (b) person who believes that a balance should be maintained between living things and the environment in which they live, and so improving the life of all organisms.

**Economist.** Person who specializes in the study of economics; agricultural economist = person who studies the economics of the agricultural industry.

**Ecoparasite.** Parasite which is adapted to a specific host; compare ectoparasite, endoparasite.

**Ecosystem.** System which includes all the organism of an area and the environment in which they live European wetlands are examples of ecosystems that have been shaped by humans. For thousands of years they have provided pasture for livestock, reeds for thatching and fuel, silage and bedding for livestock. An ecosystem can be any size, from a flower bud to the whole biosphere. The term was first used in the 193s to describe the interdependence of organisms among themselves and with the living and non-living environment.

**Ecotone.** Area between two different types of vegetation (such as the border between forest and moorland), which may share the characteristics of both.

**Edible.** Which can be eaten; edible fungi = fungi which can be eaten and are not poisonous.

**Egg.** Round object laid by female birds, with a hard calcareous sell forming a case containing albumen and yolk; the young bird grows inside the egg until it hatches; egg binding = unsuccessful attempt by a hen to lay an egg; egg classes = the grading of eggs under EC regulations, into Class A (fresh eggs). Class B (preserved eggs) and Class C (eggs for use in food processing); egg eating = action of intensively housed poultry, where birds eat their own eggs; it may be due to eggs being broken because of thin shells.

**Eggbound.** Condition of poultry where the egg is formed but the hen is unable to lay it.

The average hen's egg weighs about 60g of which about 20g is yolk, 35g white and the rest shell and membranes. Eggs contain protein, fat, iron and vitamins A, B, D was estimated at 12,000 million per annum (1988), but sales of eggs were estimated to have fallen by as much as 50 percent in December 1988 following an outbreak of Salmonella poisoning.

**Eggplant.** Plant with purple fruit (*Slanum melongena*), used as a vegetable. A native of tropical Asia, it is also called "aubergine"; its Indian name is "brinjal"

**Ejector.** Mechanism at the back of a farmyard manure spreader, which throws out the manure over a wide area.

**Electric Dog.** Electric wire at the side of the fence at the entrance to a milking parlour, which encourages the cows to go into the parlour.

**Electric Fence.** Thin wires supported by posts, the wires being able to carry an electric current; such a fence is easily moved around the farm, and makes strip grazing on limited areas possible.

**Element.** Chemical substance which cannot be broken down to a simpler substance; *essential element* = chemical element (such as carbon, hydrogen, oxygen) which is necessary to an organism's growth and function; *trace element* = substance which is essential to organic growth, but only in very small quantities.

**Elevator.** (a) Machine for carrying grain or silage to the top of a storage unit (b) very large storage unit for grain, in the US and Canadian prairies; *public elevator* = elevator which is used for storage by several farmers, and does not belong to one farmer alone (c) *elevator digger* = machine for harvesting crops such as potatoes, which can be adapted to harvest carrots, onions or flower bulbs. Most elevator diggers are semi-mounted; the soil and the potatoes are lifted onto a rod-link conveyor and the soil falls back to the ground as the conveyor passes over a series of agitators.

**Emaciation.** Becoming extremely thing scab causes emaciation in sheep.

**Embden.** A heavy white breed of goose, with blue eyes.

**Emblements.** Crops which are cultivated, as distinct from tree crops.

**Embryonic.** Referring to an embryo; (something) in the first stages of its development.

**Emergence.** Stage in the growth of a plant, when the new shoot or stalk appears through the surface of the soil.

**Emmer.** Species of wheat (*Triticum dicoccoids*) which is a natural hybrid of wild what and a goat grass; a further crossing between emmer and a goat grass produced wheat (*Triticum aestivum*).

**Emulsify.** To mix two liquids so thoroughly that they will not separate.

**Encephalopathy.** See Bovine Spongiform Encephalopathy.

**Enclosure.** The action of enclosing open land; used in England to refer open land; used in England to refer especially to the enclosure of common land in the 16th and 18th centuries, where rights to common land were removed and ditches, fences, hedgerows and walls were used to mark the boundaries of land which was owned freehold my major landowners; see also Field.

**Encroach On.** To come close to and gradually cover (something) the dunes are encroaching on the pasture land; trees are spreading down the mountain and encroaching on the lower more fertile land in the valleys.

**Encroachment.** The action of encroaching.

**Endangered Species.** Any species at risk of extinction. The categories of the degree of risk of extinction as drawn up by the IUCN are: I. Endangered: in danger of extinction and unlikely to survive if the causal factors continue to operate. 2. vulnerable; will move into the endangered category in the near future if the causal factors continue to operate. 3. Rare: not endangered or vulnerable, but at risk of becoming so.

**Endemic.** (a) (Plant or animal) that exists in a certain area the isolation of the islands has led to the evolution of endemic forms; the northern part of the island is inhabited by many endemic mammals and birds (b) (pest or disease) which is very common in a certain area this disease is endemic to Mediterranean countries. See also Epidemic, Pandemic.

**Endive.** Salad Plant (*Cichorium endiva*).

**Endoparasite.** Parasite which lives inside the host; compare Ecoparasite, ectoparasite.

**Endotoxin.** Poison from bacteria which pass into the body when contaminated food is eaten.

**Energy.** (i) Force or strength to carry out activities; (i) specifically, electricity; energy conservation = avoiding wasting energy; energy consumption = amount of energy consumed by a person or an apparatus, shown as a unit; energy crops = crops, such as fast-growing trees, which are grown to be used to provide energy; energy value or calorific value = heat value of food or the number of Calories which a certain amount of a certain food contains.

**Enhancer.** Artificial substance which increases the flavour of food, or even the flavour of artificial flavouring that has been added to food (in the EC, flavour enhancers added to food have the E numbers E620 to 637).

**Ensilage or Ensiling.** Process of making silage for livestock by cutting grass and there green plants and storing in silos.

**Enteric.** Referring to the intestine; calf enteric disease = disease of claves causing severe diarrhoea.

**Enteritis.** Inflammation of the mucous membrane of the intestine; *infective enteritis* = enteritis caused by bacteria.

**Enterobacteria.** Important family of bacteria, including Salmonella and Escherichia.

**Enterotoxin.** Bacterial exotozin which particularly affects the intestine.

**Enterovirus.** Virus which prefers to live in the intestine. The enteroviruses are an important group of viruses, and one causes Teschen disease in pigs.

**Entire.** Animal which has not been castrated.

**Entomological.** Referring to insects.

**Entomologist.** Scientist who specializes in the study of insects; *medical entomologist* = scientist who studies insects which may carry diseases environment the surroundings of any organism, including the physical world and other organism; *environment protection* = act of protecting the environment by regulating the discharge of waste, the emission of pollutants, and other human activities.

The environment is anything outside an organism in which the organism lives. It can be a geographical region, a certain climatic condition, the pollutants or the noise which surrounds an organism. Man's environment will include the country or region or town or house or room in which he lives; a parasite's environment will include the intestine of the host; a plant's environment will include a type of soil at a certain altitude.

**Environmental.** Referring to the environment; environmental protection = Environment Protection Environmental Protection Agency (EPA) = administrative body in the USA, which deals with pollution; environmental quality standards = amount of an effluent or pollutant which is accepted in a certain environment, such as the amount of trace elements in drinking water or the amount of additives in food; environmental set-aside = set-aside schemes which may improve the environment; for example, paying farmers to sow grass seed mixtures for a green cover and cutting a 15m-wide strip along the side of footpaths at the edge of cereal fields.

**Environmentalist.** Person who is concerned with protecting the environment to keep it healthy.

**Environmentally Sensitive Area (ESA).** Area designated by the Minister of Agriculture on the basis of recommendations made by the Countryside Commission and the Nature Conservancy Council.

ESAS were introduced under the 1986 Agriculture act: they are selected for their landscape and wildlife value, and where traditional farming methods would help to maintain this value, payments maybe made to farmers within these areas who agree to farm according to the practices set out in guidelines by the MAFF. ESAs are a means of slowing down and preventing agricultural landscape change, but also act as a mechanism for more positive change through the conversion of arable land to grass.

**Enzootic Disease.** An outbreak of disease among certain species of animals in a certain area; enzootic abortion = virus infection of sheep causing abortion about two weeks before lambing; enzootic bovine leucosis = a blood cancer disease of cattle; compare Epizootic.

**Enzyme.** Protein substance produced by living cells which catalyzed a biochemical reaction in living organisms.

Many different enzymes exist in organisms, working in the digestive system, in the metabolic processes and helping the synthesis of certain compounds. Some pesticides and herbicides work by interfering with enzyme systems, or by destroying them altogether.

**EPA.** Environmental Protection Agency.

**Epicarp.** The exocarp, the outer layer of skin on a fruit.

**Epidemic.** Which spreads quickly through a large number of animals; see also Endemic, Pandemix.

**Epidermis.** Outer layer of skin of plants or animals, including dead skin on the surface.

**Epiphte.** Plant which grows on another plant but does not derive nourishment from it.

**Epizootic disease.** Disease which spreads to large numbers of animals over a large area; compare Enzootic.

**Eradication.** Removing completely; eradication area = area from which a particular animal disease is eradicated, usually involving the slaughter of infected animals.

**Erect Habit.** Habit of a plant which grows upright, and does not lie on the ground.

**Erogot.** Fungus which grows on cereals, especially rye.

**Erogotamine.** The poison which causes erogotism.

**Erode.** To wear away.

**Erosion.** Wearing away of earth or rock by the effect of rain, wind, sea and the action of toxic substances grass cover provides some protection against soil erosion.
Accelerated erosion is that caused by human activity which is in addition to the natural rate of erosion. Cleared land in drough-stricken areas can produce dry soil which can blow away; felling trees removes the roots which binds the soil particles together and so exposes the soil to erosion by

rainwater; ploughing up and down slopes (as opposed to can tour ploughing) can lead to the formation of rills and serious soil erosion.

**Establish.** To come to live permanently the starling has become established in all parts of the USA; even established trees have been attacked by the disease.

**Establishment.** (a) Germination and emergence of seedings there was a good crop establishment (b) Period when a newly seeded sward is becoming established.

**Estancia.** Large farm in South America, especially in Argentina, used for ranching on an intensive scale.

**Eucalyptus.** Australian hardwood tree (Eucalyptus spp.), with strong smelling resin; the trees are quick growing and often used for afforestation. They are susceptible to fire.

**European Community (EC).** The Common Market, an organisation established in 1957 by the Treaty of Rome. The original six members were Belgium, Netherlands, France, Italy, Luxembourg and West Germany. Denmark, Ireland and the United Kingdom joined in 1973, Greece in 1981; Spain and Portugal joined in 1986. The organisation is responsible for agricultural policy among its member states. See *Common Agricultural Policy (CAP).*

**European Currency Unit (ECU).** The unit of account used as a unit for trade within the EC.

**Eutrophy.** To fill up with nutrients.

**Eutrophication.** Process by which a river or lake becomes full of phosphates and other nutrients which encourage the growth of algae, which can kill off other organisms.

**Evaporation.** Changing liquid into vapour the evaporation of water from the surface of a lake.

**Evapotranspiration.** Loss of water in an area through evaporation from the soil and transpiration by plants

**Evergreen.** (1) (Plant) which does not lose its leaves in winter (2) Tree or shrub which does not lose its leaves in winter; most conifers are evergreens; compare *Deciduous*.

**Ewe.** Adult female sheep; ewe lamb = female lamb less than six months.

**Exceed.** To be more tan (a certain limit) the concentration of radioactive material in the waste exceeded the government limits; it is dangerous to exceed the stated application rate = do not apply more than the recommended amount.

**Excess.** Too much of a substance excess phosphates run off into the river system.

**Excreta.** Waste material from the body (such as faeces)

**Excretion.** Passing waste matter (faeces or urine or carbon dioxide) out of the system; excretion rate = rate at which a substance, such as nitrogen, is excreted by an animal; compare Secrete, Secretion.

**Ex-farm.** Price for a product which does not include transport from the farm to the buyer's warehouse.

**Exhaust.** To use up completely; exhausted fallow = fallow land which is no longer fertile.

**Exmoor Horn.** Stock fat sheep, with a broad head, curled horns and dense fleece. Mainly found on exmoor, the breed has been crossed with the Devon Longwool to create the Devon closewool.

**Expander.** Device behind a mole which widens a drain.

**Experimental Farm.** Farm which is used to experiment with new farming techniques, rather than being run as a commercial enterprise; such farms can be classified as Experimental Husbandry Farms (EHF) or as Experimental Horticulture Stations (EHS).

**Exploit.** To take advantage of something large companies ruined the environment by exploiting the natural wealth of the forest; the birds have exploited the sudden increase in the numbers of insects.

**Exploitation.** Taking advantage of something to make money further exploitation of the coal deposits in not economic.

**Extender.** Food additive which makes the food bigger or heavier (without adding to its food value).

**Extensification.** Using less intensive ways of farming; payment to farmers to encourage them to farm less intensively. Less intensive use of farming involves using fewer chemical fertilizers, leaving uncultivated areas at the edges of fields, reducing sizes of herds of cattle, etc. This allows lower yields from the same area of farmland, which is necessary if production levels are too high.

**Eyespot.** Disease of cereals (*Cercosporella herpotricholdes*), which causes lesions to form on the stem surface and grey mould inside the stem; it can be treated with benomyl; compare Sharp Eyespot.

# F

**F.** (1) abbreviation for Fahrenheit (2) chemical symbol for fluorine.

**$F_1$.** The first generation of offspring; $F_1$ hybrid = plant produced by breeding two parent plants, which is stronger than the parents, but which will not itself breed true.

F1 hybrids can be crossbred to produce $F_2$ hybrids and the process can be continued for many generations.

**Factory Farming.** Highly intensive rearing of animals characterized by keeping large numbers of animals indoors in relatively small areas and feeding them concentrated foodstuffs, with frequent use of drugs to control diseases which are a constant threat under these conditions.

**Faeces or Excreta.** Dung or solid waste matter passed from the bowels of animals after food has been eaten and digested.

**Fahrenheit.** Scale of temperatures where the freezing and boiling points of water are 32° and 212°; compare Celsius, Centigrade.

**Fair.** (1) Regular meeting for the sale of goods or animals, often with sideshows and other entertainments; fairs an be specialized, such as horse fairs or cheese fairs, or can cover all types of farm animals (2) Which is reasonable; fair average quality (FAQ) = average quality of agricultural produce abased on samples taken from bulk.

**Fallow.** (1) (land) which is not used for growing crops for a period so that the nutrients can build up gain in the soil; to let land lie fallow = to allow land to stand without being cultivated (2) Period when land is not used for cultivation shifting cultivation is characterized by short cropping periods and long fallows; fallow crop = crop grown in widely spaced rows, so that it is possible to hoe and cultivate between the rows.

**Fallow Cultivation.** Type of shifting cultivation; the period under crops is increased and the length of the fallow is reduced.

**Fallow Length.** Period of time between cultivation periods (as population density increases and land becomes scarce, food supply can be increased by making the period under crops longer and the length of fallow shorter).

**Fallowing.** Allowing land to lie fallow for a period.

**False Seedbed.** Seedbed prepared in spring to allow weed seeds to germinate; these are then killed by cultivation before sowing root crops.

**False staggers.** Disease of sheep caused by maggots which cause inflammation of nostrils and head; the sheep appear dazed.

**Family.** Groups of genera which have certain characteristics in common (several families form an order).

**Famine.** Period of severe shortage of food when the monsoon failed for the second year, the threat of famine became more likely.

**Famine Relief.** Sending supplies of basic food to help people who re starving.

**Fancy Breed.** Breed reared for decoration or show, rather than for produce.

**FAO.** Food and Agriculture Organisation an agency of the United Nations established with the purpose of encouraging higher standards of nutrition and eradicating malnutrition and hunger.

**FAQ.** Fair Average Quality.

**Farm.** Area of land which may vary in size, and the buildings on it, owned or rented by one management and used to grow crops and/or raise livestock.

**Family Farm.** A farm unit which ideally supports one family.

**Farm Buildings.** Buildings on a farm: such buildings are needed to shelter animals, get stock off the ground to improve grass production, provide an artificial environment for stock or crops, improve working conditions for staff, house machinery, and protect stored materials from weather and vermin.

**Farm Consolidation.** Joining small plots of land together to form larger farms or bringing scattered units together to form large fields (consolidation is promoted by most governments to correct the inefficiencies associated with fragmentation in small scattered land holdings).

**Farm Fragmentation.** Situation where the fields of a farm are scattered over an area, so that the holding is not made up of a single unit of land; it can be the result of inheritance practices where the land of a person who has died it spoilt between all the children, of land reclamation schemes where the land is reclaimed piece by piece, or because old open-field systems have been kept.

**Farm Fresh Eggs.** Term used in the EC to describe Class A eggs.

**Farm Gate Price.** Prices which the farmer obtains for his produce.

**Farm Rent.** Rent paid by a tenant farmer to a landlord on a regular basis for the use of the farm holding.

**Farm Animal Welfare Council.** Agency established by the British government in 1979 to keep under review the welfare of farm animals on agricultural land, at markets, in transit and at the place of slaughter.

**Farm Capital Grant Scheme.** British government scheme begun in 1970, providing grants towards capital expenditure on farms for improvements such as field drainage and farm buildings.

**Farer.** Person who makes a living from agriculture by managing and cultivating a farm, whether as a tenant or owner; dairy farmer = farmer who raises cattle for milk.

**Farmer's Lung.** Form of asthma caused by an allergy to rotting hay.

**Farmers' List.** List of veterinary medicines which can be obtained from agricultural merchants with a prescription from a veterinary surgeon.

**Farmhand.** Person who works on a farm.

**Farmhouse.** House where a farmer and his family live.

**Farming.** Working a farm by growing crops or keeping animals for sale, and producing cereals, vegetables, eat, dairy products, etc.

**Farming Systems.** The classification of different farming types: such as shifting cultivation systems, ley systems, systems with permanent upland cultivation, fallow systems, grazing systems and systems with perennial crops; *contour farming* = method of cultivating sloping land, where the land is ploughed along a level across the slope, to prevent soil erosion.

**Farmland.** Cultivated land, land which is used for raising crops or animals for food.

**Farmscape.** Landscape dominated by agriculture; farmland is the main element in farmscape, though non-agricultural uses may be included; agricultural villages are part of the farmscape.

**Farmstead.** Farmhouse and the farm buildings around it.

**Farmworker.** Person who worκs on a farm.

**Farmyard.** Area around the farm buildings.

**Farmyard Manure.** Manure formed of cattle excreta mixed with straw, used as a fertilizer.

**Farmyard Manure Spreader.** Machine for spreading manure, basically a trailer with a moving floor conveyor and a combined shredding and spreading mechanism which distributes the material; there are two types, the rear ejector and the side delivery spreader.

**Farrowing.** Parturition in a sow (the act of giving oirth to piglets); farrowing crate = steel frame which holds the sow during farrowing and helps to prevent the overlying of the pilglets; farrowing rails = rails which prevent the sow from overlying the piglets.

**Fasclation.** (a) Abnormal plant growth in which several stems become fused together (b) production of several shoots from the crown of a plant, such as a pineapple; pineapples are propagated by crown slips which shoot from the base of the crown. If several are produced by fasciation, the plant's food supply is reduced and the plant should be destroyed after harvesting.

**Fat Lamb.** Lamb in condition satisfactory for slaughter. White or oily substance in the body which stores energy and protects the body against cold.

**Fat Hen.** Weed (*Chenopodium album*) which affects spring cereals, peas and row crops; found especially in rich soils and much heaps; also called "dung weed' and 'much weed"

**Fatness.** Amount of fat on an animal.

**Fastock.** Animal which are fattened for meat production.

**Fatten.** To give animals more food so as to prepare them for slaughter he buys lambs for fattening and then sells them for meat.

**Fatty.** Containing fat.

**Fatty Acid.** Organic acid (such as stearic acid) which occurs in fat; they are important substances for the maintenance of the body.

Essential fatty acid. (EFA). Unsaturated fatty acid which is essential for growth but which cannot be synthesized by the body and has to be obtained from the food supply.

**Fatal.** Which kills BSE is a fatal disorder of cattle.

**Faulta.** Proportion of rotten or diseased items in a quantity of produce sold.

**Faults.** Proportion of rotten or diseased items in a quantity of produce sold.

**Fauna.** Wild animals and birds which live naturally in a certain area.

**Fether.** (a) Growth on the skin of birds made up of a hard central stem and soft "hairs" growing along each side of it; feathers are formed at the base of follicles; a bird will moult regularly and lose its old features, growing new ones to replace them. Before moulting takes place new feathers start to grow in the follicles. Feathers are removed ("plucked") from carcasses of birds by machine (b) growths of hair round the feet of some breeds of shire horse. Feathereating or featherpecking or featherpulling. Pulling of the feathers of a bird by another bird.

**Febrile.** Referring to a fever.

**Fecundity.** Measurement of the number of offspring born and reared by a dam.

**Fee.** Money paid to a professional for a service.

**Stud Fees.** Money paid to the owner of a stud animal for servicing a female.

**Feed.** (1) Various types of food available to animals traces of pesticide were found in the cattle feed; feed additives = supplements added to the feed of farm livestock, particularly pigs and poultry, to promote growth; feed block = a block of foodstuff left out in the pasture, especially on hill farms, used by sheep to prevent loss of condition.

**Feed Preparation.** The milling and crushing of grain, mixing of the ingredients and making into cubes or pellets.

**Feed Ratio.** Ratio showing the price of an animal sold on the market against the cost of feeding it.

**Feed Wheat.** What which is used as an animal feed, and not for human consumption.

**Feeder.** Container from which livestock are fed.

**Feeder Cattle.** Cattle which are being fed to be slaughtered.

**Feeding.** Action of giving animals food to eat.

**Feeding face.** The area allowed to each animals to feed from under controlled conditions; each cow needs 150mm of feeding face, or less if continuous access is provided (this refers to the self-feeding method of silage);

**Feeding Value.** Nutritional value of feeding stuffs.

**Feedingstuffs.** Various types of food available for farm animals.

**Feedlot.** Area of land where livestock are keep at a high density, with small pens in which the animals are fattened; all feed is brought into the feedlot from outside sources.

**Feedmill.** Mill for preparing animal feed small transportable mills are being constructed for use on individual farms).

**Feed Off.** The practice of allowing stock to feed on a crop while it is still in the ground.

**Feed Ring.** A circular container for forage, from which livestock can feed.

**Fell.** High moor and mountain in the North of England. (2) To cut down (a tree); Felling licence = permission from the forestry Commission to fell trees. There are some exceptions to this; for example trees in gardens and fruit trees in orchards do not need a licence to be felled.

**Fenland.** Area of land covered by fens.

**Fenland Rotation.** A system of crop rotation developed on the fens of east Anglia using potatoes, sugar beet and wheat in rotation.

**Fenbendazole.** Medicinal substance used to worm cattle.

**Fence.** (1) Barrier put round field, either to mark the boundary or to prevent animals entering or leaving; fence post = wooden post which supports the wire of a fence (2) To put a fence round an area of land. Various methods are used to fence field boundaries, most commonly woven wire and woolen fence posts Movable electric fences are an efficient way of limiting areas of a field for grazing purposes.

**Fennel.** Aromatic herb (*Foeniculum vulgare*) of Mediterranean origin, used to flavour fish dishes and soups.

**FEPA.** Food and Environmental Protection Act.

**Ferment.** To produce alcohol and heat under the effect of yeast.

**Fermentation.** Process whereby carbohydrates are broken down by enzymes from yeast and produce heat and alcohol; in making silage, fermentation is essentially the breaking down of carbohydrates and proteins.

**Fertile.** (i) able to bear fruit; (ii) (of animal) able to produce young; (iii) (of soil) able to produce good crops.

**Fertile Crescent.** An area of South Western Asia (modern southern Turkey, Ian, Northern Iraq and Syria) with a Mediterranean climate and fertile soil, where man first settled and started to farm. This area was the centre of the domestication of what, barley, pulses and other crops which formed the basis of seed Agriculture about 10,000 years ago.

**Fertility.** (i) Being fertile; (ii) measure f the ability of a female to conceive and produce young or of the male to fertilize the female; (iii) proportion of fertile eggs which develop into young.

**Fertilization.** Joining of an ovum and a sperm to form a zygote and so start the development of an embryo.

**Fertilize.** (a) To put fertilizer on land (b) (of a sperm) to join with an ovum (c) (of a male) to make a female pregnant.

**Fertilizer.** Chemical or natural substance spread and mixed with soil to make it richer and stimulate plant growth. Artificial fertilizers or chemical fertilizers = fertilizers which are made from chemicals; nitrogen fertilizers = fertilizers containing mainly nitrogen; Compound Fertilizer or US mixed Fertilizers. Fertilizers which are made from chemicals. Nitrogen Fertilizers. Fertilizers containing mainly nitrogen.

**Fescue.** Common name for about 100 species of grasses, including many valuable pasture and fodder species.

**FFA.** Free fatty Acid.

**Fibrous.** Made of a mass of fibres; fibrous rooted plants = plants with roots which are masses of tiny threads, with no major roots like tap roots.

**Field.** (a) Area of cultivated land, usually surrounded by a fence or wall or hedge, used for growing crops or for pasture; field beans = Viciafaba, used for stock feeding, or for producing broad beans, which are the immature seeds used for human consumption. Field beans are usually grown as a break crop.

**Field Bindweed.** Deep-rooted perennial weed (*Convulvulus arvensis*) which causes great problems when combining because of its mass of clinging growths.

**Field Book.** Annual record of field utilization and other operations, kept on a farm.

**Field Botanist.** Botanist who examines plants in their growing habitat.

**Field Capacity.** The amount of water which is keep tin the soil after free drainage has taken place. The amount of moisture will vary according to the texture and structure of the soil. See also *Moisture-Holding Capacity.*

**Field Crop.** Crop grown over a wide area, such as most agricultural crops and some market-garden crops.

**Field Drainage.** Building drains in or under fields to remove surplus water.
Field observations or observations in the field. Observations taken in the open air, looking at organisms in their natural habitat (as opposed to laboratory observations).

**Field Pansy.** Widespread flower (*Viola arvensis*) increasingly found in winter crops, especially cereals, also called "corn pansy", "love-in-idleness" and "cats' faces' (b) areas of interest or study his field of study is pest control.

**Fieldman.** A farm worker whose work is mainly in the fields. Some older types of field can still be seen in the UK: *Celtic fields*, small rectangular fields, mainly on chalk uplands, surrounded by bans and walls, dating back to as early as the 6th century B.C.: *enclosure fields*, rectangular fields with regular hegerows, formed after the enclosures of the 16th to 18th centuries: open fields, the Saxons had heavier ploughs and used open fields with large furrows in strips, separated by banks of turf or walls of stone. In recent years the removal of many field boundaries in the interest of farm consolidation has led to an increase in the size of the average British field. Hedges have been removed to allow large farm machinery to be used more economically, and the loss of hedgerows has had a marked effect on the wildlife in the countryside.

**Fighting Bull.** Breed of black cattle from Spain and Portugal, bred to be aggressive and used in bull fights.

**Fill-belly.** Feed which fills the animal's stomach, without providing any useful nutrients.

**Filly.** Young female horse; so called for a year or so, after which she becomes a "mare".

**Fine Grains.** High quality grains, such a wheat and rice, as opposed to the coarse grains (oats maize, etc.)

**Fineness Count.** Scale used to assess the fineness of wool fibres.

**Fine Wool.** Wool of very good quality.

**Fingers.** Pieces of metal which project from and are attached to the cutter bar of a binder, mower or harvester. The knives pass across the fingers, cutting the grass or cereal crop as they do so.

**Finger Millet.** Important grain crop of East and Central Africa, south India and Sri Lanka. It can be stored for long periods and so is useful as a reserve grain in case of famine.

**Finish.** (1) The furrow left at the edge of a ploughed fields (2) To feed cattle or sheep at a rate of growth which increases the ratio of muscle to bone, and increases the proportion of fatty tissue in the carcasses to a level at which the animal is considered to be fit for slaughter (market prices include prices for "finished lambs", "finished pigs."

**Finishing.** Action of feeding cattle or sheep until they are ready for slaughter; finishing ration = feed given to animals to prepare them for slaughter a finishing ration includes silage, bet pulp and by-products such as outsize carrots.

**Finncattle.** Breed of dairy cattle derived from three Finnish breeds; the animals are medium-sized and brown.

**Finnish Ayrshire.** Breed of cattle found in northern Finland, similar to the Ayrshire; they are mainly reared for milk.

**Fircone.** Hard casing of the seeds of a fir tree.

**Fireblight.** Disease of apples and pears, which is characterized by dead flowers and braches; it is caused by the bacterium Erwinia amylovora.

**Firebreak.** Area where no trees are planted, so that a forest fire cannot pass across and spread to other parts of the forest. In shifting cultivation, the practice of clearing vegetation by burning is widespread. One of the simplest forms involves burning off thick and dry secondary vegetation. Immediately after burning, a crop like maize is planted and matures before the secondary vegetation has recovered. Where fire clearance methods are used, the ash acts as a fertilizer.

**Firm.** To make cultivated soil solid, before sowing a roller is used to firm the soil.

**First Calf Heifer.** A heifer which has borne its first calf.

**Fish.** Cold-blooded aquatic vertebrate, some species of which are eaten for food (fish are high in protein, phosphorus, iodine and vitamins A and D. White fish have very little fat).

**Fish Farming.** Breeding edible fish in special pools for sale as food.

**Fishmeal.** Dried fish reduced to a powder, used as an animal feed or as a fertilizer (a natural phosphate).

**Fixation.** Act of fixing something; nitrogen fixation = process by which nitrogen in air is converted by bacteria in certain plants into nitrogen compounds, and when the plants die the nitrogen is released into the soil and acts as a fertilizer.

**Fixed Costs.** Costs (such as rent) which do not increase with the quantity of a product produced.

**Flail Forage Harvester.** Type of forage harvester which uses a high-speed flail rotor; the cut crop passes through a vertical chute and its discharged into a trailer.

**Flail Mower.** Mowing machine with a high speed rotor fitted with swinging flails which cut the grass and level it bruised in a fluffy swath.

**Flat Deck Piggery.** Piggery used for rearing weaned piglets from between two and eight weeks of age; it has a mesh floor, self-feed hoppers and controlled heating and ventilation.

**Flat Rate Feeding.** A system of feeding concentrates to dairy cows, involving few changes to the level of concentrate input; it lasts from calving to turnout.

**Flatten.** To make something flat; to make plants lie flat on the ground the stems are flattened by a roller-crusher; harvesting is difficult after the entire crop has been flattened by rain.

**Flaxseed.** Seed from the flax plant, crushed to produce linseed oil.

**Flea.** Small insect which lives as a parasite on animals, sucking their blood an causing disease, such as plague.

**Flea Beetle.** A small dark beetle which causes damage to Brassica seedlings, especially during hot dry weather between April and mid-May.

**Fleece.** Coat of wool covering a sheep or goat.

**Fleeced.** Covered with a coat of wool. The fleece is both the wool growing on the animal and the wool which has been cut off, usually in one piece, when shearing.

**Flights or Flight Feathers.** The man feathers on a bird's wing, properly called the "primaries".

**Flightless Bird.** Bird (such as the penguin) which cannot fly.

**Flint.** Hard stone of nearly pure silica, found in lumps in chalk soils. Sharp-edged flints of various sizes found in some calcareous soils are very wearing on farm implements and tractor tyres; they can also cause damage to machinery if they are picked up during harvesting. Flints are very durable and are used to form a weather-resistant facing to farm buildings and walls.

**Flock.** Large group of birds or of sheep or goats; flock book = record of the pedigree of a particular breed of sheep, kept by the breed society; flock mating = mating system which uses several males to mate with the females of a flock.

**Flockmaster.** Farm worker in charge of a flock of sheep.

**Flood.** (1) Large amount of water covering land which is normally dry (caused by melting snow, heavy rain, high tide, storms, etc.) after the rainstorm there were floods in the valleys; the spring floods have washed away most of the top soils; flood alleviation or flood control measures = ways of controlling rivers which are liable to flood.

**Flood Damage.** Damage caused by floodwater.

**Flood Irrigation or Basin Irrigation.** Irrigation using water brought down by a river in flood (the floodwaters are led off into specially prepared basins).

**Floodplain.** Wide flat part of the bottom of a valley which is usually covered with water when the river floods.

**Floodwater.** Water which floods land.

**Flora.** (i) Wild plants of a certain region; (ii) Book or list describing the plants of a region; compare FAUNA.

**Floral.** Referring to plants or flowers.

**Floret.** Little flower which forms parts of a larger composite flower head.

**Flour.** Soft fine powder made from ground cereal grains, and used for making bread. Flour is made by grinding grain, and removing impurities. White flour is flour which has had all bran and germ removed; the best quality of white flour is patent flour, which is very fine. Self-raising flour is white flour with baking powder added. Brown flour is not refined, and still contains the wheat germ and parts of the bran it if contains all the grain, it is called "wholemeal", and if it contains most of the grain it is "wheatmeal". Some expensive flours are "stone-ground", that is they are made in the traditional way with millstones.

**Floury.** Soft and powdery, like flour.

**Floury Potatoes.** Varieties of potato which, when cooked, turn easily into flour.

**Flourish.** To live well and spread the colony of rabbits flourished in the absence of any predators; the island has a flourishing plant community.

**Flower.** Usually brightly-coloured reproductive part of a plant, with an external calyx, petals, stamens and pistils which bear pollen; flowers of sulphur = powdered sulphur, sulphur which is used to dust on plants to prevent mildew.

**Fluoride.** Any chemical compound of fluorine (usually found with sodium or potassium or tin).

**Fluorosis.** Condition caused by excessive fluoride in drinking water or in eaten vegetable matter (it causes discoloration of the teeth and affects the mil yields of cattle) Fluorides such as hydrogen fluoride are emitted as pollutants from certain industrial processes ad can affect plants (especially citrus fruit) by reducing chlorophyll, they also affect cattle by reducing milk yields.

**Fly.** General term for a small insect with two wings, of the order Diptera. Some flies cause diseases of plants (the frit fly) and some harm animals (the gadfly).

**Flying Flock.** A flock of sheep imported onto a farm for a time, normally for less than a year, and then sold.

**FMA.** Fertilizer Manufacturers Association.

**Foal.** A young horse (of either sex) in its first year; mare in-foal = pregnant mare.

**Foaling.** Parturition in a mare (giving birth to a foal)

**Fodder.** General term for food given to livestock, in particular straw and hay made form dried plants such as grass, clover.

**Fodder Beet.** A root crop (bred from sugar beet and mangolds) usually grown after cereals and used to feed stock.

**Fodder Crop.** A crop, such as kale, Lucerne or hay, grown for use as animal feed. See also *Forage Crop*.

**Fodder Storage.** The storing of fodder for use in winter; buildings used for storing fodder may be of the simple Dutch barn type, and can be built cheaply using pole and a galvanized iron roof.

**Foehn.** Warm dry wind which blows down the lee side of a mountain (it is caused when moist air rises up the mountain on the windward side, loses its moisture as precipitation and then goes down the other side as a dry wind).

**Foggara.** Slightly sloping underground channels, used to bring irrigation water from aquifers near the foot of mountains to neighbouring plains, especially in the Sahara.

**Foggia.** Pits or cellars used for grain storage or as cisterns for drinking water in south-eastern Italy.

**Fold.** Moveable enclosure, made of hurdles or of electric wire fencing used to keep cattle or sheep in a certain place. (2) to put sheep into a fold; Folded sheep = sheep kept in movable folds, as a means of controlling their grazing.

**Foldland.** Formerly, an area of land allotted to each manor for the purpose of grazing the manor's sheep.

**Follar.** Referring to leaves; foliar feed or foliar spray = liquid nutrient used by farmers and gardeners to spreay onto the leaves of plats which then absorb it.

**Folic Acid.** Vitamin of the B complex.

**Follicle.** Tiny hole in the skin from which a hair grows; in birds, feathers grow from follicles.

**Followers.** (a) Young cows in a dairy herd which are to yet in milk, and are being reared to replace the older stock (b) cattle put to graze a pasture after another group of animals has used it.

**Following Crop.** Crop sown by a tenant farmer before leaving the farm at the end of his tenancy; he is permitted to return and harvest the crop and remove it.

**Food.** Things which are eaten.

**Food Balance.** The balance between food supplies and the demand for food from the population.

**Food Chain.** Series of organisms which pass energy from one to another as each provides food for the next (the first organism in the chain is a producer, all the rest are consumers).

**Food Web.** Series of food chains which are linked together in a ecosystem. Two basic kinds of food chain exist: the grazing food chain and the detrital food chain in which both plant-eaters and detritus-eaters take part. In practice, food chains are interconnected, making up food webs.

**Food and Agriculture Organisation (FAO).** International organization based in Rome; an agency of the United Nations, it was established with the purpose of encouraging higher standards of nutrition and eradicating malnutrition and hunger.

**Food and Environmental Protection Act, 1986.** Legislation which brings the use of agrochemicals under statutory control 9as opposed to the previous voluntary arrangement).

**Food Poisoning.** Illness caused by eating fcod which is contaminated with bacterial or chemical agents, or by eating bacterial or chemical agents, or by eating food which is itself poisonous (such as forms of fungi). The commonest form of food poisoning is probably that caused by the salmonella group of pathogens, found in meat and animal products.

**Foodstuffs.** Different types of food.

**Foolse Parsely.** Species of hemlock (Aetusa cynapium) which looks like parsley; it is not a common source of poisoning in animals.

**Foot Rot.** A disease of the horny parts and the soft tissue of feet of sheep. It occurs particularly in wet marshy and badly-drained pastures, and is caused primarily by the organism Fusiformis necrophorus and sometimes nodosus. It makes sheep lame.

**Forage.** (1) Crops grown for consumption by livestock; Forage box = large movable container used mainly to transport forage from a silo to a trough; forage harvester = a machine which cuts, chops and lods green crops such as Lucerne into a trailer, for making silage.

**Foreleg.** One of the two front legs of an animal (as opposed to the find legs).

**Forest.** (1) (a) Natural group of plants and animals, of which the dominant organisms are trees (a large area is a forest, a small area is a wood); *high forest* = forest made up of tall trees which block the light to the forest floor; *Mixed Forest* = forest with more than one species of tree; *the forest floor* = ground at the base of the trees in a forest (b) another name for what is really a plantation (trees and shrubs planted in rows, usually for commercial exploitation); (c) Area in which a king has the right to keep deer for hunting (d) common land within a forest where deer live (2) To manage a forest, by cutting wood as necessary, and planting new trees.

**Forested.** (Land) Covered with forest.

**Forester.** Person who manages woods and plantations of trees

**Forestry.** Management of forests, woodlands and plantations of trees.

**Forestry Commission.** Government agency responsible for the management of state-owned forests in the UK.

**Fork.** Common hand implement for turning over soil, and

lifting out weeds. Forks have four square prongs each sharpened to a point. Forks with flat prongs are used for lifting potatoes; larger, five-pronged forks with round curved prongs, are used for spreading manure.

**Fortified.** With something added to make stronger.

**Fortified Food.** Food with vitamins or proteins added to make it more nutritional. Fortified wine. Wine (such as sherry or port) with extra alcohol added.

**Forward Creep Grazing.** Grazing method where grassland which has been allocated to ewes and lamb during the fattening period, is divided into paddocks, each separated by portable fencing; as one area is finished, the fencing is moved to allow the animals to move to the next.

**Four Tooth Sheep.** Sheep which is 18-21 months of age.

**Fourth World.** The poorest countries in the non-aligned Third World.

**Fowl.** The chicken, a bird (Gallus domesticus) raised for food.

**Fowl pest.** Newcastle disease, an acute contagious disease of fowls; affected birds suffer loss of appetite, diarrhoea and respiratory problems; mortality rates are high.

**Fowl pox.** A viral disease in which wart-like nodules appear on the comb, wattles, eyelids and openings of the nostrils of fowls.

**Foxglave.** Common weed (Digitalis purpurea), the plant is poisonous and harmful to animals.

**Foxtail Millet.** *Setaria italica*, the first cereal to be cultivated in China; used for silage, hay, brewing and flour in many parts of the world, in Britain it is used as birdseed.

**Fragmentation.** Farm Fragmentation = situation where the

fields of a farm are scattered over an area, so that the holding is not made up of a single unit of land; it can be the result of inheritance practices where the land of a person who has died is split between all the children, of land reclamation schemes where the land is reclaimed piece by piece or because old open-field systems have been kept.

**Freehold.** The absolute right to hold land or property for an unlimited time without paying rent.

**Freehold Property.** Property which the owner holds in freehold

**Freeholder.** Person who holds a freehold property; compare leasehold, Leaseholder.

**Freerange.** Freerange egg = eggs from hens that are allowed to run about in the open and eat more natural food (as opposed to battery hens).

**Freeze Drying.** Method of preserving food by freezing rapidly and drying in a vacuum.

**Fresh.** Not processed (i.e. no canned or frozen) Fresh vegetable are more expensive in winter, because they have to be imported; beans are grown both for the fresh market and also for preserving; fresh fruit bunch (FEB) = very large bunch of fruit lets of the oil palm tree.

**Friesland.** Breed of sheep whose milk is used in a the production of soft cheese and yoghurt.

**Frit Fly.** A small black fly (*Oscinella frit*) that attacks wheat, maize and oats.

**Frits.** Trace elements fused with silica to form glass; this is crushed into small pieces for distribution on the soil.

**Frog.** Part of a plough to which the mouldboard and share are attached.

**Frond.** Leaves of the fern group of plants (*Pteridophyta*)

**Fructose.** Fruit sugar, found in honey as well as in fruit; high fructose corn syrup (HFCS) = sweetener used in the soft drinks industry, extracted from maize.

**Fruit.** (i) ripe ovary of a plant and its contents of seeds; (ii) in general usage, the fleshy material round the fruit which is eaten as food a diet of fresh fruit and vegetables.

**Fruit Fly.** a fly which attacks fruit. To have fruit some varieties of apple fruit very early; the drought has damaged fruiting trees; the *fruiting season* = time of year when a particular tree has fruit.

**Fruitwood.** Wood from a fruit tree (such as apple or cherry) which may be used to make furniture. Fruit contains fructose which is a good source of vitamin C and some dietary fibre. Dried fruit have a higher sugar content but less vitamin C than fresh fruit.

**Full-time Farmer.** Farmer who derives his living from agriculture, as distinct from a part-time farmer.

**Full-time worker.** Farmworker engaged full-time in work on a farm.

**Fungus.** Simple plant organism with thread-like cells (such as yeast, mushrooms, mould) and without green chlorophyll.

**Fungus disease.** Disease caused by a fungus; fungus poisoning = poisoning by eating a poisonous fungus.

**Fungal.** Referring to fungi.

**Fungicidal.** (Paint) which kills fungi.

**Fungold.** Like a fungus. Some fungi can become parasites of animals and cause diseases such as aspergillosis. Other fungi cause plant diseases, such as blight. Others, such as yeast, react with sugar to form alcohol. Fungicides are available as sprays or dusts for sue on crops.

**FUW.** Farmers Union of Wales

**FWAG.** Farming and Wildlife Advisory Group a voluntary organisation, established in 1969 to encourage understanding between farmers and conservationists.

**FWT.** Farming and Wildlife Trust a trust formed to fund the FWAG and also to provide advisors in various parts of the country.

# G

**Gadfly.** A fly that bites cattle, one of the genera *Tabanus* (the horsefly) or *Oestrus* (the both fly), most common from late May onwards, and causing considerable trouble to cattle.

**Gage.** Variety of plum, especially the greengage.

**Galician Blond.** Breed of cattle from northern Spain; it is a triple-purpose breed red in colour, with yellow horns.

**Gallon.** (a) A measure of capacity, equivalent to eight pints or 4.55 litres; used both for liquids and for measuring dry goods, such as grain.

**Galloway.** A hardy breed of completely black hornless cattle. The coat is distinctive, being formed of long wavy hairs covering a soft undercoat. The Galloway originated in the wet and hilly south-west originated in the wet and hilly south-west of Scotland. It is reared mainly for beef.

**Galvanized Iron.** Iron which has been coated with zinc to prevent it rusting; galvanized iron sheeting is widely used for roofs.

**Game.** Animals which are killed for sport (and food), and listed in the UK under the Game Act which defines the shooting seasons.

**Game Birds.** Wild birds which are classified as game, and which cane be shot only during certain seasons (the most important in the UK are pheasant, partridge and grouse)

The Game Conservancy. An organization concerned with the conservation of game species; it advises on shoots and woodland management. The long-term aim of the conservancy is to increase the production of wild game by careful management of habitats. It claims that certain game birds such as the black grouse, the grey partride and capercaillie are at risk. Game, such as pheasants and partridge, I an important asset on some farms, and letting land for sport shooting is a source of high income.

**Gamma Rays.** Rays which are shorter than X=rays, given off by radioactive substances and used in food irradiation.

**Gander.** Male Goose.

**Gangrene.** Serious rot affecting potato tubers; caused by fungi, it spreads in storage.

**Gantry.** New type of farm machine consisting of a long steel beam with implement carriers. The engine and cab are at one end of the beam, and the drive wheel is at the other end; currently, gantries are 12m wide.

**Garden.** (a) Land cultivated as a hobby or for pleasure, rather than to produce an income; flower garden = garden where only flowers are grown; kitchen garden = garden with herbs and small vegetables, ready for use in the kitchen (b) market garden = farm near a town, providing fresh vegetables and salad crops for sale in the town's market

**Gardener.** Person who looks after a garden.

**Gardening.** Horticulture or looking after a garden; market gardening = growing fresh vegetables and salad crops for sale in a nearby town.

**Garl.** Coarse meal made from fermented cassava, an important food in West Africa; compare FARINHA.

**Garlic.** Plant (*Allium sativum*) with a strong-smelling pungent root used as a flavouring in cooking. The bulb consists of a series of wedge-shaped closes, surrounded by a white fibrous skin.

**Garrigue.** Dense undergrowth of armatic shrubs found in Mediterranean regions accompanying every green and cork oak.

**Gasconne.** Breed of beef cattle from the Gascony area of south-west France; the animals ar esiler-grey in colour with medium length horns.

**Gastr- or Gastro.** Referring to the stomach.

**Gastric.** Referring to the stomach; gastric acid = hydrochloric acid secreted into the stomach by acid-forming cells of the lining membrane of the stomach to help the digestion o food.

**Gastro-Enteritis.** Viral infection which causes inflammation of the membranes lining the stomach and intestines; parasitic gastro-enteritis (PGE) = infection of the stomach caused by roundworms, especially Osteragia transmissible gatro-enteritis (TGE) = very infectious form of the disease, which affects young pigs.

**Gaur.** The Indian bison; a large wild ox which is dark brown in colour with long curved horns.

**Gayal.** Ox similar to the gaur, but domesticated in north-west India to produce meat and hides.

**Geest.** Infertile sandy lowland region of North and East Germany, covered with heath.

**Gelatin.** Protein which is soluble in water, and which is extracted from animal bones and bones; it is used in laboratories as a culture medium.

**Gene.** Unit of DNA on a chromosome which governs the synthesis of one protein, usually an enzyme, and determines a particular characteristic of an organism; gene Bank = collection of seeds from wild plants, which may be found to be useful in the future for breeding new varieties; gene pool = all the best quality animals and plants which can be used for further breeding; see GENETIC.

Genes are either dominant, when the characteristic is always passed on to the offspring, or recessive, when the characteristic only appears if both parents have contributed a recessive gene.

**Generic.** Referring to a genus; generic name = the name of a genus. Organisms arê usually identified by using their generic and specific names, e.g. Homo sapiens (man) and *Felix catus* (domestic cat), The generic name is written or printed with a capital letter. Both names are usually given in italics, or are underlined if written or typed.

**Genetics.** Study of the way the characteristics of an organism are inherited through the genes.

Comparisons of today's farm animals with those of the past show considerable differences in appearance and productivity. Today's dairy cattle have no horns, and produce two or three times as much milk as their ancestors in the 19th century. This is in part due to genetic improvement of livestock by selection of superior animals for breeding.

**Genotype.** Genetic composition of an organism.

**Genus.** The second major rank in classification of living things, a group of closely-related species, the members of which are more closely related to each other than they are to members of other genera s\(several genera form a family).

**Germicide.** Substance used to kill germs.

**German Red Pied.** Breed of cattle from north-west Germany; mainly raised for meat, the animals are red and white in colour.

**Gestation.** Period when a female animal has living young in there uterus.

**Gestation Period.** The time between conception and birth. This varies with different animals; for cows it is 283 days, for mares 340 days, for ewes and goats 144 –150 days and for sows 114 days.

**Get-way Cage.** A poultry cage which is designed to provide more spare for each bird. It separates the roosting area from the laying area and provides means of feeding and drinking.

**Gezira.** Large-scale irrigation and farming are a in the Sudan; with over 100,000 tenant farmers producing cotton, sorghum, groundnuts, wheat. fodder crops and vegetables.

**Ghee.** Butter made from buffalo milk, clarified to look like oil. It is used widely in the Indian subcontinent as a cooking fat. Vegetable ghee can be made from groundnut and palm oil.

**Gherkin.** Small cucumber grown for pickling.

**Gibberellins.** Plant growth hormone which helps flower formation and accelerates germination.

**Gilt.** A young female pig.

**Ginger.** Spice plant (*Zinzibler officinle*) grown in many parts of the tropics. It grows from one to three feet high and consists of an enlarged underground stem or rhizome, with erect stems with narrow leaves above the soil. The stem is used in oriental cooking, and powdered ginger prepared from the dried rhizome is used in particular in confectionery.

**Gir.** Indian breed of cattle, raised for milk. The animals are red or grey, with horns and a pronounced hump.

**Gizzard.** The muscular stomach óf a bird, in which food is ground up, helped by the grit and small stones which collect there.

**Glasshouse or Greenhouse.** Building made of glass, used for raising plants. The most important glasshouse crop in England is tomatoes. When heated it is also called a "hothouse"

**Glaucous.** Green colour with a white bloom, giving a plant a greenblue appearance (as in some varieties of cabbage).

**Gluten.** The protein in a seed, such as wheat or maize; the nitrogenous part of flour which remains when the starch is extracted; corn gluten or maize gluten = type of animal feed made from the residues after starch has been extracted from grain.

The gluten is what makes dough elastic and bred soft; millet and rice do not contain gluten and so cannot be used- for making bread.

**Goad.** A spiked stick used to prod cattle.

**Goatling.** Female goat between the ages of one and two years, which has not yet borne a kid.

**Golden Guernsey.** Breed of goat.

**Golden Triangle.** An area of south East Asia on the borders of Burma, Thailand, Laos and China, believed to be the area where rice was first domesticated.

**Goose.** Large heavy bird, between a duck and a swan in size. Possibly this was one of the first will birds to be domesticated. Geese are raised especially for table birds at Christmas. In France, goose livers are used to make pate de foie gras.

**Gooseberry.** Softfruit, usually green in colour, from a small prickly bush; gooseberries are rarely eaten raw, but are usually cooked or preserved.

**Gourd.** Frit of a trailing or climbing plant. Many varieties re cultivated either as ornamental plants or to provide dried bottle-like containers which can be used as utensils such as water carriers.

**Gout Fly.** Small fly whose larvae hatch and feed on shoots and ears of cereals; barley is mainly affected.

**Graft.** (1) Piece of plant or animal tissue transplanted onto another plant or animal and growing there (2) To transplant a piece of tissue from one plant or animal to another.

Many cultivated plants are grafted. The piece of tissue from the original plant (or scion) is placed on a cut made in the outer back of the host plant (the stock) so that a bond takes place. The aim is usually to ensure that the hardy qualities of the stock are able to benefit the weaker cultivated scion. The scion tissue may be a sort shoot or simply a bud. The main methods of grafting are; the crown graft, here a branch of a tree is cut across at right angles, slight made in the bark around the edge of the stump, and shoots inserted into the slits; and the v-graft, where the stem of the stock is cutting is split to allow it to be fitted over the point of the stock.

**Grain.** (a) Cereal crop, such as corn, of which the seeds are dried and eaten; grain drill = machine used for sowing cereals in rows; grain drier = machine which dries moist grain, before storage; the grain is subjected to hot or warm air; grain lifters = attachments to the cutter bar of a combine harvester, which lift the stems of cerea crops which have been beaten down by bad weather, and so allow the crop to be cut and gathered; grain pan = part of a combine where the treshed grain collects and is shaken through to the bottom of the machine; grain reserves = amount of grain held in a store by a country which is estimated to be above the country's requirements for one year; grain spear = instrument for measuring the temperature and moisture of stored grain (it consists of athermometer and hygrometer at the end of a long or which is pushed into the grain); grain storage = keeping grain until it is sold or used. Most grain is stored on the farm until it is sold, and is kept in bins or in bulk on the floor of the granary. Eh system of storage depends on whether the grain is to be used for feedings tuffon the farm, or is to be sold; grain tank = storage area at the top of a combine, in which threshed grain is kept; when the tank is full, the grain is transferred to a trailer; grain weevil = reddish brown weevil; itlays eggs in stored grain; the larvae feed inside the grain where they also pupate.

**Gram.** (In India and Pakistan) the chick pea, the most important pulse grown in the Indian subcontinent; green gram = mug, an Indian pulse used as a vegetable or also to produce bean sprouts; red gram = the pigeon pea, used in India to make dhal.

**Granular.** In the form of granules.

**Grape.** Fruit of woody perennial vines (*Vitis*)

**Grapevine.** The vine on which grapes grow. Grapes are grown in most areas of the world that have a Mediterranean climate, and even in temperate areas like southern England and central Germany. They are eaten as fruit, dried to make currants and raisins, or crushed to make grape juice and wine.

**Grapefruit.** Citrus fruit of a tree (*Citrus paradisi*) similar to the orange. The fruit is lemon-yellow when ripe, about twice the size of an orange, and very juicy.

**Grass.** Flowering monocotyledon of which there are a great many genera, including wheat, barley, rice, oats; an important food for herbivores and humans; *cows at grass* = cows which are grazing in a field; *grass staggers* = hypomagnesaemia, a condition caused by lack of magnesium in he blood stream; animals shiver and stagger. Cattle may be affected shortly after being turned out onto spring pasture after having wintered indoors; see also *Gramineae*.

**Grassland.** Land covered by grasses, especially wide open spaces such as the prairies of North America or the pampas of South America. Grasis the most important crop in the UK. It occupies about two-thirds of the total crop area. Grasslands can be divided into the following types; Rough Mountain and Hill grazing: not of great value, the plants being mainly fescues, bents, nardus and molinia grasses permanent pastures; these are never ploughed, and the quality depends on the percentage of perennial ryegrass; leys; these are temporary grassland which are sown to grass for a limited period (usually one to five years). The year in which the seed mixture is sown is known as the "seeding year". At the end of the first year there is the first year harvest. Sowing the seeds mixture with a cover crop is known as "undersowing". "Direct sowing" is sowing on bare ground without a cover crop. The main species used in grasslands are: Grasses: perennial ryegrass, cocksfoot. Timothy, Italian ryegrass and meadow fescue; clovers: red clover, white clover other legumes: Lucerne, sainfoin: herbs: yarrow, chicory, rib grass, burnet. Farmers depend on reliable seed firms to supply them with standard seed mixtures.

**Gravity Feed.** System where pellets, seeds or granules, fall from a hopper into a distribution channel.

**Graze.** (a) (of animals) to feed on grass sheep grazing on the hillside will keep the grass short (b) (of a farmer) to put animals in a field to eat grass.

**Grazing.** (a) Action of feeding animals on growing grass; grazing food chain = food chain in which the energy in vegetation is eaten by animals, digested, then passed into the soil as dung and so taken up gain by plants which are eaten by animals, etc. (b) land covered with grass, suitable for animals to feed on there is good grazing on the mountain pastures; grazing systems = different methods of pasture management; see *Forward creep grazing. Paddock grazing Rotational grazing, strip grazing, zero grazing.*

**Green.** (a) the colour like the colour of grass or leaves (the green colour in plants s provided by chlorophyll); Green gram = mung, an Indian pulse used as a vegetable or also to produce bean sprouts; Green manure = rapid-growing green vegetation (such as mustard plats or rape) which is grown and ploughed into the soil to rot and act as manure; green manuring = growing green crops and ploughing them in to increase the organic content of the soil. (b) Village green = grass-covered area in the centre of a village, around which cottages are built; Green village = a nucleated village settlement. Built round a village green (c) immature; green wood = new shoots on a tree, which have not ripened fully (d) referring to an interest in ecological and environmental problems.

**Green Consumerism.** Movement to encourage people to buy food and other products which are environmentally good (such as organic foods lead-free petrol, etc.).

**Green Belt.** Area of agricultural land or woodland or parkland which surrounds an urban area.

Green belt land is protected, and building is restricted and often completely forbidden. The aim of setting up a Green Belt is to prevent urban sprawl and reduce city pollution.

**Greenfly.** Type of aphid, a small insect which sucks sap from plans and can multiply very rapidly. Greenfly attack young shoots which have a softer texture; various species of greenfly feed on cereal crops in May and June. Greenfly can carry virus diseases from infected plants to clean ones.

**Greengage.** Varity of cooking plum, which is hard and green.

**Greenhouse.** Building made mostly of glass, used to raise and protect plants.

Greenhouses are used in temperate areas to grow plants which cannot be grown out of doors; either to bring the plants on early (raising seedlings to be planed out later) or to grow plants out of season (Tomatoes can be grown in greenhouses during the winter months.) A cold greenhouse (i.e. A greenhouse without any heating)

**Greenhouse Effect.** Effect produced by the accumulation of carbon dioxide crystalsad water vapour in the upper atmosphere, which insulates the earth and raises the atmopheric temperature by preventing heat loss; greenhouse gases = gases (carbon dioxide, methane, CFCs and nitrogen oxides) which are produced by burning fossil fuels and which rise into the atmosphere, preventing heat loss.

**Green Revolution.** Development of new forms of cereal plants such as wheat and rice and the use of more powerful fertilizers, which hive much higher yields and increase the food production especially in tropical countries.

**Greens.** Green vegetables, such as cabbages; winter greens = hardy varieties of Brassica which are grown for use during the winter.

**Grey Leaf.** Disease of cereals caused by manganese deficiency.

**Grid.** Cattle grid = type of grill made of parallel bars, covering a hole dug in the road; it prevents stock from crossing the grid and leaving their pasture, but allows vehicles and humans to pass.

**Grind.** To crush or roll something until is reduced to powder wheat grain is ground in mills to make various s grades of flour.

**Grist.** (i) corn for grinding; (ii) malt crushed for brewing.

**Groom.** (10 Person who looks after horses (2) To look after animals, especially horses, by brushing cleaning and combing.

**Groundnut.** *Arachis hypogaea* the peanut, a grain legume, and one of the main oilseeds; groundnut cake = the residue left after oil extraction from groundnuts, a valuable protein concentrate for livestock.

Groundnuts (or peanuts) are used in the production of vegetable oil for cooking, in salad dressings and in the making of margarine. Poorer quality oils are used to make soap. Eaten raw or roasted or cooked in various ways, groundnuts figure prominently in West African cooking. In the USA, much of crop is made into peanut butter. The USA. Argentina, Nigeria, Sudan and Indonesia are major exporters of groundnuts, while Canada and Western Europe are the main importing countries.

**Grow.** (a) (of a plant) to exist and flourish bananas grow only in warm hum it conditions; tomatoes grow well in greenhouses (b) (of plants and animals) to become taller or bigger the tree grows a new ring each year; the plant grew three centimeters in one years; growing point = point on h stem of a plant where growth occurs (often at the tip of the stem or branch); growing season = period of the year when a plant grows; the growing season is especially important in temperate latitudes where the length of the growing season is usually limited by low temperatures alpine plants have a short growing season (c) (of people) to cultivate (plants) farmers here grow two crops in a year; he grows peas for the local caning factory; growing early vegetables is difficult because of the cold winters.

**Growth.** (a) Increase in size; amount by which something increases in size the diseases stunts the conifers; growth; the growth in the got population since 1960; the rings show the annual growth of the tree; *growth promoter* = substance which makes a plant or animal growing *growth regulator* = a chemical used to control the growth of certain plants; mainly used for weed control in cereals and grassland; growth retardant = substance used to slow or stop the growth of plant; *growth rings* = rings seen in the cross-section of the trunk of a felled tree, each one added during a single year; see also *Annual Rings*.

**Guava.** Common tree (*Psidium guajava*) originating in West Africa but now grown in tropical areas allover the world; it is easily grown and produces yellow-skinned, pink-fleshed fruits which are excellent for eating.

**Guernsey.** Breed of dairy cattle; the coat is fawn, with distinct patches of white. The Guernsey is similar to the Jersey, but larger. The breed is noted for the rich colour of the milk, the high butterfat content and the good milk yields obtained.

**Guinea Fowl.** Table bird, found wild in savanna regions of Africa. Small numbers are raised for their meat which has a delicate flavour similar to that of game birds.

**Gunter's Chain.** Chain originally used by surveyors to measure land.

**Gypsum.** Calcium sulphate, sometimes used to improve salt-affected soils.

# H

**Ha.** Hectare

**Habitat.** Area of the environment in which an organism lives.

**Hacienda.** Large agricultural estate found mainly in Spanish-speaking countries.

**Hackles.** Long feathers on the neck of a domestic cock.

**Hairworm.** Very thin worm of the species Capellaria, which infests poultry.

**Half-breed.** Animal of mixed breed, mainly applied to crossbred sheep.

**Half-Hardy.** (Garden plants) which can stand a certain amount of cold.

**Half-Standard.** Type of fruit tree, with a stem trunk which is shorter than for a full standard (about 1.2m from the ground to the first branches)

**Halomorphic Soil.** Soil which contains large amounts of salt.

**Halophyte.** Plant which lives in salty soil.

**Hamlet.** Group of Farmhouses. Cottages and farm buildings in a rural area.

**Hammer Mill.** Machine used in the preparation of animal feed by grinding cereals into meal.

**Hampahire Down.** Short stocky early-maturing sheep, originating from Berkhire ewe flocks and Southdown rams.

**Hardwood.** Slow-growing broad-leaved tree (such as oak or teak) which produces a hard wood with a fine grain; hardwoods = forests of hardwood trees.

**Haricot Bean.** Dry ripe seed of the French bean.

**Harmattan.** Hot drywinter wind which blows from the north-east and causes dust storms in the Sahara.

**Harrow.** (1) Farm implement, made of a series of spikes or tines which is dragged across the surface of ploughed soil to prepare seed bedsand to destroy weeds. Harrows arealso usedtocover seeds with soil. There are a number of different types, including chain, disc, dutch, power and spike tooth harrows. (2) to level the surface of ploughed soil, covering seeds which have been sown in furrows.

**Harvest.** (i) Action of gathering a crop (ii) time when a crop is gathered; (iii) the crop which is gathered we think this year's rice harvest will be a good one. To gather a crop which is ripe they are harvesting the rice crop; clear cutting is one of the methods of harvestings timber.

**Harvester.** Machine which harvests a crop; most crops are now harvested by machines such as combine harvesters or sugar beet harvesters; see also *Forage Harvester*.

**Haryana.** Breed of cattle found in the Indian sub-continent.

**Hatch.** Brood of chicks.

**Hatchery.** Unit which specializes in the hatching of eggs. A hen will naturally sit on her eggs until they hatch, Incubators are used to hatch large numbers of eggs by artificial means.

**Haulm.** Stalks and stems of peas, beans and potatoes.

**Hawthorn.** Small tree (*Crataegus monogyna*) with spiny shoots, used for hedges round grazing areas.

**Hayloader.** Implement for loading hay from the field into a trailer.

**Haymaking.** Conserving a grass crop for use as fodder.

**Hay-sweep.** Implement used to collect hay from swaths and carry it to a stack. Hay is cut before the grass flowers; at this stage in its growth it is a nutritious fodder. If it is mowed after it has flowered it is called straw, and is of much less use as a food, an so is used for bedding. Haymaking normally needs three to our days of fine weather in early season and two to three days when the humidity falls as temperatures rise. The critical period for hay occurs when the crop is partly dried in the field. The object should be to dry the cp as much as possible without too much exposure to sun, and the least possible movement after the crop is partially dry. Field-dried hay is normally baled, and further barn drying is common.

**Hazel.** A nut-bearing tree (*Corylus avellana*); the Kentish cob or filbert is a commercially grown hazel.

**Head Corn.** Largest grain in a sample of cereal.

**Headland.** Land at the edges of a field where the plough is turned; it is the last part of the field to be ploughed.

**Headrail.** Rail across the front of a cubicle, to which a halter can be attached.

**Heartwood.** The central hard dead wood in a tree trunk, as opposed to the sapwood.

**Heat.** (a) Warmth which is produced by electricity or hot air or warm pipes; to sow lettuces under heat= to sow lettuce seed in a heated greenhouse; heat-sealing = method of closing plastic food containers; air is removed from a plastic bag with the food inside and the bag is then pressed by a hot plate which melts the plastic and seals the contents in the vacuum (b) the oestrus period, when a female will allow mating; an animal on heat = female animal in the oestrus period, when she will accept a male.

**Heathland.** Wide area of heath largely waste ground, though it may provide some grazing.

**Heather.** Plant (*Calluna vulgaris*) found on acid soils, common in upland Heaves. Condition of horses, where spores from mouldy hay block the animals lungs, making breathing difficult.

**Heavy Grains (HG).** Cereal crops such as maize, rye and wheat (as opposed to the light grains, barley and oats).

**Hebridean Sheep.** A rare breed of small black sheep of Scandinavian origin; the fleece is jet-black in colour, and the animals have one pair of horns curling downwards and another pair almost upright.

**Hedgelaying.** Traditional method of cultivating hedges, where tall saplings are partly cut through near the base, and then bent over so that they lie horizontally and make a thick barrier.

**Hedgerow.** Line of bushes forming a hedge.

**Hedging.** Art of cultivating hedges. It is said that you can judge the age of a hedgeby counting the species in it and multiplying by 100: the more species there are, the older the hedge is About three-quarters of the farms in England and Walves have hedges, with an estimated total length of 500,000 km. In the last years. 8,000km of hedges have been removed and about 4,000m. have been planted.

**Hen.** (A) female of the common domestic fowl (b) also any female bird, such as a hen pheasant; see also *fat hen.*

**Henhouse.** Small wooden building for keeping hens.

**Herb.** (a) plant which has no perennial stem above the ground during the winter period (b) plant which can be used as a medicine or to give a certain taste to food or to give a certain scent.

**Herbaceous.** (Plant) without perennial stems above the ground; herbaceous border = bed of herbaceous plants growing aong the edge of a lawn.

**Herdsman.** Male farm worker who looks after a herd of livestock.

**Herringbone Parlour.** Type of milking parlour with no stalls and where the operator works from a central pit. The cattle stand side by side at an angle on each side of the central pit.

**HFCS.** High Fructose Corn Syrup.

**Hg.** Chemical symbol for mercury.

**HG.** Heavy Grains.

**HGCA.** Home grown Cereals Authority.

**Hide.** Animal skin, which is important commercially both in its raw state and as leather.

**Highland.** Hardy breed of beef cattle, with a long shaggy hair hiding a dense undercoat; the breed is small, with very long horns, and matures slowly; it is native to the Highlands and Western Isles of Scotland.

**Hill Farms.** Farms in mountainous country, with 95% or more of their land classified as rough grazing, depending mainly on breeding ewe flocks.

**Hill Grazing.** Grassland used for sheep and cattle grazing in hilly and mountainous areas. The main plants grown are fescues, bents, nardus and molinia grasses, as well as cotton grass, heather and gorse.

**Hind.** Referring to the back part of an animal.

**Hoe.** (1) Implement pulled by a tractor to turn the soil between rows of crops, and so to control weeds; Hand hoe = garden implement, with a small sharp blade, used to break up the surface of the soil or to cut off weeds (2) to cultivate land with a hoe.

There are several types of hand hoe, including the Dutch hoe, where the blade is more or less straight and is pushed by the operator, the draw hoe has the blade set at right angles to the handle and is used for drawing drills at seed-sowing time. The Canterbury hoe does not have a lade, but is like a three-pronged fork, with the prongs set a right angles to the handle.

**Home Farm.** Farm on a large estate, usually farmed by the owner.

**Home Grown Cereals Authority (HGCA).** Organization established to improve the production and marking of home-grown what, barley, maize oats and rye; the authority promotes research into cereal growing; it is also engaged in intervention buy in and selling of cereals.

**Homogenized Milk.** Milk which is made more digestible by breaking up the fat droplets into smaller particles which are evenly distributed through the liquid.

**Honey.** Sweet yellow fluid collected by bees from nectar in flowers, and store din a beehive.

**Honey Bee.** Common hive-bee.

**Honeycomb.** Construction of wax, made by bees for storing honey.

**Hoot.** Horny casing of the foot of a horse, a cow or other animals.

**Hopper.** Container with a hole at the bottom, for holding seed or fertilizer granules; the seed drops from eh hole onto the ground or into channels taking it to drills.

**Orizon.** Layer in the soil. In general, the topsoil is called the "A" horizon, the subsoil the "B" horizon, and the underlying rock the "C" horizon.

**Hornless.** Without horns a hornless breed of cattle.

**Hornbeam.** *Carpinus betulus*, tree which produces a very hard wood, formerly used in making wheels for farm carts.

**Horse.** Hoofed animal with a flowing mane and tail, used on farms as a working animal, now mainly replaced by tractors.

**Horse.** Hoofed animal with a flowing mane and tail, used on farms as a working animal, now mainly replaced by tractors. The main groups of horses are: the Heavy Draught class, such as the shire horse; the Light Draught Class, such s the Cleveland Bay; the Saddle and Harness Cass, such as the hackney,; the Pony Class, such as the Shetland.

**Horticulture.** Gardening, the growing of fruit, flowers and vegetables for food or decoration.

**Horticultural.** Referring to horticulture allotment holders show their vegetables at the local horticultural show.

**Horticulturist.** Gardener, person who specializes in horticulture.

**Hosier System.** System of dairy cattle management, where the milking of crows is down in the field using a milking pail.

**Hull.** (i) outer covering of a cereal seed (hulls form bran); (ii) the pod of peas or beans.

**Huller.** Kind of threshing machine which removes seeds from their husks.

**Hybrid.** (a) Cross between two varieties or species of plant or animal; Hybrid vigour = increase in size or rate of growth or fertility or resistance to disease found in offspring of a cross between two species. (B) The first generation of a cross between two species or two which differ in one or more genes.

**Hydridization.** Production of hybrids.

**Hydridize.** To produce hybrids by crossing varieties of plants or animals.

**Hydroponics.** Science of growing plants without soil but in sand or other granular material using a liquid solution of nutrients to feed them.

# I

**IACR.** Institute of Arable Crops research.

**IAH.** Institute for Animal Health.

**ICA.** International Coffee Agreement, agreement between countries to stabilize the price of coffee.

**ICCA.** International Cocoa Agreement, agreement between countries to stabilize the price of cocoa.

**ICCO.** International Cocoa Organization international organisation set up to stabilize the international market in cocoa by holding buffer stocks to offset seasonal differences in production quantities.

**ICO.** International Coffee Organisation International organisation set up to stabilize the international market in coffee by holding buffer stocks to offset seasonal differences in production quantities.

**IFR.** Institute of Food Research.

**IGAP.** Institution for Grassland and Animal Production.

**IHR.** Institute of Horticulture research.

**IITA.** International Institute of Tropical Agriculture.

**ILCA.** International livestock Centre for Africa.

**ILRAD.** International Laboratory for Research on Animal Diseases. Immunization. Making an animal immune to an infection, either by injecting an antiserum (passive immunization) by giving the body the disease in such a small dose that the body does not develop the disease, but produces antibodies to counteract it.

**Implement.** Tool, piece of equipment used for a certain job. Agricultural Implements. Tools, such as billhooks, scythes, which are used on farms; garden implements = implements such as forks and spades which are used in the garden.

**Importer.** Person or company which imports produce a grain importer.

**Impoverish.** To make poor over farming has impoverished the soil.

**Improve.** To make better; improved varieties = new species of plants which are stronger, or more productive than old species.

**Inbreeding.** Breeding between a closely related male and female, who have the same parents or grandparents, which strengthens he dominant trait in the breed, but also increases the possibility of congenital defects.

**Inbreeding Depression.** Reduction of characteristic strong traits by inbreeding; compare Outbreeding.

**Inbred.** Suffering from inbreeding. Inbreeding sorts out some of the best qualities in stock and has been used to establish uniform flocks or herds carrying distinctive traits.

**Incorporate.** (i) To apply chemicals, such as slug pellets, by spreading them in rows at the same time as the seed is sown, as opposed to broadcasting; (ii) to plough back straw or green manure into the soil.

**Incorporation.** Introducing chopped straw, green manure, etc. into the soil as it is being ploughed.

**Incubation.** Hatching of eggs either by a sitting bird or by artificial means in an incubator; incubation period = (i) the length of time take for a chick to hatch; (ii) length of time between the infection of an animal by a disease and the appearance of the first symptoms.

**Incubator.** Special unit providing artificial heat used to hatch eggs; available as small trays, or as large rooms for large-scale producers.

**Indefinite Inflorescence.** Inflorescence where the stems bearing the flowers continue to grow.

**Indian Buffalo.** Domesticated water buffalo used as a draught animal in Indian and Sri Lanka; the animals are grey, black or dark brown in colour, with large horns. Buffalo milk is used for making butter.

**Indian Game.** Breed of table poultry, often black with yellow legs.

**Indigenous.** Which is native to a place oas are indigenous to the British Isles; the government encourages the planting of Indigenous hardwoods where possible.

**Indigo.** Blue dye extracted from species of the Indigofera bush.

**Infect.** To contaminate with disease producing microorganisms or toxins; to transmit infection; infected area = place where animals must be kept in isolation as a result of a notice issued by the Animals Inspector when an animal is suspected or known to have a notifiable disease.

**Infection.** Entry of microbes into the body, which then multiply in the body.

**Infectivity.** Being infective.

**Infertile.** (i) Not able to bear fruit; (ii) (of animal) not able to produce young; (iii) (of soil) barren or not able to produce good crops.

**Infertility.** Not being fertile or not being able to reproduce. An infertile soil is one which is deficient in plant nutrients. The fertility of a soil at any one time is partly due to its natural makeup, and partly to its condition, which is largely dependent on the management of the soil in recent times. Application of fertilizers can raise soil fertility; bad management can decrease it. Infertility in cattle can be a serious problem and may e caused by disease such as contagious abortion, or by lack of or imbalance in minerals in the diet.

**Infest.** (of parasites) to be present in large numbers pine forests have been infested with beetles; infested plants should be dug up and burnt.

**Infestation.** Having large numbers of parasites the crop showed serious infestation with greenfly.

**Infestation.** Having large numbers of parasities the crop showed serious infestation with greenfly.

**Infiltration.** (i) Passing of waste water into the soil or into a drainage system; (ii) irrigation system where water passes through many small channels to reach the fields; Infiltration capacity = rate at which water is absorbed by soil.

**Inflorescence.** A flower or group of small flowers, together with the stems called spikelets.

There are two types of inflorescence: indefinite inflorescence is where the branches bearing the flowers continue to grow; where the main stem ends in a singe flower and then stops growing is known as definite inflorescence.

**Inject.** To put a liquid into an animal's body under pressure, by using a hollow needle inserted into the tissues the cow was injected with antibiotics.

**Injection.** (a) Act of injecting a liquid into the body; Intramuscular Injection. Injection of liquid into a muscle (as for a slow release of a drug); Intravenous injection = injection of liquid into a vein (as for fast release of a drug); hypodermic injection or subcutaneous injection = injection of a liquid beneath the skin (As for painkilling drugs) (b) liquid introduced into the body the vet gave the bull an injection of antibiotics.

**Inoculate.** To introduce vaccine into an animal's body in order to make the body create antibodies, so making the animal immune to the disease the animals are inoculated against pneumonia.

**Inorganic.** (substance) which does not come from animal or vegetabele sources and does not contain carbon inorganic substances include acids, alkalis and metals; inorganic fertilizer = artificial synthesized fertilizer (as opposed to manure, compost and other organic fertilizers which are produced from bones, blood and other parts of formerly living matter); inorganic pesticide or fungicide or herbicide = pesticide or fungicide or herbicide made from inorganic substances such as sulphur.

**Insecticide.** Natural or synthetic substance which kills insects. Insects form the class Insecta. The body of an insect is divided into three distinct parts: the head, the thorax and the abdomen. The six legs are attached to the thorax. There are two antennae on the head. Most insect bites are simply irritating, but some people can be extremely sensitive to eh bites of certain types of insect (such as bee stings). Other insect bites can be more serious, as insects can carry the bacteria which produce typhus, sleeping sickness, malaria, filariasis, etc. natural insecticides (i.e. those produced from plant extracts) are less harmful to the environment than the synthetic insecticides which, though effective, are often persistent and kill not only insects but also other large animals when they get into the food chain. In agriculture, most pesticides are chemically based; they re either chlorinated hydrocarbons, organophosphorous compounds or carbamate compounds. Insecticides are used in a number of ways, including spraying and dusting, or in granular forms as seed dressings. In the form of a gas, insecticides are used to fumigate greenhouses and granaries.

**Inspector.** Official whose job is to examine animals or soil or buildings, etc., to see if they are in conformity with government regulations; Animals Inspector = official whose job is to inspect animals to see if they have notifiable disease, are being kept in acceptable conditions, etc.

**Intake.** (a) Amount of a substance taken into an organism (either eaten or absorbed) a study of food intake among grassland animals; the bird's daily intake of insects is more than half its own weight (b) hill pasture which has been improved and fenced in.

**Intensity.** Degree to which land is used; Low-intensity land = land one which crops are not intensively cultivated.

**Intensification.** Doing something in an intensive way intensification of farming has contributed to soil erosion.

**Intensive.** Intensive Agriculture = system of farming characterized by a high level of inputs, especially capital, labour and fertilizer, per unit area of land; intensive beef production = production of a young lean production = production of a young lean beef animal in a period of less than a year; Intensive cultivation or intensive farming = (farming) in which as much use is made of the land as possible (growing crops close together or growing several crops in a year or using large amounts of fertilizer); Intensive livestock production = specialized system of livestock production where the livestock are housed indoors; this system can be started up at any time of the year; disease hazards are those related to diet and permanent housing for the whole of the animal's life.

**Intensively.** In an intensive way.

**Interbreed.** To breed together (individuals from the same species can interbreed; those from different species cannot) Interbreeding of close relatives can sometimes give a concentration of desirable traits. This was much used by breed pioneers, but it can also increase the frequency of inherited physical defects and breeding plants based on interbreeding are now rare.

**Intercrop.** (1) Crop which is grown between the rows of other crops, such as barley and mustard or pigeon pea and black gram (2) To grow crops between the rows of other crops.

**Interculture.** The practice of mixed cropping, where two or more different crops are grown together on the name area of land.

**Intermediate.** Between two extremes; intermediate host = host on which a parasite lives for a time before passing on a to another; intermediate technology – technology which is between the advanced electronic technology of industrialized countries and the primitive technology in underdeveloped countries.

**Intermuscular Fat.** Fat between muscles (as opposed to intramuscular fat)

**Internal Lying.** Condition in hens caused by a fault in the oviduct, which results in the yolks not being passed along the oviduct for covering with membranes and shell.

**International.** Between countries; International Union for the Conservation of Nature (IUCN) = international organization which coordinates the protection of species throughout the words; International Cocao Organization (CCO) = international organization set up to stabilize the international market in cocoa by holding buffer stocks to offset seasonal differences in production quantities; International Coffee Organization (ICO) = international organization set up to stabilize the international market in coffee by holding buffer stocks to offset seasonal differences in production quantities; International

Crops Research Institute for the Semi-Arid Tropics (ICRISAT). organization established in 1972 at Hyderabad, India.

**International Institute of Tropical Agriculture (IITA)** . Organization established at Ibadan, Nigeria in 1965.

**International Livestock Centre for Africa (ILCA).** Organization established in 1974 at Addis Ababa, Ethiopia; International Laboratory for Research on Animal Disease (IILRAD) = Organization established at Nairobi, Kenya in 1974; International Rice Research Institute (IRRI) = Organization established at los banos, Philippines in 1959; International Sugar Organization (ISO) = International organization formed of sugar-exporting countries; International Wheat Council (IWC) = group of wheat-exporting countries; International Wool Secretariat (WS) =group which represents countries which export wool.

**Interrelay Cropping.** Cropping system in which the crops are grown in quick succession, so much so, that the succeeding crop is sown in the standing one, some time before it is harvested.

Studies conducted at the Punab Agricultural University suggest the possibility of intersowing wheat in the furrows between the consecutive potato ridges at the time of earthing up; summer mung bean (green gram) can then be intersown in the standing wheat crop a few days before harvest, using the space released by the potatoes.

**Intervention.** Acting to make a change; Intervention Board = body set u in 1972 to implement the regulations of the Common Agricultural Policy in the UK; the Board is mainly concerned with compensatory payments.

**Intervention Buying.** A feature of the Common Agricultural Policy, whereby governments or their agents offer to buy surplus agricultural produce at a predetermined price; it is subject to a minimum quality standard; intervention price

= price at which the EC will buy farm produce which farmers cannot sell, in order to store it; Intervention stocks = the various amounts of commodities held by the EC in store; to sell into intervention = to sell to a government agency at an intervention price because the market price is too low.

**Introduction.** (a) Bringing something to a new place before the introduction of grey squirrels, the red squirrel was widespread (b) plant or animal which has been introduced to a new area it is not an indigenous species but a 19th century introduction.

**Iodine.** Chemical element which is essential to the body, especially to the functioning of the thyroid gland, found in seaweed.

**Iodophor.** Disinfectant used to disinfect teats of cows to prevent mastitis.

**Ion.** Atom which has an electric charge (ions with a positive charge are called cations, and those with a negative charge are anions); ion exchange = exchanging of ions between a solid and a solution.

**Irish Molled.** A rare reed of medium-sized dual-purpose cattle; the animals have a distinctive white back strip.

**Iron.** Metallic element essential to biological life and an essential part of human diet (found in liver, eggs, etc.). Iron is an essential part of the red pigment inred blood cells. Lack of iron in haemoglobin results in iron-deficiency anaemia. It sroel in the physiology of plants appears to be associated with specific enzymatic reactions and the production of chlorophyll.

**Irongrass or Ironweed.** Popular names for the knotgrass.

**Irradiate.** (i) To subject something to radiation; (ii) To treat food with radiation to prevent it going bad.

**Irradiation.** (a) spread from a centre, as nerve impulses (b)

Use of rays to kill bacteria in food.
Food is irradiated with gamma rays from isotopes which kill bacteria. It is not certain, however, that irradiated food is safe for humans to eat, as the effects of irradiation on food are not known. In some countries irradiation is only permitted as a treatment of certain foods.

**IRRI.** International Rice Research Institute.

**Irrigate.** To supply land with water.

**Irrigation.** The artificial supplying and application of water to land with growing crops new areas of land must be brought under irrigation to meet the rising demand fro food; basin irrigation –irrigation technique where water is trapped in basins surrounded by low mud walls (as in trice fields); flood irrigation = irrigation system where water is allowed to flood over the land; furrow irrigation == irrigation techniques where water is allowed to flow along furrows.

**Irrigator.** Device for irrigating, such as the Baars irrigator. Irrigation can be carried out using powered rotary sprinklers, rain guns, spray lines or by channeling water along underground pipes or small irrigation canals from reservoirs or rivers. Irrigation water can be more effectively used than the equivalent amount of rainfall, because a regular supply is ensured. Basin or flood irrigation is a primitive form of irrigation, where flood waters from rivers are led to prepared basins. Perennial irrigation allows the land to be irrigated at anytime. This may be by primitive mans such as shadufs, or by distributing water from barrages by canal and ditches. It is usually to measure irrigation water in millimeters: 1mm on the hectare equals $10m^5$ or ten tones. Irrigation is not necessarily always advantageous to the land, as it can cause salinization of the soil. This happens when the soil becomes waterlogged so that salts in the soil rise to the surface. At the surface, the irrigated water rapidly evaporates. Leaving the salts behind in the form of a saline crust. Irrigation also has the further disadvantage of increasing the spread of disease. Water insects easily spread through irrigation canals and reservoirs.

**Isobar.** Line on a map linking points of equal barometric pressure at the same time.

**Isohyet.** Line on a map linking points of equal rainfall.

**Isolation.** Keeping infected animals away from others.

**Isoleucine.** Essential amino acid.

**Itallan ryegrass.** Short lived ryegrass (Lolium multiflourum); it is won in spring and is very quick to establish; it produces good growing in its seeding year and early graze the following year; it is commonly used for short duration leys.

**IUCN.** International Union for the Conservation of Nature.

**Ivy.** Parasitic plant.

**IWC.** International Wheat Council.

**IWS.** International Wool secretariat.

# J

**Jack Bean.** Tropical legume (*Canavalia ensiformis*) grown as a fodder crop.

**Jacon.** Rare breed of sheep with multi-coloured fleece; it is medium-sized and multi-horned, with a white coat and brown or black patches.

**Jamaica Hope.** Breed of dairy cattle developed by the Jamaican government from Jersey cows and Sahiwal Indian bulls; the colour is fawn or brown.

**Japanese Millet.** Grain crop (*Echinochloa Frumentacea*) cultivated in Japan and Korea for human consumption; grown in the USA as a forage crop.

**Java Cotton.** Important breed of dairy cattle, originally from the island of Jersey; Jersey cows are smaller tan most other breeds and produce high yields of high butterfat content milk. The cattle are variously coloured from light fawn to red and almost black.

**Jhum.** Form of slash-and-burn shifting cultivation practiced in Nagaland and Arunachal Pradesh, India.

**Juice.** Liquid insive a fruit or vegetable; liquid inside cooked meat;

**Juice extractor.** Device for extracting juice from a fruit or vegetable.

**Jumna Pari.** Breed of goat found in India; a large animal with long lop ears, it is reared for its milk.

**June Agricultural Census.** In Great Britain, the annual farm returns on 4th June each year provide the basis for a census of agriculture carried out by the MAFF; the census covers crop areas, numbers of livestock, production and yields, number and size of holdings, numbers of workers, farm machinery, prices and incomes.

**June Drop.** The fall of small fruit from applies and pears, which takes place in summer as the fruit begin to grow; some fruit fall off, allowing the remaining fruit to mature more easily.

**Juniper.** Coniferous tri tree of the genus Juniperus; the berries are used for flavouring especially in making gin.

**Jute.** Coarse fibre from a plant (*Corchorus sp*), used to make sacks coarse cloth and cheap twine. The main producers of jute are Bangladesh (which produces over 50 per cent of the total world production), India and Brazil.

# K

**Kaffir Corn.** Variety of grain sorghum, rather similar to maize; grown for food and animal forage in tropical Africa.

**Kainit.** Potash fertilizer, made of a mixture of potassium and sodium salts, with sometimes magnesium salts added, used mainly on sugar beet and similar crops.

**Kale.** Type of brassica, sometimes used as a green vegetable for human consumption, but mainly grown as animal forage.

Kale can be fed to animals in the field, or made into silage for use during winter. The main types of kale are the marrowstem, which produces heavy crops but is not winter hardy; the thousand-headed, which is hardier; and dwarf thousand-head, which produces a large number of new shoots late in the winter. Other hybrid varieties are also available. Kale is the commonest of green crops other than grass. The highest feeding value is in the leaf rather than the stem.

**Karst.** Terrain typical of limestone country, with an uneven surface and holes and cracks due to weathering, usually with underground drainage and cave systems.

**Kashmir.** Breed of goat with a white or black and white coat; the breed is valued for the fineness of its long hair. Found in Tibet, Iran, Turkey and the USSR.

**Kauri Gum.** Resin obtained from a coniferous tree found in New Zealand.

**Ked.** The sheep tick; a bloodsucking fly (*Melophagus ovinus*) which is a parasite of sheep and causes extreme irritation.

**Keep.** (1) Grass or fodder crops for the grazing of livestock (2) (of produce) to remain in good condition after harvest Conference pears will keep until spring.

**Keeper.** (a) Person who looks after deer, pheasants or other animals and birds which are reared to be hunted (b) fruit which keeps well.

**Keleserite.** Magnesium sulphate powder, used as a fertilizer where magnesium deficiency is evident, especially in light sandy soil.

**Kennel.** (a) Small hut for a god (b) Kennels = commercial establishment where does are reared or kept for their owners (c) cow kennels = wooden building with stalls for cows.

**Kentish Cob.** Commercially grown variety of hazel nut.

**Keny.** Rare breed of dairy cattle which is native to Eire; the animals are black, sometimes with white patches on the udder, and are small with upturned horns.

**Kerry Hill.** Breed of small hill sheep originating in the Kerry hills of Powys in Wales. It has a soft white fleece and speckled face and legs. The ewes are crossed with Down rams for lam production.

**Kg.** Kilogram kg/ha = kilograms per hectare.

**Khesal.** High-yielding vetch grown as a catch crop with linseed, lentils, peas or mustard in paddy fallows in India.

**Khillari.** Indian breed of cattle; the animals are grey or white in colour, with long pointed horns. They are mainly found in Maharashtra State, and are primarily used as draught animals.

**Kholmogor.** Breed of dairy cattle found in the USSR; the animals are mainly coloured black and white.

**Kid.** Young goat of either sex, up to one year old.

**Kid-snatching.** Taking a new-born kid away from its mother to prevent her from licking it and so passing on CAE.

**Kidding Pen.** Pen in which a doe is kept when giving birth to kids.

**Kip.** Hide of a young animal, used for leather.

**Kitchen Garden.** Garder, near a house, where fruit, vegetables and sald crops are grown for use by the household.

**Kiwi.** (fruit). Subtropical woody climbing plant (Actinidia chinesis) which bears brownish oval fruit with a green juicy flesh the plant has been developed in New Zealand, and is now grown in many subtropical regions; also called "Yang Tao" or "Chinese gooseberry"

**Knacker.** Person who slaughters casualty animals, particularly horses.

**Knife.** Attachment on the cutter bar of a mower or combine harvester, there are two types; one with smooth sections which need frequent sharpening, and the other with serrated sections which need no sharpening.

**Knotgrass.** Common weed (Polygonum aviclare) which affects spring cereals, sugar beet and vegetable crops; its spreading habit prevents other slower-growing plants from growing; also known as IRONWEED, IRONGRASS.

**Knotter.** The mechanism on a baler which ties the bales; it has three basic parts; billhook, retainer disc and the knife.

**Kohirabl.** Variety of cabbage with a swollen stem, used as a fodder crop, and also sometimes eaten as a vegetable; the leases may be green or purple; also know n as "turnip-rooted cabbage"

**Kuri.** Breed of cattle found in the Lake Chad region of West Africa; the animals are white or grey in colour, with very large dark horns. Mainly reared for meat and milk.

**Kwashlorkor.** Malnutrition of small children, mostly in tropical countries, causing anaemia, wasting of the body and swollen liver; it is caused by protein deficiency in the diet, especially where cassava is the staple foodstuff, since the protein content of cassava is almost nil.

**Kyloes.** Breed of small long-horned shaggy Highland cattle.

# L

**Label.** (1) Piece of paper attached to produce, showing the price and other details.

**Labourer.** Person who does heavy work; agricultural Labourer = person who does heavy work on a farm, formerly a rural worker with no land, and sometimes still a worker with a special skill, such as ditching or hedging; casual labourer = worker who can be hired for a short period, usually at harvest time.

**Lactate.** To produce milk.

**Lactation.** (i) Production of milk; (ii) suckling, the period during which young are nourished with milk from the mother's mammary glands.

Lactation is stimulated by the production of the hormone prolaction by the pituitary gland. In cows, goats and sheep kept for milk production, the lactation period is made longer by regular milking. For a dairy cow, the period is ten months, followed by a two-month rest before calving again.

**Lactic Acid.** An organic acid formed by the action of bacteria on lactose, causing milk to go sour, used in the production of sourced cream, cheese and yoghurt. Lactic acid is also produced in silage by bacteria present in the green cop acting on he crbohydrates and converting it from sugars present in the crop or added to it. Lactic acid and bacteria are also added to silage to assist the preservation process.

**Lactose.** Milk sugar, the sugar found in milk ladder farm. Farm with a series of small long narrow fields.

**Ladybird.** Beetle of the Coccinellidae family, which is useful to the farmer because it feeds on aphids which would damage plants if they were not destroyed.

**LAI.** Leaf area Index.

**Laid Crop.** Crop which has been flattened by rain and wind.

**Laid Hedge.** Hedge that has been made by bending over each stem and weaving it between stakes driven into the ground.

**Lamb.** (1) (a) young sheep under six months of age (b) meat from a lamb (meat from an older sheep is called "mutton", though this is not common) (2) To give birth to lambs most ewes lamb without difficulty, but some may need help.

**Lambing.** The action of giving birth to lambs.

**Lambing Pen.** Pen in which a ewe is kept when giving birth to lambs.

**Lambing Percentage.** The number of live lambs born per hundred ewes.

**Lambing Season.** Period of the year when a flock of ewes produces lambs, usually between December and January; the object is to produce lambs for the market when the price is highest, usually between February and May.

**Lamina.** (a) The blade of a leaf (B) the sensitive membrane lying beneath the outer horny layer of an animal's hoof.

**Laminitis.** Inflammation of the lamina in a hoof, causing swelling, and often leading to deformed hooves; possibly caused by too much grain feed.

**Land.** (a) Solid part of the earth's surface (as opposed to the sea) the family have worked the land for generations; back to the land = encouragement given to people who once lived in the country and moved to urban areas to find work, to return to the country.

**Land Agent.** Person employed to run a farm or an estate on behalf of he owner.

**Land Consolidation.** The bringing together of small scattered plots of land into large single units, often helped by government grants, as in France and the Netherlands : Land Reclamation. The process of bringing back areas of desert, heath, marsh or other unproductive land to being productive for agricultural purposes; land service = a former division of the agricultural Development and advisory Service with the responsibility for advising farmers on farm management and resource planning; land tenure = the way in which land is owned and possessed; this may be by an individual owning the freehold, by a tenancy agreement between freeholder and tenant, or by a form of community ownership (b) section of a field, divided from other sections by a shallow furrow (term used in systematic ploughing)

**Land Capability.** An estimate of the potential of land for agriculture, mad eon purely physical environmental factors, such as climate and soil; compare Land suitability.

**Land Classification.** Classification of land into categories, according to its value for a broad land use type.

**Land Drainage.** Removing surplus water form land. Land Drinage Service. Former division of the Agricultural Development and Advisory Service, with the responsibility to advisory Service, with the responsibility to advise farmers on land drainage.

If surplus water is prevented from moving through the soil and subsoil, it soon fills all the pore spaces in the sol and this will kill or stunt the growing crops. Well-drained land is better aerated, and crops are loss likely to be damaged by root-destroying fungi; also aerated soil warms up more quickly in spring. Plants form deeper and more extensive roots systems. Grassland is firmer, and disease risk from parasites is reduced. The main methods of draining land are underground pipe drains, mole drains and ditches.

**Landfill site.** Area of excavated land (such as an old gravel pit) in which refuse is placed.

**Landlord.** Owner of land or building who lets it to a tenant for an agreed rent.

**Landowner.** Persón who owns land freehold, and may et it to a tenant, or may farm it himself.

**Landrace.** (a) Native species of plant or animal which has not been cultivated (b) Landrace = breed of pig, native to Scandinavia; the animals have small heads, lop ears and long bodies; when crossed with the Large White it produces vigorous hybrid sows; almost all indoor and outdoor hybrid sows in the UK are 50 per cent landrace.

**Landscape.** (1) The general shape and appearance of an area of land (2) To change the appearance of a garden or park by planting trees, creating little hills, making lakes, etc.

**Landscape Gardener.** Gardener who creates a new appearance for a garden.

**Land Suitability.** The suitability of land for a certain agricultural purpose.

Land suitability is similar to land capability, but defines its usefulness for a particular purpose; Suitability tends to emphasize the positive value of land, while capability emphasizes its limitations.

**Land Use.** Way in which the land I used by humans they are carrying out a study of land use in northern area; land use classification = the classification of land according to the way it is used.

**Large Black.** Dual-purpose hardy breed of pig; he animals are black with long lop ears. Formerly it was a useful outdoor breed, because it could stand extreme weather, but is now less common. A large Black sow when mated with a white boar produces hardy blue-and-white hybrids.

**Large White.** Important commercial breed of pig; the animals are white with pricked up ears; it is the most popular UK boar breed and forms part in almost all indoor hybrid sows (usually 50 per cent ) and hybrid boars. It has a large mature size and has been improved to produce good fecundity, growth ad carcass characteristics.

**Larva.** Stage (caterpillar or grub) in the development of an insect. After the egg has hatched but before it becomes adult.

**Lateral.** Shoot which branches off from the leader or main branch of a tree or shrub.

**Laterite.** Substance which when it dries out forms a hard material which cannot be wetted again; it is highly weathered and consists mainly of iron and aluminium oxides in some countries houses are built of laterite.

**Laterize.** To create laterite by exposing tropical soil to weather. When tropical rainforests are cleared, the soil beneath rapidly turns to laterite as nutrients are leached out by rain. Laterized land cannot be cultivated and such areas turn to desert.

**Latex.** (i) White fluid from a plant such as the poppyl (ii) White substance in the fluid from the rubber tree, which is treated and processed to make rubber.

**Latifundium.** Large landed estate, common in South America;

latifundia are often spolit into small units which are rented out to peasants.

**Latosol.** Tropical soil in savanna and rainforest areas; its colour is most commonly red, though brown and yellow occur. The soil is rich in hydroxides of iron, aluminium and manganese, and it heavily leached.

**Laurics or Lauric Oils.** Oils from palm seed and coconut.

**Lavender.** Shrub (*Lavandula officinalis*) with small lilac-coloured flowers and narrow leaves, cultivated for perfume; once cut, the bloom is either dried or distilled: this is the traditional process for the extraction of lavender oil.

**Laver.** Welsh name for a variety of seaweed which is edible.

**Laxative.** Substance which encourage movements of the bowel succulent food such as root crops have a laxative effect.

**Laxton's Superb.** Variety of dessert apple formerly grown commercially in eh UK.

**LAY.** (1) hen in lay = bird which is laying eggs (2) (of a bird) to produce an egg.

**Layer.** (1) (a) bird that is in lay; layers' ailments = disorders of fowls in lay, especially birds that are in heavy production; disorders lf layers include egg binding, internal laying and layer's crampl layer's cramp = condition found in pullets after the first few weeks of their laying life; the bird appears weak, but the trouble usually is appears after a few days (b) stem of a plant which has made roots where it touches the ground (2) To propagatea plant by bending a stem down until it touches the soil and letting it form roots there.

**Layering.** (a) Method of propagation where the stem of a plant is bent until it touches the soil, and is fixed down on the soil surface until roots form; air layering = method of propagation where a stem is partially cut, then surrounded with dampmoss, the whole being tied securely; roots will grow from the cut at the point where it is in contact with the moss (b) bending over the half cut stems of hedge plants, and weaving them around stakes set in the ground, to forma new hedge.

**Laying.** The action of producting eggs; laying cage = specially built cage for laying hens; the cages are arranged in tiers and each cage should allow the birds to stand comfortably, allow the eggs roll forward and permit access to food and water, easy cleaning and easy handling of the birds; laying period = period during which a hen will continue to lay eggs; this begins at 22 weeks of age and normally lists for 50 weeks; internal laying = condition caused by a fault in the oviduct, which results in the yolks not being passed along the oviduct for covering with membranes and shell.

**Lazy-bed.** Small arable plot used for growing potatoes, cereals and other crops, found in the West Highlands of Scotland; if the soil is thin, seed potatoes are placed on the surface of the soil and covered with turf.

**Lea.** Open ground left fallow or under grass.

**Leach.** To wash something out of soil by passing water through it excess chemical fertilizers on the surface of the soil leach into rivers and cause pollution; nitrates have leached into ground water and contaminate the water supply.

**Leachate.** (i) Substance which is washed out of the soil; (ii) liquid which forms at the bottom of a landfill site.

**Leaching.** Process by which plant nutrients such as NPK are lost from the soil by water percolating through soil in humid climates; soils gradually become mineral-deficient and sour; leaching field = area round a septic tank with pies which allow the sewage to drain away underground.

**Led.** Very heavy soft metallic element, which is poisonous in compounds; lead pointing = the poisoning of animals which have eaten or licked paint; it is common in cattle and can be fatal.

**Leader.** Animal which goes first, which leads the flock or herd.

**Leader-follower System.** System of grazing where priority is given to a group of animals (the leaders) and the crop is later grazed by a second group of animals (the followers); so first-ear heifers might be followed by second-year heifers.

**Leaf.** Green, usually flat, part of a plant, growing from a stem, whose purpose is to activate photosynthesis, the means by which the plant gets energy from sunlight.

**Leaf Area Index (LAI).** The area of green leaf per unit area of ground.

**Leaf Blotch.** Disease of cereals (*Rhynchosporium secal is*) where dark grey lesions with dark brown margins occur on the leaves.

**Leaf Roll.** Viral disease of potatoes, transmitted by aphids; the leaves rollup and become dry, and the crop yield is affected.

**leaf Spot.** Fungal disease of brassicas, where the leave develop brown and black pathes.

**Leaf Stripe.** Disease of barley and oats (*Pyrenophora graminea*) where the young leaves show pale astripes and seedlings often die.

**Lean Meat.** Meat with very little fat animals are bred to produce lean meat; venison is a very lean form of meat.

**Lease.** (1) Legal contract for letting a building or piece of land for a period of time against payment of a rent (2) (A) to let or rent land or machinery for a period be leases workshops on his farm to small craft studios; we lease large pieces of equipment such as combines (b) to use land or machinery for a time and pay a fee to the landlord or lessee he leases his farm from insurance company; all our farm equipment is leased.

**Leaseback.** Arrangement where property is sold and then taken back by the former owner on a leased.

**Leaseback.** Arrangement where property is sold and then taken back by the former owner on a lease.

**Leasehold.** Possessing property on a lease, for a fixed time to purchase a property leasehold; the property is for sale leasehold.

**Leaseholder.** Person who holds a property on a lease.

**Leasing.** Which leases or working under a lease all the farm's tractors are owned, but the combines are leased.

**Leather.** The skin of an animal, tanned and prepared for use.

**Leatherjacket.** The larva of the cranefly (Tipuda paludosa) which hatch from eggs laid on the ground and feed on the young crop in spring; when grass is ploughted for cereal crops, the larvae feed on the seedling wheat, damaging the plants at or just below ground level.

**Leek.** Hardy winter vegetable (*Allium ameloprasum*) with a mild onion taste; to produce high-quality leeks, the lower parts of the stems need to be blanched. The stems are used in soups and stews.

**Leghorn.** Excellent laying breed of hen; a hardy bird, coloured black, brown and white. Leghorns produce good-sized white eggs.

**Legume.** (a) Any member of the plant family Leguminosae which produce seeds in pods grass and legume associations are common in European pastureland (b) Dry seed from a single carpel, which splits into two halves (such as a pea).

**Leguminosae.** Family of plants (including pea and bean plants) which produce seeds in legume pods.

**Lhmann System.** System of pig breeding developed in Germany, where build food such as potatoes and fodder beet are fed after a basic ration of meal.

**Leicester Longwool.** Breed of large hornless white faced sheep, used a lot by Robert Bakewell, now rare; see also Border Leicester, blue-faced.

**Lemma.** The outer bract which encloses the flowers of grass.

**Lemon.** Yellow edible frit of an evergreen citrus tree (*Citrus lemon*); lemons have a very tart flavour and are used in flavouring and in making drinks.

**Lentil.** Important pulse crop, growing in he warmer temperate and subtropical regions of the world. Indian is the largest producer of lentils. The dried seeds are often processed into dal.

**Leptospirosis.** Disease of cattle caused by bacteria, which causes abortions and low milk yields; it can be carried by sheep or in running water.

**Lesion.** Open wound on the surface of a plant or on the kin of an animal, caused by disease or physical damage.

**Less Favoured Area.** Former name for landing mountainous and hilly areas, which is capable of improvement and use as breeding and rearing land for sheep and cattle; now called Disadvantaged or Severely Disadvantaged Areas; the EC now recognizes such areas and given financial help to farmers in them.

**Lettuce.** Salad vegetable (Lactuca sativa) which comes in a variety of forms and leaf textures; the commonest are cos lettuce, cabbage lettuce, crisphead and loose-leaved lettuces; cabbage lettuces have roundish heads, while cos lettuces have longer leaves and are more upright.

**Levada.** Irrigation anal leading to small irrigated plots on terraces.

**Level.** (1) Flat or horizontal the mountains give way to miles of level grassy plain (2) (a) amount forest will gradually die if pollution levels remain content; present levels of water pollution are not acceptable (b) fat low-lying area of usually marshy land, often reclaimed by artificial drainage in parts of Fen Country in Eastern England round the Wash.

**Levy.** Money which is demanded and collected by a government; import levy = tax on farm produce which is imported into the EC.

**Ley.** (a) Land which has been sown to grass for a time (b) field in which crop are grown in rotation with periods when the field is under pasture; ley farming = farming system in which fields are left to pasture in rotation.

Strictly speaking, ley farming is a system where a farmer group of fields is cropped completely with leys which are reseeded at regular interval; alternatively, any cropping system which involves the use of leys is called ley farming. Ley farming is an essential part of organic farming; pasture land is fertilized by the animals which graze on it, and then is ploughed for crop growing. When the land has been exhausted by the crops, it is put back to pasture to recover.

**Lichen.** Primitive plant which grows on the surface of stones or trunks of trees and can survive in arctic climates.

Lichens are formed of two organisms; a fungus which provides the outer shell and algae which provide chlorophyll and give the plant its colour. Lichens are very sensitive to pollution. Especially sulphur dioxide, and act as indicators for atmospheric pollution. They also provide food for many arctic animals.

**Lift.** To harvest root crops, such as potatoes, by digging them out of the ground; potatoes can be lifted form the soil and, using a spinner or an elevator digger, left in rows for hand-picking.

**Liftings.** Crops which have been lifted.

**Lifting Unit or Lifter.** Pair of wheels or a triangular-shaped share, used on a harvester to lift the roots and pass them to the main elevator. The roots are lifted by being squeezed out of the ground in between the two wheels. The distance between the two wheels or shares can be adjusted to suit the size of the crop. The wheels should be set quite close together at the bottom when harvesting small roots. The wheels run at an angle to each other so that their rims lie close together when in the soil and farther apart at the top.

**Light Grains.** Cereals such as barley and oats.

**Light Soil.** Soil consisting mainly of large particles which are loosely held together because of the relatively large pore space; light soil is usually easier to cultivate than heavy soil, but may dry out too quickly.

**Light Sussex.** Dual-purpose breed of poultry; the Light Sussex is one of the several varieties of the Sussex breed; the birds are white, with black stripes to the feathers of the neck and black feathers on the wings and tail.

**Lignin.** Complex woody tissue deposited in plants and resulting in reduced level sof digestibility.

**Lignify.** To become hard and woody plants are less digestible as they become lignified.

**Limb.** Leg of an animal.

**Lime.** (a) Calcium compounds used to spread on soil to increase the pH level and correct acidity; lime is usually applied as simple chalk or limestone; also a s quicklime or slaked lime (b) common European hardwood tree (*Tulia sp*) (c) *Citrus aurantifolia*, a citrus fruit tree, with green fruit similar to, but smaller than, a lemon.

**Limestone.** Common sedimentary rock.

**Lincoln Longwool.** Rare breed of sheep, with white faces and long shiny wool; the animals are very large and slow to mature; the breed is now found mainly in Lincolnshire.

**Lincoln Red.** Breed of cattle bred from the shorthorn; the animals are deep red in colour; originally the breed was dual-purpose, but now is mainly used for crossing with dairy cows to produce beef calves.

**Linebreeding.** Mating of related animals with offspring. The purpose of line breeding is to try to preserve in succeeding generations the mix of genes responsible for a particularly excellent individual specimen.

**Link.** (a) Measurement, forming one loop of a chain (one-hundredth of a surveying chain, or 7.92 inches) (b) something which joins two things.

**Linkage.** Association of genes that appear to be inherited together

**Linseed.** Variety of flax (*Linum usitatissimum*), with a short straw; it produces a good yield of seed used for producing oil.

**Liquid.** Matter (like water) which is not solid and is not a gas.

**Liquid Manure.** Manure consisting of dung and urine in a liquid form (manure in semi-liquid form is slurry).

**Liquid Fertilizers.** Non-pressurized solutions of normal solid fertilizers; liquid fertilizers are easier, quickly and cheaper to handle and apply then solid fertilizers.

**Liquor.** Concentrated liquid substance; silage liquor = liquid which forms in silage and drains away from the silo.

**Liquorice.** Root of a plant (*glycyrrhiza glabra*) used in making sweets and soft drinks; it also has medicinal Properties (formerly grown in Pontefract, Yorkshire, but now not common there).

**Litter.** (a) Bedding for livestock; straw is the best type of litter, although bracken, peat moss, sawdust and wood shavings can be used (b) group of young mammals born to one mother at the same time a pig litter of 34 has been recorded, although about 12 is average 2 verb to have a litter of young.

**Livestock.** Domesticated farm animals, which are reared to produce meat or milk or other precuts livestock production has increased by 5 percent; pastoralists move their livestock from place to place to find new grazing;

**Livestock Records.** each farm has to make simple records of all livestock, and these are then available for the MAFF returns which are compiled each year.

**Livestock Unit.** Part of a farm, where livestock are reared.

**Liveweight.** The weight of a live animal (as opposed to deadweight, the weight of the carcasss); liveweight marketing = the marketing of live animals.

**Loader.** Machine used to load crops, manure, etc, into trailers or spreaders; the front-end tractor-mounted loader is the mot common.

**Loam.** (a) Good dark soil, with medium-sized grains of sand, which crumbles easily and is very fertile and easily cultivated. Loam is intermediate in texture between clay and sandy soil. Loams warm up quite early in spring, and are fairly resistant to drought (b) (in horticulture) mixture of clay, sand and humus, used as a potting compost.

**Loamy.** Crumbly fertile dark (soil).

**Locks.** Small tufts of wool separated from the fleece during shearing.

**Locust.** Flying insect of the grasshopper family (Locusta migratotoria) which occurs in subtropical areas, flies in swarms and eats large amounts of vegetation; locust bean = the broken-down pods of the carob tree, used as animal feed.

**Lodging.** The tendency of cereal crops to bend over, so that they lie more or less flat on the ground. Loading can be caused by wet weather or high winds, and also by disease such as eyespot; it can cause problems for harvesting the crop.

**Loganberry.** Soft fruit, a cross between a raspberry and a blackberry.

**Lome Convention.** An agreement reached in 1975 betwen the European Community and 66 developing nations (the ACP states); it gives entry into the EC for certain agricultural product withut duty, with sections on guaranteed price.

**Long-grain Rice.** Varieties of rice with long grains, grown in tropical climates, such as India, (as opposed to short-grain rice grown in colder climates such as Japan)

**Loue.** Smallisect of the Pediculus genus, which sucks blood an lives on the skin as a parasite on animals and humans.

**Low.** Depression, area of low atmospheric pressure a series of lows are crossing the Atlantic towards Ireland.

**Lowlands.** Area of low land where conditions are usually good for farming (as opposed to hills and mountains, or highlands) vegetation in the lowlands or in the lowland areas I sparse.

**Low Loader.** Farm trailer with its flat floor near the ground to make loading easier.

**Lugs.** Projections from the tyres of tractor wheels; they increase traction by digging into the soil and by keeping the tyre in contact with solid surfaces in muddy conditions.

**Lump Lime.** Another name of burnt lime or quicklime.

**Lymph.** Colourless liquid containing white blood cells, which circulates in the lymph system from all body tissues, carrying waste matter away from tissues to the veins.

**Lynchet.** (a) strip of land formed as the result of a movement of soil down a slope as a result of cultivation; negative lynchets form at the top of the slope and positive lynchets at the bottom. (b) unploughed strip of land forming a temporary boundary between fields.

**Lysine.** Essential amino acid in protein foodstuffs, essential for animal growth. It is the most important and often the first limiting amino acid in protein.

# M

**Macronutrient.** A nutrient which is needed by a plant in relatively large amounts, such as nitrogen, phosphorus, potassium, calcium, magnesium and iron.

**MAFF.** Ministry of Agriculture, Fisheries and Food.

**Magnesium.** Chemical element, a white metal which is used in making alloys, and is also an essential element in biological life (in human diets, it is hound in green vegetables). Magnesium is a necessary part of chlorophyll. If soil is deficient in magnesium, it can be added in the form of ground limestone, magnesium sulphate or farmyard manure.

**Maiden.** Tree in this first year after grafting or budding, when it is formed of a single stem.

**Maincrop Potatoes.** Varieties of potato grown as a main crop, as opposed to "earlies"; see also Potato.

**Maintenance Ration.** The amount of food needed by an animal to keep in good condition.

**Maize.** Widely grown cereal crop (*Zea mays*) maize gluten = animal feeding stuff obtained after maize has been milled; it is high in protein.

Maize is a tall annual grass plant, with a strong solid stem. The male flowers forma tassel on the top of the plant and the females some distance away in the axils of some of the middle stem leaves. After wind pollination of the filament-like styles or silks, the grain develops into long "cobs" of tightly packed seeds. In Great Britain the crop sis grown for making silage, or for harvesting as ripened grain; some is grazed or cut as a forage crop, while a small proportion is sold for human consumption as "corn on the cob". Maize needs rich deep well-drained soils and ideally a frost-free growing season with a lot of sunshine before harvest. Maize is the only grain crop which was introduced from the New World into the old World, and it owes its name of Indian corn to the fact that it was cultivated by American Indians before the arrival of European settlers. It is the principal crop grown in the United States, where it is used as feed for cattle and pigs.

**Malt.** (1) Best-quality barley grains which have been through the malting process and are used in breweries to make beer and in distilleries to make whisky. (2) To teat grain, such as barley, by allowing it to sprout and the drying it; the malted grain is used for making beer.

**Malt Culms.** Roots and shots of partly germinated malting barley; a by-product of the malting process, the culms are used as a feeding stuff for livestock.

**Malted Meal.** Brown wheat flour mixed with flour made from barley.

**Maltase.** Enzyme present in germinating grains, in saliva and in intestinal juices in the small intestine; it converts maltose into glucose.

**Malting.** The process by which barley grain is soaked in water, then sprouted on a floor to produce an enzyme; it is then dried in a kiln and the roots and shoots are removed to leave the malt grains.

**Malting Barley.** Best-quality barley used for malting.

**Maltose.** Sugar formed by digesting starch or glucose.

**Maltster.** Person who makes malt for salt to breweries.

**Mammal.** Animal of the class Mammalia (such as the human being) which gives birth to live young, secretes milk to feed them, keeps a constant body temperature and is covered with hair. All farm livestock with the exception of poultry are mammals.

**Mammary Glands.** Glands in females that produce milk; in cows, sheep and goats, the glands are located in the udder.

**Manage.** To control; to be in charge of the department is in charge of managing land resources; managed woodland = woodland which is controlled by felling, coppicing, planting, etc.

**Management.** Organized use of resources or materials.

**Pasture Management.** The control of pasture by grazing, cutting, reseeding, etc.; woodland management = controlling an area of woodland so that it is productive (b regular feeling, coppicing, planting, etc.)

**Manganese.** Metallic trace element which is essential for biological life as an enzyme activator.

**Mange.** Skin disease of hairy or woolly animals, caused by mites, including Sarcoptes, the itch mite.

**Manger.** A trough in a stable, from which horses and cattle feed.

**Mango.** Tropical tree (*Mangifera indica*) and the fruit it produces; the tree originated in India, but is grown widely in tropical countries; the fruit is large yellow or yellowish-green, with a soft orange pulp surrounding the very large seed; the seeds and bark are also used medicinally.

**Mangosteen.** Tree (*Garciniaa mangostana*) which is native of malayasia, but which is native of Malaysia, but which is now cultivated in the west Indies; the fruit has a dark shinyrind and a soft sweet white flesh.

**Manx Loghtan.** Rare breed of sheep, which is native to the Isle of Man. The wool is moue-brown and the animals are multi-horned.

**Maple.** Hardwood tree (Acer sp), of northern temperate regions, some varieties of which produce sweet sap which is used for making sugar and syrup.

**Mapping.** The process of collecting information and using it to produce maps; soil mapping = making maps showing different types of soil in an area.

**Marbling.** Appearance of muscle with intramuscular fat, seen on the cut surface of meat.

**Marginal.** At the edge of cultivated land (such as edges of fields, banks beside roads, etc.); land of poor quality which results from bad physical conditions, such as poor soil, high rainfall, steep slopes, and where farming is often hazardous cultivating marginal areas a can lead to erosion.

**Mariculture.** Farming in the sea or in a marine environment. Mariculture refers to aquaculture in seawater, such as raising oysters, lobsters and fish in special enclosures.

**Market Garden.** Place for the commercial growing of plants, usually vegetables, soft fruit, salad crops and flowers, found near a large urban centre which provides a steady outlet for the sale of its produce.

**Market Gardening.** Growing vegetables, salad crops, fruit for sale.

**Market Gardener.** Person who runs a market garden.

**Marketing Boards.** In the UK certain commodities are marketed by boards set up by Acts of Parliament, such as the Potato marketing Board.

**Marota.** Breed of goat found in brazil; the animals are white or light grey, and a reared both of milk and for their skins.

**Marram Grass.** Type of grass (*Ammopila arenaria*) which is planted on sand dunes to stabilize them and prevent them being extended by the wind.

**Marrow.** Large vegetable (*Cucurbita pepo*) of the pumpkin family, which may be grown as bush or trailing varieties.

**Marshy Soil.** Very wet soil. A marsh usually has a soil base, as opposed to a bog or fen which is made up of peat. Many former areas of marshal and have been reclaimed and have been artificially drained by an system of ditches and sluices which allow surface water to escape to the sea, but prevent salt water entering the area. The drained soils are usually fertile and some of these areas are important for agriculture.

**Mash.** Mixture of feeding meals mixed to provide all he necessary elements for a balanced diet; wet mash= mash fed mixed with water.

**Mast.** (a) Seeds of the beech tree, used as food by pigs and other animals. (b) Mast cell = large cell n connective tissues which carries histamine and reacts to allergens (c) mast swine = German term for fattening pig.

**Mastitis.** Common Bacterial disease affecting dairy animals in which the udders become inflamed and swollen, and the passage of the milk is blocked.

Common causes are staphylococci such as *Staphylococcus aureus* (staphylococcal mastitish), streptococci (*Streptococcus uberis*) or other bacteria (E. coli mastitis). The condition can be treated with antibiotics.

**Matted.** With many fibres woven together.

**Maturity.** (a) time when a plant's seeds are ripe (b) time when an animal has become an adult; time when an animal is ready for slaughter.

**Meadowgreass.** Varieties of grass of the genus Poa annual *meadowgrass* = widespread weed (Poa annua) found in all arable and grass crops; smooth-stalked *meadowgrass* = species of grass which can withstand quite dry conditions; a perennial grass with smooth grayish-green leaves and green purplish flowers.

**Meal.** Finely ground compound feeding stuff for poultry and pigs, containing all the elements necessary for good health and steady growth.

**Mealwor.** Larva of various beetles of the genus *tenebrio* that infests and pollutes grain products. Meat. Animal flesh which is eaten as food; meat is formed of the animal's muscle.

**Meat-eating animals.** Carnivores, animals (such as the cat family) which eat almost exclusively met; meat extender = any foodstuff or mixture of foodstuffs died to meat preparations to increase their bulk; meat and bone meal = meal made from waste meat and bones, very rich in protein.

**Meat.** Showing the flesh of an animal used in particularly in the EC).

**Meat and Livestock Commission.** Organisation which provides services to livestock breeders, including the evaluation of breeding stock potential, carcass grading and classification; the Commission also carries out various research projects. Its staff also provide services for abattoirs and livestock auction markets. The Commission promotes the sale of British meat.

**Melshan.** Breed of pig imported into the UK from China; it is a fast-maturing breed and remarkably prolific and is one of the Taihu breeds; animals commonly have 18 to 20 teats.

**Metabolize.** To change the nature of something by metabolism the liver metabolizes proteins and carbohydrates.

**Metamorphosis.** Change, especially the change of a larva into an adult insect.

**Methane ($CH_4$).** Marsh gas, colourless gas, produced naturally from rotting organic waste; methane converter = process which takes the gas produced by rotting waste in landfill sites and processes it into a form which can be used.
Methoane is produced naturally from rotting vegetation in marshes, where it can sometimes catch fire, creating the phenomenon called will o' the wisp, a light flickering over a marsh. Large quantities may also be formed in the rumen of cattle. It occurs as the product of animal excretions in livestock farming. Excreta from livestock can be passed into tans where methane is extracted leaving the slurry which is then used as fertilizer. The methane can be used for heating or as a power source. Methane is also a greenhouse gas, and it has been suggested that methane from rotting vegetation, from cattle excreta, from water in paddy fields, and even from termites' nests, all contribute to the greenhouse effect.

**Methanol ($CH_3OH$).** Alcohol, manufactured from coal, natural gas or waste wood, which can be used as fuel.
Methanol can be used as a fuel in any type of burner; its main disadvantage is that it is less efficient than petrol and can cause pollution if it escapes into the environment as it mixes easily with water. Production of methanol from coal or natural gas, does not help fuel conservation, since it reduces the earth's fossil fuel resources.

**Metritis.** An infection of the lining of the womb in cattle; the symptoms are a white discharge and/or a high temperature; sows can also have mastitis.

**Microclimate.** Climate found in a very small area, such as a pond or a tree or a field; compare Macroclimate.

**Micronutrient.** Substance (such as iron, zinc, copper etc.) which organisms only need in very small quantities, i.e. as trace elements.

**Middle White.** Breed of white pig which comes from a cross between the Large White and the Small White. A short compact breed with long upright ears and a turned-up snout; now a rare breed.

**Midwest.** Region of the USA, between the Rocky Mountains on the west and the Alleghenies on the east, comprising the main farming area of the country.

**Milch Cow.** Cow which gives milk or is kept for milk production.

**Mildew.** Plant disease caused by a fungus which produces a fine powdery film on the surface of the infected parts; downy mildew = particularly strong form of mildew which affects lettuces and rots their leaves and stems.

**Milk.** Opaque white liquid secreted by female mammals during lactation; milk composition = the percentages of protein, lactose, fat, minerals and water which make up milk; the composition varies according to the breed of cow, but average percentages are; protein (3.4%), milk sugar (4.75%), fat (3.75%), minerals (0.75%), water (87.35%); milk compositional quality scheme = a scheme organized by the Milk Marketing Board, which categorizes milk and pays farmers according to the quality of milk produced.

**Milk Cooler.** Stainless steel bulk storage tan, in which milk is cooled by running water passing over the outside of the tank.

**Milk Producer.** Farmer who is registered with the MAFF, and produces milk in compliance with the regulations concerning clean milk production; he is also registered with the area MMB. In 1989 there were 32,500 milk producers in England and Wales; milk produced from it, which are sold for human consumption; the main milk products are liquid milk (homogenized, pasteurized, sterilized or UHT), butter, cheese, cream, condensed milk and milk powder.

**Milk Recording.** Keeping a record of the milk given by each cow at each milking; milk ripe stage or milky stage = stage in the development of grain, such as wheat, where the seed has formed but is still soft and white and full of white sap.

**Milk Sinus.** The space in each teat into which the milk is secreted.

**Milk Teeth.** First temporary teeth of young animals.

**Milker.** (a) Cow which is giving milk; cow which is kept for milk (b) farm worker who supervises the milking of cows (c) Part of the milking machine which is attached to the cow' s teats with teat cups.

In the UK, most milk comes from Friesian cows, and has been heat treated, pasteurized, sterilized or ultraheat treated before it is sold to the public, I may also be calcium enriched or lactose reduced. Milk is sold in cartons, either as homogenized, semi-skimmed or skimmed. In bottles it is sold with various coloured metal tops; "silver top" is pasteurized with an average 3.9% fat; it has a noticeable cream line; "red top" is similar to the silver, but the milk is homogenized to distribute the cream throughout; "gold top" is pasteurized milk from Guernsey or Jersey breads of cow, and has an average fat content of 4.9%; "red and silver striped top": pasteurized semi-skimmed milk with average 1.6% a fat content; "blue and silver checked top": pasteurized skimmed milk, with an average 0.1% fat content: "green top": untreated whole milk, with an average 3.9% fat (no longer sold in the UK). Sterilized whole milk with fat content of. 3.9% is sold in bottles with crown caps or blue foil tops. UHT milk is also availabie s whole, semi-skimmed or skimmed: it is milk with a shelf life of 6 months, though when opened it should be kept cold and used as ordinary pasteurized milk.

**Milk Fever.** Disease of milk cows, milk goats and ewes. In spite of this name, the disease is not a fever, and may affect a dairy cow just before calving or during the seven days which follow calving. The first symptoms are restlessness, moving the hind feet up and down white standing; these symptoms are followed by loss of balance and later loss of consciousness. The disease is common at the third, fourth or fifth time of calving, an is caused by a metabolic disturbance or imbalance in the system, due to a low calcium content in the blood. The disease is treated by injections of calcium borogluconate.

**Milk Goat.** Goat which is reared for its milk.

**Milking Machine.** Machine which imitates the sucking action of a calf, used to extract milk from the cow's udder. It uses a pulsator mechanism to apply pressure to the teats, causing the release of the milk. The milk is then passed into a collecting jar or may pas by pipeline to a large tank.

**Milking Parlour.** Building in which cows are milked, and often are also fed, washed and cleaned.
There a four basic designs of parlour; the herringbone parlour, where the cow stands at an angle of 45° to the milker, is commonest for large herds; the abreast parlour, where there cows stand side by side with their backs to the milker; the tandem parlour where they stand in line with their sides to the milker; the most expensive and complex of the four systems is the rotary parlour, where the cows stand on a rotating platform with the milker in the middle.

**Milk Marketing Board (MMB).** Board which organizes the

collection and buying of milk from farmers and its sale to buyers. The milk is collected in the board's bulk tankers and taken to dairies or creameries. The government is responsible for fixing the wholesale and retail price of milk; it is also responsible for the setting of quotes for milk production, according to the directives of the EC commission. The MMB provides a variety of services, such as artificial insemination, as well as organizing the promotion for the retail sale of milk.

**Milk Quota (MQ).** System by which farmers are only allowed to produce certain amounts of milk, introduced to restrict the overproduction of milk in member states of the EC. Quotas were introduced in 1984, and were based on each state's 1981 production, plus 1%. A further 1% was allowed in the first year. A supplementary levy or super levy, was introduced to penalize milk production over the quota level. Reductions in the quota amount were made in 1986/7 and 1987/8.

**Milk Sheep.** Sheep which is reared for its milk.

**Milk Sugar.** Lactose, the sugar found in milk.

**Milk Yield.** The quantity of milk produced each year by a cow.

**Mill.** (1) Factory where a substance is crushed to make powder, especially one for making flour from the dried seeds of corn; watermill or windmill = mills driven by water or wind; mill race = channel of water which turns the wheel of a watermill; mill wheel = large wheel (with wooden bars) which is turned by the force of water (2) to process grain into a another form (wheat into flour, brown rice into white rice).

**Milling Quality.** Calculation of how easy it is to separate the white endosperm from the brown seed coat or bran, in the milling process; in general hard wheats are of higher milling quality than soft wheats.

**Milling Wheat.** Best-quality wheat used to make flour for making bread.

**Millstone.** Heavy round slab of stone, used to grind corn.

**Millet**. Common cereal crop (*Panicum miliaceum*) grown in many of the hot, dry regions of Africa and Asia, where it is a staple food.
The two most important species are finger millet and bulrush millet. Millet grains are used in various types of food. It can be boiled and eaten like rice; made into flour for porridge, pasta or chapattis; mixed with whet flour to make bread. Millet can also be malted to make beer. Millets are also grown as forage crops, and the seed is used as a poultry feed. The main producers of millet are Nigeria, Mali and Niger.

**Mineralization.** Breaking down of organic waste into its non-organic chemical components.

**Minimal.** Very small; minimal area = smallest area for sampling in which specimens of all species can be found; minimal disease herd = herd of livestock with a very low level of infectious diseases.

**Minimal Cultivation.** System of cultivation which subjects the land to shallow working and minimizes the number of passes of machinery. No ploughing is needed.
Although suitable for cereal production, minimal cultivation is not suitable for all crops or soil conditions. Crops like sugar beet and potatoes need a deeper tilth than that obtained by minimal cultivation.

**Ministry of Agriculture, Fisheries and Food (MAFF).** British government department concerned with agriculture.

**Minorca.** Breed of poultry, originating in the Mediterranean; the birds are black or white in colour.

**Miranda.** Breed of cattle found in Portugal; the animals are dark brown in colour, with horns coloured white with black tips; they are bred for meat and for draught.

**Mite.** Tiny animal of the spider family (*Arachnidae*) which maybe free-living in the soil or parasitic on animals or plants.

**Mole Drain.** Underground circular channel formed by a mole plough as it is pulled across a field; mole drains are normally drawn 3 to 4 metres apart, and are best used in fields with a clay subsoil.

**Molehill.** Small heap of earth pushed up to the surface by amole as it makes its tunnel.

**Mole Plough.** Implement used to draw mole drains; the plough is pulled by a tractor, and consists of a vertical blade below which there is a torpedo or bullet-shaped mole. Behind this mole is an expander which widens the drain as it is cut.

**Molinia.** Poor type of grass found in round mountain or hill grazings; it is of little value as grazing.

**Molybdenum.** Metallic trace element, essential to biological life; excess molybdenum in grazing can, however, lead to insufficient copper uptake in sheep.

**Mongolian.** Breed of cattle, usually reddish-brown in colour; the animals are small and kept for milk and meat. Now not very common.

**Monocropping or Monoculture.** System of cultivation where only one crop is grown on the same piece of land over a period of years; conifer monoculture = system of afforestation where only one type of conifer is grown.

**Monogastric.** Animals with only one stomach, such as pigs, as opposed to ruminants.

**Monsoon.** Season of wind and rain in tropical countries; monsoon forest= tropical rainforest in an area where rain falls during the monsoon season.

**Moorland**. Area of land covered with moor of low agricultural value; it is a habitat for game birds.

**Morbidity.** Being diseased; morbidity rate = number of cases of disease per hundred thousand of population.

**Mosaic Virus.** Virus disease of plants which makes spots on the leaves and can seriously affect some crops.

**Mosquito.** Insect which sucks blood and passes viruses or parasites into the bloodstream.

**Moss.** Very small plant without roots, which grows in damp places and forms mats of vegetation; *moss peat* = dried and sterilized peat formed from the remains of mosses, sold in bags for horticultural purposes.

**Mountain.** (a) High land (b) commodity mountain = surplus of a certain agricultural product produced in the EC, for example the "butter mountain".

**Movement Record.** Record kept by a farmer of all movements of animals on and off the farm premises (compulsory in the UK since 1925).

**Mower.** Machine used to cut grass and other upright crops. The cut crop is left in a swath behind the cutting mechanism for further treatment in the process of making hay or silage. The main types of mowers are; cutter bar mowers, which are rear-mounted and consist of a framework with a hinged cutter bar; the cutter bar has a number of fingers with a cutting edge on each side; these support the knife; rotary mowers are made with two or four rotors, each having two, three or four turning blades: Flail mowers have a high-speed rotor fitted with swinging flails which cut the grass and leave it bruised in a fluffy swath; cylinder mowers, used for lawns, but rarely used on farms.

**Muddy.** Covered with mud.

**Mudflats.** Areas of flat mud, usually near the mouths of rivers.

**Mule.** (a) Hybrid (and usually sterile) offspring of a male ass and a mare (b) crossbred sheep from a Blue-faced Leicester ram and a Swaledale ewe; mules have speckled faces and a high lambing rate.

**Mull.** Well decomposed humus mixed with mineral matter; it occurs under neutral or alkaline conditions, such as under deciduous forests.

**Multi-cropping.** Multiple cropping, growing more than one crop on the same piece of land in one year wet rice is often multi-cropped.

**Multigerm Seed.** Seed which occurs as a cluster of seeds fused together and which produces more than one plant when it germinates; a common example is the sugar beet seed; the multiple plants must be reduced to one by a process called "singling".

**Murray Grey.** Breed of beef cattle, silver grey in colour; a polled early-maturing hardy breed; the carcass has a high proportion of lean meat.

**Mustard.** Species of brassica (*Sinapsis*), whose seeds are among the most important species; also used as green manure. Much of the mustard grown commercially is rape (*Brassica napus*); the seeds of black mustard (*Brassica nigra*) are ground to produce the yellow spice; while white mustard (*Brassica alba*) is grown as a salad crop (used in mustard and cress).

**Mutation.** Change in the DNA which changes the gene.

**Mycelium.** Mass of threads which forms the main part of a fungus.

**Mycology.** Study of fungi.

**Mycorrhiza.** Types of fungi which are associated with plant roots and help in nutrient uptake.

**Myrtaceae.** Family of Australian plants, including the eucalyptus.

**Myzomatosis.** Usually fatal virus disease affecting rabbits, transmitted by fleas.

# N

**NAC.** National Agricultural Centre.

**Nanny Goat.** Female goat.

**National Agricultural Centre (NAC).** The site of the annual Royal show (at stoneleigh, in Warwickshire), owned by the RASE.

**National Farers' Union (NFU).** Organization representing the interests of British farmers in negotiations with the government and other agencies.

**National Institute of Agricultural Botany (NIAB).** Organization which tests all new varieties of crops; after successful testing, the varieties are made available to farmers.

**National List.** List of Agricultural crop varieties tests by the NIAB and available for sale; under EC regulations all seeds sold to farmers or horticulturists must be tested and certified.

**National Union of Agricultural and Allied Workers (NUAW).** Independent section of the Transport and General Workers Union representing the interests of farm workers in negotiating terms and conditions of their employment.

**Nature.** (i) Essential quality of something; (ii) kind or sort; (iii) plants, animals and their environment in general.

**Nature Conservation.** Active management of natural resources to ensure their quality is maintained and that they are wisely used.

**Nature Conservancy Council (NCC).** Official body is the UK which is responsible for the conservation of nature.

**Nature Reserve.** Special area where the wildlife is protected (National Nature Reserves are designated by the NCC).

**Nature Trail.** Footpath with signposts and explanatory notices, designed to explain the fauna and flora of a piece of countryside to the general public; some farms have designed trails as a means of supplementing farm income.

**Nematicide.** Substance which kills nematode worms.

**Nematodirus Disease.** Disease of lambs caused by paraitic roundworms; the animals suffer diarrhoea and loss of condition.

**Nemoriculture.** Primitive stage of human culture, concerning mainly food-gathering in forests.

**Nest.** Construction built by birds and some fish for their eggs; construction made by some social insects, such as ants and bees, for the colony to live in.

**Nest Box.** Open fronted box in which a hen lays eggs; the box may be single unit or part of a series of boxes.

**Nettle.** Plant, especially one of the genus *Urtica* which possesses stinging hairs.

**New Blood.** New strain of a breed introduced by outcrossing.

**Newcastle Disease.** Fowl pest, an acute febrile contagious disease of fowls; affected birds suffer loss of appette, diarrhoea and respiratory problems. Mortality rates are high.

**Nemoriculture.** Primitive stage of human culture, concerning mainy food-gathering in forests.

**NFE.** Nitrogen-free Extract used in the chemical analysis of animal feeding stuffs; the nitrogen-free extract consists mainly of soluble carbohydrates (sugars) and starch.

**NFU.** National Farmers' Union.

**NIAB.** National Institute of Agricultural Botany.

**Nicotiana.** Name for the tobacco plant.

**Nightshade.** Plants of the family Solanaceae which, if eastern by stock, are likely to cause sickness or death deadly. Nightshade = poisonous plant (*Atrropa belladonna*) which is sometimes eaten by animals.

**Night Soil.** Human excreta, collected and used for fertilizer in some parts of the world, particularly in China and the far East.

**Night Soil.** Human excreta, collected and used for fertilizer in some parts of the world, particularly in can and the Far East.

**Nitrate.** (i) Anion with the formula $NO_3$; (ii) natural constituent of plants; beets, cabbage, cauliflower and broccoli can contain up to 1mg/kg; (iii) chemical compound containing the nitrate ion such as sodium nitrate; nitrate-sensitive area (NSA) = region of the country where nitrate pollution is likely, and where the use of nitrate fertilizers is strictly controlled.

Nitrates are a source of nitrogen for plants; they are used as fertilizers but can run off into rivers and as they are highly soluble in water easily enter the water supply.

**Nitrogen.** Chemical element which is essential to biological life (a gas which is the main component of air and is an essential part of protein).

**Nitrogen Cycle.** Process by which nitrogen enters living organisms (the nitrogen is absorbed into green plants in the form of nitrates, the plants are then eastern by animals, and the nitrogen is returned to the ecosystem through the animal's excreta or when an anima or a plant dies).

**Nitrogen Deficiency.** Lack of nitrogen in soil, found where organic matter is low; it results in thin, weak grown of plants, especially grasses, cereals, kales and cabbages.

**Nitrogen Fertilizers.** Many straight and compound fertilizers contain nitrogen, but it is quickly changed by bacteria in the soil to the nitrate form.

**Nitrogen Fixation.** Process by which nitrogen in air is converted by bacteria in certain plants into nitrogen compounds, and when the plants die the nitrogen is released into the soil and acts as a fertilizer.

**Nitrogen-fixing Plants.** Plants, such as Lucerne or beans, which form a association with bacteria which convert nitrogen from the air into nitrogen compounds which pass into the soil.

**Nitrogenous Fertilizers.** Fertilizers (such as sulphate of ammonia) which are based on nitrogen.

**Nitrogen-free Extract (NFE).** Used in the chemical analysis of animal feeding stuffs, the nitrogen-free extract consists mainly of soluble carbohydrates (sugars) and starch.

Nitrogen is taken into an animal's body by digesting protein-rich foods; excess nitrogen is excreted in urine. When the intake of nitrogen and the excretion rte are equal the body is in nitrogen balance or protein balance. Nitrogen is supplied to the soil by fertilizers, organic matter, nodule bacteria on legumes, and by nitrogen-fixing microorganisms in the soil. The nitrogen cycle is the series of processes by which nitrogen is converted into nitrates which are absorbed into green plants. The plats are then eaten by animals, which themselves are eaten by other animals. The nitrates are returned to the ecosystem in excreta or when animals or plants die.

**Nodule.** Small node found on the roots f leguminous crops; the nodules contain types of bacteria which can convert nitrogen from the air into nitrogen compounds.

**Nomadic.** Referring to nomads the herdsmen in the area lead a nomdic existence; nomadic pastoralists move their livestock aroudnto eed on available grazing.

**Nomadian.** Habit of certain animals which move around from place to place without having fixed habitat.

**Non-Centrifugal Sugar.** Dark semi-solid sugar made by boiling the juices obtained from crushed sugar cane; India is the principal producer.

**Non-persistent Pesticide.** (Pesticide) which does not remain toxic for long so does not enter the food chain.

**Normandy.** Breed of cattle from north-west France; the coat is white with red-brown patches. The animals are reared for meat and milk, from which the camembert cheese is made.

**Northern Dairy Shorthorn.** Dairy breed o cattle, which comes from the old Teeswater cattle, with perhaps a little Ayrshire blood; now established as a pure breed. The most popular colour is light roan, but red, white and mixtures of shades are found. The animals are thrifty, hardy and suitable for harsh upland conditions.

**Notify.** To report something officialy the MAFF must be notified of any outbreak of foot and mouth disease.

**Notifiable Disease.** (a) Serious infectious disease of animals and poultry which in Great Britain has to be reported to the police when an outbreak is confirmed on a farm (b) diseases and pests of plants which must be notified to the MAFF.

**NPK.** For a compound or mixed fertilizer containing nitrogen, phosphorus and potassium.

**NUAAW.** National Union of Agricultural and Allied Workers.

**Nubian Goat.** Breed of goat of mixed Egyptian an d Indian origin, now crossed with British goats to produce the Anglo-Nubian breed.

**Nucleus.** Central body in a cell, containing DNA and RNA, and controlling the function and characteristics of the cell.

**Nurse Cow.** Cow used to suckle the calves of others.

**Nurse Crop.** Crop grown to give protection to young plants of a perennial crop which is being established; nurse crops provide shade and act as windbreaks; in the tropics, bananas can be used as a nurse crop for cocoa.

**Nursery.** Place where plants are grown until they are large enough to be planted in their final positions; tree nursery = place where trees are grown from seed until they are large enough to be planted out.

**Nursery Bed.** Bed in which seedlings are planted out for the seedbed until they are large enough to be put in permanent positions.

**Nut.** (a) The seed of certain trees (a fruit with a single seed in a hard woody shell) (b) any hard edible seed contained in a fibrous or woody shell (such as groundnuts) (c) small cube of compressed meal; a convenient form of animal feed.

**Nutrient.** (i) Substance (such as protein or fat or vitamin) in food which is necessary to provide energy or to help the body grow, repair and maintain itself; (ii) substance which a plat needs to allow it to grow and produce seed the major nutrients needed by plants are carbon, hydrogen, oxygen, nitrogen, phosphorus, potassium, calcium, magnesium and sulphur, minor nutrients are trace elements such as boron, copper or manganese; nutrient.

**Nutrition.** (a) Nourishment or food which an animal eats (b) Studyof diet.

**Nutritional.** Referring to nutrition the nutritional quality of meat.

**Nutritional Disorder.** Disorder related to food and nutrients.

**Nymph.** Stage following the larval stage in certain flies, such as the dragonfly.

# O

**Oak.** Common hardwood tree of the genus Quercus found in temperate regions; it provides valuable timber.

**Oarweed.** Common seaweed (*Laminaria digitata*) used as food.

**Oasthouse.** Building containing a kiln of or drying hops; it is a circular or square building with a characteristic conical roof.

**Oats.** Hardy cereal crop (*Avena saiva*) grown in most types of soil in cool wet northern temperate regions; best quality oats can be used for making biscuits, oatcakes and porridge, Mainly used for animal feed.

**Oatmeal.** Feeding stuff produced when the husk is removed from the oats kernel by a rolling process; oatmeal is particularly good for horses and valuable for cattle and sheep, but not as suitable for pigs because of its high fibre content.

**Oestrogen.** Hormone produced in the ovaries of animals which stimulates the reproductive system; also produced in small a mounts by the testis; also called "bulling hormone".

**Offal.** (a) Inside parts of an animal, such as liver, kidney or intestines, when used as food (as opposed to meat, which is muscle)(b) wheat offals = the embryo and seed coat of the wheat grain, used as animal feed.

**Off-going Crop.** Crop sown by a tenant farmer before leaving the farm at the end of his tenancy; he is permitted to return and harvest the crop and remove it.

**Oil.** Liquid which cannot be mixed with water; corn oil =vegetable oil obtained from maize grains, used for cooking and as a salad oil; essentials oils = oils from scented plants used in cosmetics and as antiseptics; Palm kernel oil = vegetable oil produced from the kernels of the oil palm nut, used for making margarine, and cooking fat; the residue after extraction of the oil is used as a livestock feed; palm oil = edible oil produced from the seed or fruit of an oil palm; red in coulour, with only 5-12% polyunsaturated fatty acids, it is widely used in cooking fats and margarines; the residue after extraction is used as livestock feed; sunflower oil = oil extracted from sunflower seeds; seeds contain between 25 and 45% of semi-drying oil which is high in unsaturated fats.

**Oil Palm.** *Elaeis guineensis*, a tree indigenous to West Africa, which yields large supplies of oil; the fruit produces two distinct oil, palm oil from the pericarp and palm kernel oil from the hard kernel.

**Oilseed Cake.** A Feedingstuff concentrate, high in protin, made from the residue of seeds which have been crushed to produce oil.

**Oilseeds or Oilseed Crops.** Crops from which vegetable oils are extracted from the fruit or seed.

**Oilseed Rape.** Important oil-yielding crop; the seed contains about 42% of oil, whchis extracted by crushing and is used in making margarine, cooking fats and salad oils. The residual cake is used for stock feeding. Oilseed rape will grow in a wide range of soil and climatic conditions; there are both spring and winter varieites; it is also useful as a break crop between cereals. See also *Double Lows*.

There are three types of oil: Fixed veetable and animal oils; essential volatile oils; and mineral oils. The most important oil-producing crops are the coconut palm, the oil palm, groundnuts, linseed, soya beans, maize nd cotton seed. Other sources are olives, rape seed, lupin; seasame and sunflowers. After the nuts or seed have been crushed to extract the oil, the residue may be used as a ivestock feed or as a fertilizer.

**Olive.** Mediterranean tree (*Olea europaea*), with fruit from which edible oil can be produced; a considerable quantity offritis grown for direct consumption; olive oil = oil pressed from the olive, said to be the finest of the edible oils. The first crushing gives the highest grade oil for cooking and medicinal purposes; the residue gives oil used in making soap and other industrial uses.

**Onion.** Vegetable crop (*Allium cepa*), grown either for cooking or for eating in saads; the ripe onion consists of the edible swollen leaf bases surrounded by scale leaves. It is harvested when the growing tops have fallen over; it is the dormant bulbs which are harvested and eaten; onion fly = an insect pest (*Hylemyia antiqua*) which causes damage to onions by the maggots which eat into the developing bulb; onion set = a seed onion, a small onion grown from seed, which has been dried, and which is planted the following year so that it will root and grow on to maturity.

**Open fields.** Fields which are not separated by hedges or walls, but by banks of earth; formerly, fields were divided into strips, each worked by a farmer; the system was used originally by the Saxons.

**Orange.** Fruit of the *Citrus aurantium*, a native tree of China; its nutritional value is due mainly to its high vitamin C content; grown in semi-tropical and Mediterranean regions, it is eaten as fresh fruit or used for juice and for making preserves. The USA, Brazil, Spain, Morocco and Israel are large exporters of oranges.

Blood oranges are coloured by the presence of anthocyanims; mandarin oranges such as satsumas and tangerines have loose peel, The Seville orange is a bitter orange, grown in Spain and used by marmalade anufacturers.

**Orchard area of land used for growing fruit treed.** Orchards were once a common feature of most farms, but now fruit is commercially produced by specialized commercial growers. The modern orchard consists of trees grafted onto dwarfing rootstock, shaped by pruning and closely planted in rows which are separated to allow room for tractors and sprayers to pass. Applies, plums, pears and cherries are the most important tree fruits in Britain with Kent, worcestersire ad parts of East Anglia being the most important growing regions. In the USA, oranges and other citrus fruits are grown in orchards in the Southern States, in particular in Florida and California.

**Organic.** (i) (substance) which comes from an animal or plant; (ii) chemical compound which contains carbon; (iii) (food) which has been cultivated naturally, without any chemical fertilizers or pesticides; organic fertilizers = plant nutrients which are returned to the soil from dead or decaying plant matter and animal wastes, such as compost farmyard manure and bone meal.

**Organically.** (Food) grown using natural fertilizers and not chemicals.

**Organic Farming.** Method of farming which does not involve using chemical fertilizers or pesticides.

Organic farming uses natural fertilizers and rotates stock farming (i.e. raising of animals) with crop farming; soil nutrients are maintained by the addition of plant and animal manures, and pest control is achieved by he use of naturally derived pesticides, and by crop rotation. Which allows natural predation to take place. Organic farming may produce lower yields than traditional or intensive farming, but the lower yields may be offset by the high cost of the chemical fertilizers used in intensive farming; it may become more economic than conventional farming due to premium prices which are paid for organic products. In areas of over production, organic farming has the advantage of reducing crop production without loss of quality-and without taking land out of agricultural use. At the preset time, less than 10% of Britain's farmland is organically cultivated. The main factor in controlling conversion to organic farming is the capital cost.

**Organochlorine.** Chlorinated hydrocarbon, any of several chemical compounds containing chlorin, used as an insecticide (such as aldrin, dieldrein, etc.).

Organochlorine insecticides are very insistent, with a long half-life of upto 15 years, while organophosphorous insecticides have a much shorter life. Chlorinated hydrocarbon insecticides not only kill insects, but also enter the food chain and kill small animals and birds which feed on the insects.

**Orphaned Animal.** Young animal whose mother has died, and is therefore either fostered onto another animal or has to be hand-reared.

**Osmotic Pressure.** The force exerted to enable the flow of water through a cell wall in the process of osmosis.

**Outbreak.** Series of cases of a disease which start suddenly there is an outbreak of foot and mouth disease in the area.

**Outbreeding.** Breeding of animals that are less closely related than the average of the population from which they come.

**Outcrossing.** Bringing some new genetic variation ("new blood") into a flock or herd; usually done by introducing a new male.

**Outfields.** In hill farms, the fields furthest from the homestead, cropped only from time to time and allowed to life allow for long periods.

**Outhouse.** Farm building which is not attached to the main farmhouse, and may be used for storage or for keeping poultry.

**Oven-ready Poultry.** Poultry which has been slaughtered and dressed so that it can be cooked without any further preparation.

**Over cropping.** Growing too many crops on poor soil, which has the effect of weakening the soil still further.

**Overcultivated.** (Land) which has been too intensively cultivated and so is exhausted.

**Overexploitation.** Action of exploiting land too much overexploitation has reduced yields by half.

**Overfeed.** To give animals too much feed.

**Overgraze.** To graze a pasture so much that it is no longer rich enough to provide grazing for cattle.

**Overgrown.** (Seedbed or field) which is covered with weeds or other unwanted vegetation.

**Overtopping.** Cutting too much off the top of plant when preparing it (as it the case of sugar beet)

**Ox.** Male or female domestic cattle, and also the castrated male, especially when used as a draught animal.

**Oxford Down.** The largest of the down breeds of sheep, produced by crossing Southdown improved stock with the longwoolled Cotswold; it has a dark-brown face and legs and a conspicuous topknot.

**Oxidases.** Enzymes that oxidize compounds by removing hydrogen and adding it to oxygen to form water.

**Oxygen.** Chemical element, a common colourless gas which is present in the air, essential to biological life and is widespread in rocks.

**Oxygenate.** To treat (blood) with oxygen.

**Oxygenation.** Becoming filled with oxygen.

Oxygen is an important constituent of living matter, s well as water and air. Oxygen is absorbed from the air into the bloodstream through the lungs and is carried to the tissues along the arteries; it is essential to normal metabolism. Oxygen is formed by plants from carbon dioxide in the atmosphere during photosynthesis and released back into the air.

**Oxytoxin.** Hormone which activates the release of milk in the udder and the contractions in the uterus during birth; also possibly important in contracting the uterus during mating. Its action is blocked by the release of adrenalin.

# P

**Packhouse.** Building used for grading, cleaning and packing produce on a farm, before it is sent to the customer.

**Paddock.** Small enclosed field, usually near farm buildings; Paddock grazing = rotational grazing system which uses paddocks of equal area for grazing, followed by rest period.

**Paddy or Padi.** (i) Growing rice crop, a cultivated grass, crop of the monsoon area of south-east Asia; (ii) Rice grains which have been harvested, but not processed in any way; paddy (field) = field filled with water, in which rice is grown paddies are breeding grounds fro mosquitoes scientists believe that paddy fields contribute to the methane in the atmosphere.

**Palatable.** Which is good to eat some types of grass are less palatable than others; big bales preserve the grass in an almost cut state which is very palatable.

**Palm.** Large tropical plant growing as tall as a tree, with branching fern-like leaves producing fruits which give oil and other foodstuffs; coconut palm or date palm = palms which produce coconuts or dates; palm kernel oil = vegetable oil produced from the kernels of the oil palm nut, used in the manufacture of margarine, and cooking fat; the residue after traction of the oil is used as a livestock feed.

**Palm Oil.** Edible oil produced from the seed or fruit of an oil palm; red in colour, with only 5-12% polyunsaturated fatty acids, it is widely used in cooking fats and margarines; the residue after traction issued as livestock feed.

**Pampas.** Temperate grasslands of south America, found in Argentina and Uruguay.

**Pan.** (a) wide shallow pot for growing seeds (b) hard cemented layer of soil, impervious to drainage, lying below the surface; it is formed by the deposition of iron compounds or by ploughing at the same depth every year; pan may be broken up by using a subsoiler.

**Papaya.** Native of tropical South America, but now found in all tropical regions. The greenish-yellow melonshaped fruits have a soft pulp which is eaten raw; the fruit is also a valuable source of papain, which is used in brewing and in tenderizing meat. The leaves are also used in cooking to make meat tender.

**Parasite.** Plant or animal which lives on or inside another organism (the host) and draws nourishment from it; See also *Ecotoparasite, Endoparasite*.

**Parasiticide.** Which kills parasites.

**Parasitism.** State in which one organism (the parasite) lives on another organism (the host) and derives its nourishment and other needs from it.

**Parasitize.** To live as a parasite on (another organism) sheep are parasitized by flukes.

**Parasitold.** Animal which is a parasite only at one stage in its development.

**Parathion.** Organophosphorous compound used to control insect pests.

**Parent.** Parent cell or mother cell = original cell which splits into daughter cells by mitosis; parent material rock = the unweathered base rock which breaks down o form a constituent part of the surface soil.

**Park.** Area of open land used as a place of recreation; country park= area in the countryside set aside for the public to visit and enjoy; national park = large area of unspoilt land, owned and managed by a special planning authority which has control over agriculture as well as the normal planning powers. Parks exist for people to enjoy and for scenery. Flora and fauna, and were established forming is effectively maintained.

**Parkland.** Grassland with scattered trees, typical of large landed estates.

**Parlour.** Milking parlour = building in which cows are milked, and often are also fed, washed and cleaned; parlour systems = the four basic designs of parlour; the herringbone parlour, the abreast parlour, the tandem parlour and the rotary parlour.

**Parship.** Plant (*Pastinaca sativa*) whose long white root is eaten as a vegetable.

**Parthenais.** Breed of cattle originating in France; it produces calves for a suckler herd, and is known for easy calving and high growth rate.

**Parthenocarpy.** The production of fruit without seeds.

**Partial Drought.** In the UK, period of at least 29 consecutive days when the mean rainfall does not exceed 2.54mm.

**Part-time Farming.** Type of farming, where the farmer ha a regular occupation other than farming; common throughout much of central and Eastern Europe. In the UK, part-time farmers are mainly wealthy people who farm as a hobby or as a second form of business.

**Parturition.** Giving birth to offspring, when the foetus leaves the uterus, called by different names according to the animal.

**Passion Fruit or Granadilla.** Passiflora edulis, a climbing plant with purple juicy fruit. It is native to Brazil.

**Pasta.** Food made from flour from durum wheat, such as spaghetti, lasagne, etc.

**Pasteurization.** Heating of food or food products to destroy bacteria, but without affecting palatability.

**Pasteurize.** To kill bacteria in food by heating it the government is telling people to drink only pasteurized milk.

Pasteurization is carried out by heating food for a short time at a lower temperature than that used for sterilization; the two methods used are heating to 72°C for fifteen seconds (the high temperature short time method) or to 65° for half an hour, and then cooling rapidly. This has the effect of killing tuberculosis bacteria. Pasteurization is used principally in the preservation of milk for human consumption.

**Pastoral.** Available for pasture.

**Pastoralist.** Farmer who keeps grazing animals on pasture the people most affected by the drought in the Sahara are nomadic pastoralists.

Pastoral farming ranges from large-scale highly scientific systems such as cattle or sheep-ranching to primitive systems of domadism. In relatively dry or inhospitable regions, the need to find pastures for grazing animals causes the farmers to lead a nomadic existence.

**Pasture** (1) Grassland grown for or used for the grazing of livestock, as opposed to meadows which are grown for hay or silage the cows are in the pasture or the cows are put to pastures; alphine pastures = grass fields in high mountains which are used by cattle farmers in the summer; pasture management = the control of pasture by grazing, cutting, reseeding, etc. (2) To put animals in a pasture their cows are pastured in fields high in the mountains.

**Pasturage.** Place where animals are pastured.

**Pastureland.** Land which is given over to pasture.

**Patent Flour.** Very fine good-quality wheat flour.

**Pathogen.** Germ, virus, etc.; a microorganism which causes a disease.

**Pathogenesis.** Origin or production or development of a disease.

**Pathogenicity.** Ability of a pathogen to cause a disease.

**Pause.** Rest period in a bird's laying cycle.

**Pb.** Symbol for lead.

**Pea.** Pisum sativum, an important grain legume; pea and bean weevil = pest (Sitona sp) affecting peas, beans and other legumes. The eggs are laid in soil near the plants, allowing the larvae to feed on the roots. The adult weevils feed on the leaves, making U-shaped notches in the edges of the leaves.

Peas are grown for pulses and for their immature seeds which are eaten fresh as a green vegetable and are also often frozen; occasionally the young pods are eaten as mangetouts. Peas are also grown for forage and may be used for hay and silage; they are often grown following a cereal crop in rotation, and enrich the soil with nitrogen. Most peas are harvested, transported and processed on the same day ad the majority are taken for freezing and canning. Vining peas are Britain's most important contract vegetable crop.

**Peach.** Small deciduous tree (*Prunus persica*) found particularly in Mediterranean areas, though it will grow as far north as southern england. The fruit are large and juicy, with a downy skin; they cannot be kept for any length of time. Peaches are divided into two groups; the freestone (where the flesh is not attached to the stone), and the clingstone. The nectarine is a form of peach with a smooth skin.

**Peach-leaf curl.** Fungal disease which affects peaches, where the leaves swell and become red.

**Pear.** A pome fruit of the genus Pyrus used for dessert fruit, cooking or for fermenting to make perry; in the UK, William's Bon Chretien, Conference and Doyenne du comice are popular dessert varieties, while William'sis also commonly used for canning.

**Peat.** Wet, partly-decayed mosses and other plants which form the soil of a bog.

**Peatland.** Area of land covered with peat bog.

**Peck.** (1) Measure of capacity of dry goods, equal to a quarter of a bushel or two gallons (used as measure of grain) (2) To pick up food with the beak; pecking order = the order of social dominance in a group of birds and also animals (the equivalent in cattle is the "bunt order").

**Pectin.** Cellulose substance which is found in cell walls of certain fruit, and which forms a jelly when heated with sugar; this is important in making jam.

**Pedigree.** The ancestra line of animals bred by breeders, or of cultivated plants; pedigree market = the market for animals sold for breeding, not for slaughter (as opposed to the commercial market); Pedigree records= records of pedigree stock kept by the breeder and by breed societies; pedigree animals are registered at birth and given official numbers; pedigree selection = the selection of animals for breeding based on the records of their ancestors.

**Pedology.** The study of the soil.

**Pedologist.** Scientist who has specialized in the study of the soil.

**Pekin.** Breed of table duck; it has buff coloured feathers and bright orange feet, legs and bill.

**Pellet.** Form of feeding stuff (usually mash) which has been moistened and pressed to form small grains.

**Pelleted Seed.** Seed coated with clay to produce pellets of uniform size and density; pelleting is done to make the sowing of very fine seed easier.

**Penicillium.** Fungus from which penicillin is derived.

**Pepper.** (a) Spice (either black or white) from the fruit of the pepper vine (b) fruit of the Capsicum, either red, yellow or green (c) Chilli peppers = small red fruit of the Capsicum frutescens which are very pungent; the dried fruit are used to make Cayenne pepper.

**Peppermint.** Aromatic herb (*Mentha Piperata*) which is cultivated to produce an oil used in confectionery, drinks and toothpaste.

**Perch.** (1) Wooden rail on which a bird sites (2) To sit on a branch or wooden rail.

**Percheron.** Heavy breed of horse, developed in Normandy; it is grey in colour.

**Performance Test.** Record of growth rate in an individual animal over a given period of time, when fed on a standard ration. Performance testing gives the breeder a better chance of identifying generically superior animals.

**Pericarp.** Fibrous layers next to the outer husk of a cereal grain, removed during milling. It is the major constituent of bran.

**Permanent.** Which exists always; permanent hardness = hardness of water, caused by calcium and magnesium, which remains even after the water has been boiled; permanent pasture = and which remains solely as grassland over a long period of time, and is not ploughed.

**Permeability.** Ability to allow water to pass through; (of a membrane) ability to allow fluid containing chemical substances to pass through.

**Permeable.** Which allows a liquid to pass through; (membrane) which can allow substances dissolved in fluids to pass through.

**Perpetual-flowering.** Variety of plant which bears flowers more or less all year round.

**Persimmon.** Native tree (Diospyros kaki) of Japan and China, which produces reddish-orange fruit, similar in appearance to tomatoes; the fruit are eaten either as dessert or ma be cooked; they are very rich in vitamins.

**Persist.** To continue for some time; to remain active for some time some substances persist in toxic forms in the air for weeks; plants which persist for more than two years are called perennials.

**Persistence.** Ability of a pollutant to remain active for a period of time.

**Persistency.** Ability of a plant to survive for a long time, even when the soil is cultivated ryegrasses are used for leys where persistency is not important.

**Persistent.** Which continues for some time; persistent insecticide = insecticide that remains toxic (either in the soil or in the body of an animal) and is passed from animal to animal through the food chain.

**Pervious.** Which can allow substances dissolved in fluids t pass through.

**Pest.** (a) Living organism which is in any way disruptive to the growth of crops or animals, or which may cause trouble to stored produce a spray to remove insect pests; peast control = the control of pests (by killing them) (b) name given to some diseases, such as fowl pest.

The word is a relative term; a pest to one person may not be a pest to another, so foxes are pests of chicken farmers, but not to naturalists. It has been estimated that around 50% of the total potential world harvest is lost through the activities of pests, and losses are significantly higher than this in poorer countries where pesticides are less readily available.

**Pesticide.** Toxic agent used to control a wide variety of plant, animal and microbial organisms which might have an adverse effect on growing or harvested crops, or on livestock.

**Pesticide Safety Precaution Scheme (PSPS).** Agreement between the agrochemical industry and the government, supported by Health and Safety regulations, which designates products as safe to use, provided recommended precautions are taken during their use.

There are three basic types of pesticide. I. Organochlorine insecticides, which have a high persistence in the environment of up to about 15 years (DDT, diedrin and aldrin); (2). Organophosphates, which have an intermediate persistence of several months (parathion, carbaryl nd malathion); (3). Carbamates, which have low persistence of around two weeks (*Temik, Seetran and Zineb*). Most pesticides are broad-spectum, that is they kill all insects in a certain are and may kill other animals like birds and small mammals. Pesticide residue levels in food in the UK are generally low. Pesticide residues have been found in bran products, bread and baby foods, as well as in milk and meat. Where pesticides are found, the levels are low and rarely exceed international maximum residue levels.

**Petal.** Outer coloured part of the corolla of a flower.

**Phacelia.** Plant used as a ground cover crop (introduced into the UK from the USA.)

**Phagocyte.** Cell (such as a white blood cell) which can surround and destroy other cells, such as bacteria cells.

**Phaseolus.** Latin name for beans, such as the French bean and butter bean.

**Phenoxyherbicide.** Herbicide, based on 2, 4, 5-T.

**Pheromones.** Sex attractants produced by female insects to attract males. Artificial pheromones are used to disorientate male insects and prevent mating. Synthetic boar pheromones can be used both to stimulate and detect oestrus in sows and gilts.

**Phloem.** Living tissue in a plant which carries organic substances from leaves to other parts of the plant (as opposed to xylem, which is dead tissue).

**Phosphate.** Salt of phosphoric acid, which is an essential plant nutrient and which is formed naturally by weathering of rocks.
Phosphates escape into water from sewage, especially in waste water containing detergents, and encourage the growth of algae by eutrophication. Natural organic phosophates are provided by guano and fishmeal; otherwise, phosphates are mined (especially in the USSR, the USA and Mexico). Artificially produced phosphates are used in agriculture; the main types of phosophate fertilizer are ground rock phosphate. Hyperphosphate, superphosphate, triple superphosphate and basic slags. Phosphate deliciency is one of the commonest deficiencies in livestock, and gives rise to osteomalacia.

**Phosphoric Acid.** Acid which forms phosphates.

**Phosphorus.** Toxic chemical element which is essential to biological life, being present in bones and nerve tissue (pure phosphorus will cause burns if it touches the skin and can poison if swallowed); phospharus cycle = cycle by which phosphorus atoms are circulated through living organisms.

Phosphorus is an essential part of DNA and RNA, and when an organism dies, the phosphorus contained in its tissues returns to the soil and is taken up by plants in the phosphorous cycle. Phosphorus deficiency in plants causes stunted growth, discoloration of leaves and small or misshapen fruit.

**Photoperiodicity.** Way n which plants and animals react to changes in the length of the period of daylight from summer to winter.

**Photorespiration.** Respiration that occurs in plants in the light; in $C_4$ plants photorespiration is very low.

**Photosynthesis.** Process by which green plants convert carbon dioxide and water into sugar and oxygen using sunlight as energy.

**Phytotoxicant.** Substance which is poisonous to plants.

**Pick.** To take ripe frit or vegetables from plants.

**Picker.** Person who picks fruit or vegetables a strawberry picker.

**Pickle.** To preserve food by keeping it in vinegar; pickling cabbage or pickling onions = cabbage or onions specially grown for preserving.

**Pick-up Attachment.** Attachment used on combine to lift grass swath and feed it into the main elevator; it is fitted over the combine cutter bar.

**Pick-up Baler.** Machine which picks up cut grass and makes small bales; the machine which makes big bales is called a “big baler”

**Pick-up Reel.** Part of a combine harvester with spring tines, used to improve cutting efficiency in tangled crops.

**Pick-your-own (PYO).** System where customers are allowed onto the farm, to pick what they need from the field; it is used with most types of soft fruit and many vegetables. Plebald. Whose coat has two colours, especially black and white, in irregular shapes.

**Piecework.** Work for which workers are paid for the products produced or for the piece of work done, and not at an hourly rate; potato pickers and strawberry pickers are paid in this way.

**Pledmontese.** Breed of beef cattle from north-west Italy; the animals are light or dark grey, with block horns, ears and tail.

**Pig.** Animal of the *Suidae* family kept exclusively for met production.

**Pig future.** Sales on the commodity market of pigment for future delivery.

**Pig Improvement Scheme.** Scheme Introduced by the Meat and Livestock Commission to improve pig stock; the scheme involves extensive performance testing.

**Pigeon.** Bird which is regarded as a pest, and can cause severe damage to small plants; the wood pigeon nets cereal seed and causes damage to young and mature crops of peas and brassicas. Destruction of nests and pigeon shoots are the only effective way of keeping these birds under control.

**Pigeon Pea.** Tropical legume (*Cajanus cajan*) native to Africa; a drought-resistant plant producing seeds which are eaten cooked. In Indian it is known as "red gram" and used to make dhal.

**Piggery.** Place where pigs are housed.

Pigs can be kept successfully under allsorts of conditions, but housing systems must provide efficient feeding facilities. Individual feeding of sows is essential, and confining dry sows in stalls is common. Farrowing sows and their litters need careful housing; farrowing should take place in a special crate which prevents overlying of piglets (where the sow crushes the piglets by lying on them). Breeding pigs may be reared outsdoors and housed in moveable arks. Fattening pigs can be housed in yards, usually covered with straw edding and provided with a shelter, but more commonly they are kept in special buildings with controlled environments and ventilation, feeding, watering and efficient disposal of dung through special channels. There are many systems of pig housing, ranging from the traditional cottage piggery, with its low-roofed pens and open yard; the Danish type, a totally enclosed building with a controlled environment; the flat deck type, used for rearing young pigs, with special heating and ventilation controls; the Solari piggery, with fattening pens on each side of a central feeding passage, housed in an open-sided Dutchbarin; and the monopitch type incorporating artificially controlled natural ventilation.

**Pigman.** Term formerly used for a male farm worker who looks after pigs (now replaced, in advertisements, by "pigperson")

**Pigmeat.** Term used in the EC for meat from pigs.

**Pig Production.** Commercial farming of pigs.
Sows are mature enough to breed at around six months of age. They are usually mated with the boar every 140-150 days. After a gestation period of 114 days a litter is born and is usually allowed to suckle for 21-28 days. Four to seven days after separating the sow from her piglets, she comes into oestrus and allows the boar to mate. Each of the resulting litters will consist of about ten piglets, an over her lifetime the sow will other six to eight litters. Sows may be kept in stalls, sometimes completely closed, and sometimes open-ended. Sows are tethered in open-ended stalls. Sows

are also kept in covered yards on straw. New systems are being introduced, such as the use of a collar for each sow, with its computer code number; the number is relayed to a computer which allocates a measured amount of feed to the sow. Herds of sows are also kept in open fields, using arks for shelter.

**Pine** (a) Pine tree = evergreen tree of the genus *Pinus* growing in temperate latitudes the north of the country is covered with pine forests; pine kernels = seeds of the Mediterranean pine (*Pinus pinea*) eaten raw or roasted and salted, and also used in cooking and confectionery.

**Pineapple.** Fruit of a tropical plant *Ananas comosus*, native to South America and now grown in many tropical areas; the fruit are eaten both raw and canned, or in the form of juice extracted by crushing; Mexico, the Philippines, Coted'Ivoire, Malasia and Hawaii are major producers.

**Pining.** Disease of sheep, caused by shortage of cobalt; the animals lose condition, and have poor fleece, dull eyes and general weakness.

**Pinzgauer.** Breed of cattle from Austria; the animals are coloured reddish or dark brown with a distinctive white strip along the back; both a meat and draught breed.

**Pioneer Crop.** Crop grown to improve general soil fertility, prior to the sowing of another more valuable crop; pioneers crops are grazed by livestock with the result that dunging improves the soil's fertility.

**Pipe.** To bring water to an area in pies (as opposed to irrigation canals) water is piped to fields to provide irrigation.

**Pippin.** Name given to several dessert apples.

**Pistachio.** Small tree ((*Pistacia vera*) native of central Asia and now cultivated in Mediterranean regions; the nuts are eaten salted or in confectionery.

**Pistil.** The female part of a flower.

**Pitted.** Fruit with the stones removed.

**Placement Drill.** Machine which drills seeds and fertilizer at the same time, and places the fertilizer close to the side of and below the rows of seeds.

**Placenta.** Tissue which grows inside the uterus in mammals during pregnancy and links the embryo to the mother.

**Placental.** Referring to the placenta.

The placenta allows an exchange of oxygen and nutrients to be passed from the mother to the embryo. It does not exist in marsupials.

**Plain.** Wide are of level or gently rolling country, usually at a low altitude.

**Plane Tree.** *Platanus acerifolia*, a common temperate deciduous hardwood tree, frequently grown in towns because of its resistance to air pollution.

**Plant.** (1) Organism containing chlorophyll with which it carries out photosynthesis botanists discovered several new species of plant in the jungle; plant breeding = development of new and improved varieties and strains of plants; plant food ration = ratio of nitrogen to phosphate and potash in a fertilizer; plant nutrients = minerals whose presence in the soil is essential for the healthy growth of plants; plant population = the number of plants in an area, such as the number of plants per hectare (2) To put a plant into the earth the ground needs to be dug over carefully before the young trees are planted.

**Planter.** (a) Person who plants; especially a person who plants and looks after a plantation (b) Device for planting.

**Plantain.** (a) Name given to various types of banana, used for cooking and brewing; it has a lower sugar content than dessert bananas (b) common weed (*Plantago major*).

Plantains are an important crop in Nigeria. Zaire and the Cameroons.

**Plough.** (1) Agricultural implement used to turn over the surface of soil into ridges and furrows in order to cultivate crops. (2) To turn over the soil with a plough; deep ploughing = ploughing very deep into the soil (used when reclaiming previously virgin land for agricultural purposes)

**Plough Body.** The main part of the plough, consisting of the frog, mould board, share and landside.

**Plough In.** to cover a cop, stubble or weeds with soil, by turning over the surface with a plough.

**Ploughland.** Arable or cultivated land.

**Ploughman.** Man who ploughs.

**Plough Pan.** Hard layer in the soil caused by ploughing at the same depth every year.

**Ploughshare.** Heavy metal blade of a plough, which cuts the bottom of the furrow.

**Plough Up.** To plough a pasture, usually in order to use it for growing crops.

The modern plough is usually fully monted on a tractor's hydraulic system; some are semi-mounted, with the rear supported by one or more wheels and some maybe trailed. The principal parts of a plough are the beam or frame, made of steel, to which are attached a number of parts which engage the soil, such as the disc coulter, the share and the mouldboard which turns the furrow slice. There are three main types of plough: conventional, with right-handed mouldboards, reversible, with left and right-handed mouldboards, and disc ploughs, which are used for deep rapid cultivation of hard dry soils, and are not common in the UK. There are many designs of plough body, the amin ones being the general purpose plough, the semi-digger the digger and the Bar point. The three main methods of ploughing are: systematic, where the field is divided into lands by shallow furrows.

Round and round ploughing, in which fields are ploughed from the centre to the outside or from the edge to the centre.

**Pluck.** (a) To remove the feathers from a bird's carcass (usually done by machine, but still also done by hand); dry pluck = removing the features when the bird is dry, so avoiding harming the skin; wet Pluck = removing the feathers when the carcass is wet (easier than dry plucking, but may harm the skin) (b) to remove the internal organs from an animal carcass after slaughter (c) to remove the leaves from a plant (such as the tea plant.

**Plum.** Stone fruit (*Prunus domestica*). There are many varieties of cultivated plums, and they vary in colour, shape, size and flavour, Pond's seeding. Monarch and Pershore are cooking varieties, while the rich-flavoured dessert varieties include Victoria, Laxton and Kirke's Blue. American varieties include Chickasaw and the Oregon Plum. In the UK, plums are grown mainly in the south and in the west midlands; in the USA, they are common in the pacific states.

**Poach.** (a) (of cattle) to trample the ground in wet weather; heavy soils such as clays are particularly susceptible to poaching (b) to state game or fish which as privately owned.

**Poacher.** Person who takes game or fish illegally.

**Pod.** (1) Legume, the long casing for several seeds (as for peas or beans) (2) To pod up = to begin to develop pods.

**Podsol or podzol.** Type of acid soil where iron and aluminium oxides and/or humus have been leached from the bleached top layer into a lower layer which is characterized by bight colours due to iron.

**Podzolic Soil.** Soil from which iron and aluminum oxides have been leached from the topsoil in moist cool climates from the topsoil in moist cool climates.

**Podzolization.** Process by which iron and aluminium oxides leach from the top layers of acid soil.

On the whole pozols make poor agricultural soils, due to their low nutrient status and he frequent presence of an iron pan; large areas of the coniferous forest regions of Canada and the Soviet Union are covered with podzols.

**Polder.** Piece of low-lying land which has been reclaimed from the sea, and is surrounded by earth banks to protect it from encroachment. In the Netherlands polders are fertile and form valuable agricultural land or pasture for cattle.

**Poll.** (1) The top of an animal's head; Poll Doret = Australian breed of sheep similar to the Dorset Horn, but with no horns (2) To dehorn an animal; polled stock = (i) Animals which are naturally hornless; (ii) animals which have had their horns removed.

**Pollination.** Action of pollinating a flower; self-pollination = pollination where the pollen from an anther goes to a stigma on the same plant; see also *Cross-pollination.*

**Pollinator.** Organism such as a bee or bird or other plant, which helps pollinate a plant some apple trees need to be planted with pollinators as they are not self-fertile; birds are pollinators for many types of tropical plant.

**Pollute.** To discharge harmful matter in abnormally high concentrations into the environment, often done by people but can occur naturally polluting gases react with the sun's rays polluted soil must be removed and burled.

**Polluter.** Person or company which pollutes certain industries are major polluters of the environment; polluter pays principle = principle that if pollution occurs, the person or company responsible should be made to pay for consequences of the pollution.

**Pollution.** Presence of abnormally high concentrations of harmful substances in the environment, often put there by people pollution of the atmosphere has increased pollution of the atmosphere has increased over the last 50 years; soil pollution round mines poses a problem for land reclamation; atmospheric pollution = pollution of the air.

**Polyculture.** Rearing or growing of more than one species of plant or animal on the same area of land at the same time; compare Monoculture.

**Polyphagous.** (Animal) which eats more than one type of food.

**Pork.** Fresh meat from pigs (as opposed to cured meat, which is bacon or ham). See also *Pigmeat*.

**Portland.** Rare breed of sheep; both sexes are honed, with brown or tan faces and legs.

**Post.** Solid wooden or concrete pole, placed in a hole in the ground, and used to support a fence or a gate; post hole digger = implement driven by a tractor, shaped like a very large screw which bores holes in the ground in which posts are placed.

**Pot.** (1) Flower pot = container in which a plant is grown; pot-bound plant = plant which is in a pot which is too small and which its roots fill (2) To put a plant into a pot; potting compost = special prepared compost for plants in pots.

**Pot On.** To take a plant form one pot and repot it in a larger one so that it can develop.

**Potash.** General term used to describe potassium salts; potash salts are crude minerals and contain much sodium chloride; potash fertilizers = fertilizers based on potassium.

The main types of potash used are muriate of potash (potassium chloride), kainit, nitrate of potash (potassium nitrate) or saltpere, and potash salts; the quality of a potash fertilizer is shown as a percentage of potassium oxide $K_2O$ equivalent. Potash deposits are mined in the USSR, the USA, Germany and France.

**Potassium.** Metallic element, essential to biological life; potassium nitrate = fertilizer recommended for horticultural crops; potassium permanganate = purpose-coloured salt, used as a disinfectant.

Potassium is one of the three major soil nutrients needed by growing plants (the

Others are nitrogen and phosphorus); potassium also plays an important part in animal physiology and occurs in a variety of plant and animal foodstuffs. Potassium deficiency causes spotted leaves, weak growth and small fruit.

**Potato.** Tuber of *Solanum tuberosum*, a most important starchy root crop; apart from being grown for human consumption, potatoes also are used to produce alcohol and starch, and are used as stock feed; potato blight = fungus disease (*Phytophthora infestans*) which kills potato foliage and rots the tubers; potato clamp = heap of stored potatoes covered with straw and earth; potato harvester = machine which lifts the crop onto a sorting platform, where up to six pickers sort the potatoes from soil and stones; the potatoes are then raised onto a trailer.

The potato originated in Sough America; its introduction into almost every country of the world has proved of great importance on account of its extreme productiveness, its easy cultivation and its remarkable powers of acclimatization. Varieties of potato can be cultivated from the tropics to the furthest him its of agriculture, even further than the polar limit of barley. Huge quantities are grown in the USSR, Poland, Germany, and the USA. Potatoes vary in shape: they may be round, oval, kidney-shaped or just irregular. They also vary in colour, from cream to brown or red. In the UK, varieties are classified as the first and second earlies (harvested from May to August), and early and late main crop (harvested in September/October). About 20% of the potatoes grown in the UK are earlies. Seed potatoes are grown under a certification scheme. In the UK, potatoes are grown mainly for human consumption, either in tubers, or for processing into chips, crisps, for canning or dehydration.

**Potato Elevator Digger.** Machine which lifts potatoes.

A wide flat share runs under the potato ridge and lifts the soil onto a rod-link conveyor. Most of the sol is returned to the ground and the potatoes move on to a second elevator, which returns the potatoes to the ground for hand picking.

**Potato Marketing Board (PMB).** Government oganisation in the UK, which regulates the area of land to be planted with potatoes; all potato growers must register with the board and the board implements guaranteed price arrangements and support buying when necessary.

**Potato Planter.** Machine for planting potatoes.

A coulter makes a furrow and the seed potatoes are carried forward by a conveyor mechanism from the hopper and placed are regular intervals in the row. Potatoes are carried in self-filling cups from the hopper to the ground. Many potato planters have a fertilizer attachment, Automatic planters are best for handling unchitted seed.

**Potato Spinner.** Machine for lifting the potato crop.

A spider wheel rotates and the loosened potato ridge is pushed sideways. The potatoes hits a net at the side of the spinner and fall to the ground, where they are left for the hand pickers.

**Potential Transpiration.** The calculated amount of water taken up from the soil and transpired through the leaves of plants; the amount varies according to the climate and weather conditions.

**Poultry.** General term for domestic birds kept for meat and egg production; chickens are he most common; turkey and geese are mainly kept as meat birds; ducks and guinea fowl also produce significant quantities of meat and eggs.

**Poultry Man.** Farm worker who looks after and raises poultry.

**Pound.** Unit of currency used in the UK and several other countries; green pound = value of the British pound as used for calculating agricultural subsidies and prices in the EC.

**Power.** Energy which makes substances move.

**Power Harrow.** Harrow with two tine bars driven from the power take-off; the tines move alternately in a rotary manner. Power harrows are used to prepare seedbeds of fine tilth.

**Power Take-off.** Mechanism providing power to drive field machines from a tractor.

**Powder.** Material which has been reduced to very fine grains.

**Powdered Sulphur.** Sulphur which is used to dust on plants to prevent mildew.

**Powdery Mildew.** Fungal disease (*Erysiphe graminis*) affecting cereals and grasses; another form also affects sugar beet and brassicas.

**Precision Chop Forage Harvester.** Type of harvester which cuts the crop with flails, chops it into precise lengths and blows it into a trailer; it maybe self-propelled, off-set trailed or mounted. It is used for harvesting green material for making silage.

**Precision Drill.** Seed drill which sows he seed separately at set intervals in the soil.

**Preservation.** Keeping of something in the same condition food reservation allows some types of perishable food to be eaten during the winter months when fresh food is not available; tree preservation order (TPO) = order from a local government department which prevents a tree from being felled.

**Prick Ears.** Ears of an animal which stand up straight (as opposed to lop ears).

**Prick Out.** To transplant seedlings from trays or pans into pots or flowerbeds.

**Primed Seed.** Seed which has been moistened to start the germination process before sowing.

**Process.** To treat produce in a way so that it will keep longer or become more palatable; processed meats = met products such as bacon, sausages, etc.

Food can be processed in many different ways; some of the commonest are drying, freezing, canning, bottling and chilling.

**Prod.** Spiked metal rod, used to make cattle move forward.

**Produce.** Foodstuffs such as vegetables, fruit, eggs, etc., which are produced commercially; farm produce = foodstuffs grown on farms.

**Production.** (a) Production diseases = metabolic disorders of animals which are caused by high levels of production (b) act of producing something; Primary production = amount of organic matter formed by photysynthesis; production ration = quantity of fodder needed to make a farm animal produce a product such as milk or eggs (always more than the basic maintenance ration).

**Productivity.** Rate at which something is produced with new strains of rice, productivity per hectare can be increased; primary productivity = (i) rate at which plants produce organic matter through photosynthesis; (ii) amount of organic matter produced in a certain area over certain period of time (such as a crop during a growing season); net productivity = difference between the amount of organic matter produced by photosynthesis ad the amount of organic matter used by plants in their growth.

**Profusion.** Mass a profusion of small whit flowers.

**Progeny.** Offspring of an animal or plant.

**Progeny Test.** The evaluation of the breeding value of an animal or plant variety by examining the performance of its progeny.

**Progesterone.** Female sex hormone which stimulates the uterus prior to fertilization and maintains the animal in a state of pregnancy.

**Prolactin.** Hormone produced by the pituitary gland which stimulates lactation.

**Prolific.** (Animal or plant) which produces a large number of offspring or fruit.

**Protect.** To seep something safe from harm; protected cropping or protected cultivation = crops grown under some form of protection, such as in greenhouses, or under polythene sheeting; in the UK, the main areas are in Guernsey and along the south coast; commonest protected crops are tomatoes, cucumbers, lettuces and mushrooms.

**Protectant Fungicide.** Fungicide applied to the leaves of plants (it can be washed off by rain, so removing the protection).

**Protein.** Nitrogen compound which is present in and is an essential part of all living cells in the body, formed by the condensation of amino acids.

**Protein Balance.** Situation when the nitrogen intake in protein is equal to the excretion rate (in the urine).

**Protein Deficiency.** Lack of enough proteins in the diet; protein efficiency ration = measure of the nutritional value of proteins carried out on young growing animals; defined as the gain in weight per gram of protein eaten.

**Protein Equivalent.** Measure of the digestible nitrogen of an animal feeding stuff in terms of protein.

**Protein Quality.** Measure of the usefulness of a protein food for various purposes, including growth, maintenance, repair of tissue, formation of new tissue and production of eggs, wool and milk.

**Proteolysis.** Breaking down of proteins in food by proteolytic enzymes.

**Proteolytic.** Referring to proteolysis; proteolytic enzyme or protease= digestive enzyme which breaks down proteins in food.

Proteins are necessary for grown the repair of the tissue of animals bodies; they are mainly formed of carbon, nitrogen and oxygen in various combinations as amino acids, Certain foods (such as beans, meat, eggs, fish and milk) are rich in protein. Although ruminant animals can make use of cellulose and non-protein nitrogen (which human beings cannot metabolize), animal feeds are often supplemented with grains, pulses and other foods that contain protein.

**Protoplasm.** Living material which makes up the largest part of the cells of plants and animals.

**Proximate Analysis.** Method of chemical analysis used on animal feeding stuffs, which measures the amounts of ash, crude fibre, crude protein, there extract, moisture content and nitrogen-free extract.

**Prune.** (1) Black-skinned dried plum (2) To remove pieces of a plant, in order to keep it in shape, or to reduce vigour.

**Pruning Knife.** Special knife with a curved blade, used for pruning fruit trees.

**Pruners.** Type of secateurs, used for pruning fruit trees.

**Prunus.** Latin name family of trees including the plum, peach, almond, cherry, damson, apricot.

**Puddling.** Preparing the land in rice fields to prevent the water from percolating through the soil.

**Pullet.** Young female fowl, from hatching until a year old.

**Pulling Peas.** Peas harvested by removing the pods when fresh and sold as young peas in pods.

**Pulp.** The soft flesh of a fruit

**Pulpy Kidney Disease.** Disease caused by a strain of the same bacteria which cause lamp dysentery; it occurs in older lambs and can be fatal.

**Pulsator.** Part of a milking machine which causes the suction action and release of the milk from the udder.

**Pulses.** General term for certain seeds that grow in pods; the species of vegetable which have this type of fruit are very numerous and include trees as well as tender plants; the term is often applied to edible seeds of leguminous plants (lentils, beans and peas) used as food for human or animal consumption.

**Pumpkin.** Large round yellow vegetable, eaten both as a vegetable and in pies as a dessert.

**Pungent.** With a Sharp taste or smell (as, for example, mustard).

**Pure Breeding.** Mating together of pure bread animals of the same breed.Purebred animals of the same breed.

**Pyrethrum.** (a) Annual herb, grown for its flowers which are used in the preparation of an insecticide (b) organic pesticide, developed from a form of chrysanthemum, which is not very toxic and non-persistent.

# Q

**Quadrat**. Area of land measuring one square metre, chosen as a sample for research into plant populations the vegetation of the area was sampled using the quadrant method.

**Quail.** Small game bird (*Coturnitx, coturnix*), now reared to produce oven ready birds and also for their eggs.

**Quality Grain.** Application of quality standards when selling grain; good quality is indicated by a high specific weight.

**Quarantine.** (1) Period (originally forty days) when an animal or person or ship just arrived in a country has to e kept separate in a country has to be kept separate in case it carries a serious disease, to allow the disease time to develop and so be detected the animals were put in quarantine on arrival at the port; a ship in quarantine shows a yellow flag called he quantine flag (2) To put a person or animal in quarantine.

Animals coming into Britain are quarantined for six months because of the danger of rabies. People who are suspected of having an infectious disease can be kept in quarantine for a period which varies according to the incubation period of the disease. The main diseases concerned are cholera, yellow fever and typhus.

**Quick-Feeze.** To preserve food products by freezing hem rapidly.

**Quicklime.** Calcium oxide, chemical used in many industrial processes, and also spread on soil to reduce acidity.

**Quota.** Fixed amount of something which is allowed the government has imposed a quota on the fishing of herring; quota system = system where imports or supplies are regulated by fixing maximum amounts; milk quotas = system by which farmers are only allowed to produce certain amounts of milk, introduced to restrict the overproduction of milk in member states of the EC.

Quotas were introduced in 1984, and were based on each state's 1981 production, plus 1%. A further 1% was allowed in the first year. A supplementary levy or super levy, was introduced to penalized milk production over the quota level.

# R

**Rabbit.** Common furry herbivorous rodent (*Oryctolagus cuniculus*)

Rabbits are raised for meat and for their fur: wild rabbits are a major pest in some parts of the world.

**Race.** (a) General term for a breed or variety of plant or animal; (b) improvised wooden way along which animals are made to walk, such as when being loaded into a van (also called a "raceway")

**Rack.** Frame of wooden or metal bars which holds fodder, and from which animals can eat.

**Radish.** *Raphanus sativus*, small plant with red or white roots used mainly in salads.

**Radnor.** Breed of small hill sheep similar to the Welsh Mountain.

**Ragwort.** A weed (*senecio jacobea*) found in grassland; it can cause poisoning of cattle and sheep, and must therefore be controlled.

**Rain.** Water which falls from clouds as small drops; acid rain = rain which contains a higher level of acid than normal; artificial rain = rain which is made by "seeding" clouds with crystals of salt and other substances.

**Rainfall.** Amount of water which falls as rain on a certain area over a certain period.

**Rainforest.** Thick tropical forest which grows in regions where the rainfall is very high poor farmers have cleared hectares of rainforest to grow cash crops.

**Rain Guns.** One of the means of applying irrigation water; water is applied under pressure by a series of widely-spaced guns, which can be either fixed or mobile and are used for grassland or sugar beet irrigation.

**Rainmaking.** Attempting to create rain by scattering carbon dioxide on clouds.

**Rainwater.** Water which falls as rain and is collected and used for irrigation.

Rain is normally slightly acid buy becomes more acid when pollutants from burning fossil fuels are released into the atmosphere.

**Ram.** Male sheep or goat, that has not been castrated.

**Rambutan.** Tropical fruit (*Nephelium lappaceum*) grown in South-East Asia; the fruit is similar to the litchi.

**Ranch.** (a) Large farm specializing in raising cattle, sheep or horses; Cattle ranch = very large grassland farm where cattle are raised governments have encouraged the conversion of rainforest to livestock ranches.

**Rancher.** Owner of a ranch; worker on a cattle ranch.

**Ranching.** Agricultural system based on commercial grazing on ranches.

**Range.** Open space, particularly for poultry; eggs produced on a range are called "freerange eggs"

**RAS.** Royal Agricultural Societies.

**RASE.** Royal Agricultural Society of England.

**Rat.** Brown rat or *Norway rat* = Rattus norvegius a pest which eats and damages growing and stored crops; rats also carry infection to cattle and pigs.

**Ratoon Crop.** The second and later crops taken from the regrowth of a crop that has been harvested once (for example, sugar cane plants can be harvested many times)

**Reafforestation.** Planting trees again in an area which was once covered by forest.

**Rear.** To look after young animals until they are old enough to look after themselves.

**Reclaim.** To take virgin land or land which has already been developed and make it available for agricultural or commercial purposes.

**Red Currant.** Soft fruit, growing on bushes, and used mainly for making jams.

**Red Data Book.** World catalogue of species which are rare or in danger of becoming extinct.

**Red List.** List of pesticides issued by the Department of Environment, which are due for review on grounds of stricter safety measures.

**Red Poll.** Dual- purpose breed of cattle, which originated in East Anglia; deep red in colour, with a white swish at the end of the tail.

**Red Sindhi.** Breed of dairy cattle founding Pakistan; the animals are small, hardy and deep red in colour. The breed is now found in Malaysia, Burma, Japan and Brazil.

**Redwater.** Parasitic disease of cattle transmitted by the common tick; the affected animal becomes very dull, feverish, salivates freely and often staggers and falls; the acute form of the disease is often fatal.

**Redwood.** American conifer, often growing to a very large size.

**Reel.** Part of the mechanism of a combine harvester, which holds the crop against the cutter bar for cutting; the reel directs the crop after it has been cut onto the cutter bar table or platform; most combines have a pick-up reel which can be adjusted to deal with inlaid or tangled crops.

**Reference Price.** The minimum price at which certain fruit and vegetables can be imported into the EC.

**Refrigerate.** To cool produce and keep it at a cool temperature; refrigerated lorry = special lorry which carries produce under refrigeration.

**Refrigeration.** Method of prolonging the life of various foods by storing them at very low temperatures.

**Regenerate.** To replace by new growth a forest takes about ten years to regenerate after a fire.

**Regeneration.** Growing again (of vegetation on land which has been cleared) grazing by herbivores prevents the regeneration of forests destroyed by fire.

**Regrowth.** New growth after a plant has been cut down or burnt.

**Regulations.** (i) Rules laid down by a government or official body; (ii) rules laid down by the Council of Ministers or the Commission of the EC, which have legal force in all member countries.

**Regulator.** Thing which controls development; growth regulator = a chemical used to control the growth of certain plants; mainly used for`weed control in cereals and grassland.

**Remembrement.** French term of the enlargement of Agricultural holdings.

**Replant.** To plant again after the trees were felled, the land was cleared and replanted with mixed conifers and broadleaved species; replant disease = condition affecting apple trees planted in an orchard which has been grubbed out.

**Repot.** To take a plant out of its pot and plant it in another, changing or adding to the soil at the same time.

**Reproduce.** (a) To produce offspring; (of bacteria, etc.) to produce new cells (b) to do a test again in exactly the same way.

**Reproduction.** Process of making offspring or derived cells, etc.; organs of reproduction = Reproductive Organs asexual reproduction = reproduction by taking cuttings of plants or by cloning.

**Reseed.** To reestablish a ley b sowing seed again.

**Reservoir.** Area of water made by man, used for storing after for domestic or industrial use.

**Resistnce.** (i) Ability of an organism not to get a disease; (ii) ability of a germ not to be affected by antibiotics; (iii) ability of a pest or weed not to be affected by a pesticide or herbicide the bacteria have developed a resistance to certain antibiotics; after living in the tropics his resistance to colds was low; increasing insect resistance to chemical pesticides is a major problem.

**Resistant.** Able not to be affected b something the bacteria re resistant to some antibiotics; fungus-resistant genetic material was found in genetic stocks from Mexico; resistant strain = strain of an insect which is not affected by pesticides or of bacterium which is not affected by antibiotics.

**Respiration.** Action of breathing; external respiration = part of respiration concerned with oxygen in the hair being exchanged in the lungs for carbon dioxide from the blood; internal respiration = part of respiration concerned with the passage of oxygen from the blood to the tissues, and the passage of carbon dioxide from the tissues to the blood.

**Rest.** To rest land = to let land lie fallow, without growing any crops ad to remove grazing animals from pasture to allow it time to recover.

**Reticulum.** Series of small fibres forming a network in the second stomach of ruminants, connected to the rumen; its acts as a sort of filter and holds water and hard objects which have been swallowed (also known as the honeycomb stomach); see also *Abomasum, omasum, Rumen.*

**Reversible Plough.** Plough with left-and right-handed mould boards, which made it possible to plough up and down the same furrow; this gives a level surface and reduces the headland; very little marking is needed before the start of ploughing.

**Rhizome.** Fleshy plant stem which lies under the ground, and contains leaf buds (as opposed to a root which lies under the ground but is not a stem).

**RHS.** Royal Horticultural Society.

**Rib Grass.** Palatable deep-rooting herb with a high mineral content, which may benefit pasture.

**Ricefield.** Field for growing rice. Wet rice is by far the commonest method of cultivation: the paddies are enclosed by low banks and are kept flooded during the growing season. They are allowed to dry out before the crop is harvested. Dry land rice is cultivated in a similar way to wheat or barley. Rice is classified according to the length of the grains: long-grain rice is grown in tropical climates, such as India, while short-grain rice is grown in colder climates such as Japan. There are over 120,000 varieties of rice grown world wide; in India alone, more than 40,000 varieties are cultivated. Rice is an important crop in most countries of Asia, and is becoming increasingly important in Africa, South America, the USA and Australia. In Europe, Italy, France and Hungary grow considerable amounts of rice. The world's leading rice exporters are the USA and Thailand.

**Rickets.** Disease of young animals due to deficiency of Vitamin D. Bones fail to ossify and joints become swollen.

**Ridge.** (1) Long raised section of earth; a ridge is made by ploughing up and down on either side of the furrow. In systematic ploughing, ridges first mark out land in a field before the plough is reset for normal work and the field is ploughed (2) To make a ridge while ploughing.

**Ridger.** Type of plough used to form ridges for earthing up crops such as potatoes.

**Ripen.** To become ready for eating unripe bananas are shipped in special containers and will ripen in storage.

**River.** Large flow of water, running from mountains or hills down to the sea; river system = series of small streams and rivers which connect with each other; river terrace = flat plain left when a river cuts more deeply into the bottom of a valley, usually fertile and used for cultivation.
Robot Milkers system of completely automated milking parlour; lasers, mirrors and cameras are used to put all four caps n the teats simultaneously.

**Robusta Coffee.** The coffer Canephora, grown chiefly West Africa.

**Roceiro.** A subsistence farmer who cultivates a "roca".

**Roe Deer.** Capreolus capreolus, one of the breeds of deer which are found wild in the UK.

**Rolled Grain.** Grain which has been through a roller mill before it is fed to livestock; rolled grain (usually barley) is more easily digested.

**Romney.** Hardy breed of sheep found in large umbers on Romney Marsh; it has heavy fine-quality long wool fleece; the Romney half-breed has been developed by crossing Romney ewes with North Counter Cheviot rams, The breed has been widely exported. It is also called the "Kent"

**Rookery.** Breeding place for a colony of rooks.

**Root.** (1) Part of a plant which is normally under the ground and absorbs water and nutrients from the surrounding soil; root crops= plants which store edible material in a root, corm or tuber; root crops used as food vegetables or fodder include carrots, parsnips, Swedes and turnips; starchy root crops include potatoes, cassavas and yams. The foliage of some root crops is valuable fodder, and sheep are often "folded" on them. No continent depends as much on root crops and food legumes as does Africa; root cutting =cutting taken from a rhizome which can be planted and used to propagate a plant; root harvester = machine for lifting root crops out of the ground, such as a sugar beet harvester; root system = all the roots of a plant.

**Rootstock.** (a) Rhizome, plant stem which lies under the ground and contains buds, as opposed to a simple root which is not a stem. (b) stock on which a scion is grafted; dwarfing rootstock = stock which is normally low-growing so making the grafted tree grow smaller than normal.

**Rosewood.** A tropical hardwood (*Caesapinia*) used in furniture making.

**Rosemary.** Aromatic herb (*Rosemarinus officinalis*) used for flavouring; also a source of oil used in soaps and cosmetics.

**Rotary Cultivator or Rotavator.** Mounted or trailed machine with a shaft bearing a number of L-shaped blades; used for stubble-clearing, seedbed work and general land reclamation and cleaning; rotary mower = machine used for cutting grass and other upright crops. Rotary mowers have two or four rotors each with three or four swinging blades; the rotors contra-rotate and leave a single swath of cut grass; rotary milking parlour = the most expensive and complex of the four milking systems, where the cows stand on a rotating platform with the milker in the middle; the operator may work on the inner or outer side of the circle; rotary sprinkler = machine used for irrigation purposes; sprinklers can be fitted with fine spray nozzles for protection of fruit crops and potatoes against frost damage.

**Rotational Grazing.** Movement of livestock around a number of fields or paddocks in an ordered sequence.
The advantages of rotating crops are firstly that pests particular to one crop are discouraged form spreading, and secondly that some crops actually benefit the soil. Legumes (peas and beans) increase the nitrogen content of the soil if their roots are left in the soil after harvesting. If the rotation includes a ley, the system is known as alternative husbandry or mixed farming. One of the best-known rotations was the Norfolk four-course system. A rotation should increase and maintain soil fertility control weeds and pests, decrease the risk of crop failure and employ labour throughout the year.

**Row Crop.** Crop planted in rows wide enough to allow cultivators between the rows (most farm crops are drilled in rows, in preference to broadcasting); row crop tractor = tractor used by market gardeners and farmers who grow row crops; a lightweight tractor with a narrow turning circle and adjustable wheel track widths.

**Royal Agricultural Society of England (RASE).** Organization whose main task is running the annual Royal Show.

**Royal Horticultural Society (RHS).** National society which organizes the Chelsea Flower Show and has permanent gardens at Wisley in Surrey.

**Rubber.** (a) Material which can be stretched and compressed, made from a thick white liquid (latex) from a tropical tree; Malaysia is the leading world producer of rubber, followed by Indonesia and Sri Lanka (b) *Hevea brasilliensis*, the rubber tree, a tropical tree grown for its latex; in commercial practice, trees are grafted onto suitable rootstock.

**Runholer.** Farmer who owns a sheep run.

**Runt.** Small individual animal, one that it is smaller than average for its kind; the smallest animal in a litter.

**Rural.** Referring to the country, as opposed to the town many rural areas have been cut off by foods; the government is planning an electrification project for rural areas.

**Rust.** Type of fungus disease which gives plants a powdery surface; some types are particularly serious among cereal crops, such as yellow rust on barley; see also Brown Rust.

**Ryeland.** Rare breed of sheep; a medium-sized animal, white faced and without horns; the sheep has a very symmetrical shape and a tick growth of wool.

# S

**Saddle.** Leather seat for a rider placed on the back of a horse.

**Saddle Bow.** High part of a saddle in front of the rider.

**Saddleback.** A breed of pig now known as the British Saddleback.

**Safety Cab.** Protective cab fitted to a tractor to prevent injury to the driver if the tractor turns over; it also reduces the noise levels affecting the driver.

**Safflower.** An oilseed crop (*Carthamus tinctorius*) grown mainly in India; the oil is used in the manufacture of margarine, and the residual oilseed cake has a limited use as a livestock feed.

**Saffron.** Spice obtained form the dried flowers of the Crocus plant *Crocus sativus*.

**Sage.** Aromatic herb (Salvia officinalis); the leaves are dried and used for flavouring.

**Sageo Palm.** Metroxylon sage, tree native of South-East Asia; the seeds give sag flour and pearl sage used I desserts.

**Sahlwal.** Type of cattle found in Bangladesh.

**Salivation.** Production of saliva. Saliva is a mixture of a large quantity of water and a small amount of mucus, secreted by the salivary glands.

**Salt.** (1) Common salt = sodium Chloride (NACL), used as a cheap fertilizer for sugar beet and carrots; also used to preserve food; Salt lick = block of salt given to cattle to lick in hot weather; salt marsh = marsh near the sea, formed with sea water; salt pan = area where salt from beneath the soil surface rises to form crystals on the surface (2) To preserve food by keeping it in salt or in salt water; cabbage, gherkins, ham and many types of fish are salted for preservation.

**Salty.** Fully of salt; tasting of salt excess minerals in fertilizers combined with naturally saline ground to make the land so salty that it can no longer produce crops.
Salt forms a necessary part of diet, as it replaces salt lost in sweating and helps to control the water balance in the body. It also improves the working of the muscles and nerves. An adequate intake of sodium chloride is necessary to all animals. Grass is relatively poor in sodium and its high potassium content induces secretion of sodium in urine; this loss causes a craving for salt which may be supplied by salt licks.

**Sand.** Fine grains of weathered rock, usually round grains of quartz, and a constituent of soil.

**Sandstone.** Type of sedimentary rock, formed of particles of quartz.

**Sandy Soils.** Soil containing a high proportion of sand particles (approximately 50 per cent). Sandy soil feels gritty. These soils drain easily and are naturally low in plant nutrients through leaching. They are often called "light" soils, as they are easy to work and also "hungry" soils since they need fertilizer. Market gardening is particularly well-suited to sandy soils.

**Santa Gertrudia.** Breed of beef cattle developed in Texas, USA. A cross between the Brahman and Shorthorn stock; the animals are red in colour. The breed is now found in many tropical countries.

**Sap.** Liquid which flows inside a plant carrying nutrients and water.

**Sapwood.** Outer layer of wood on the trunk of a tree, which is younger than the heartwood inside and carries the sap; see also *Heartwood.*

**Saprophyte.** Organism (such as a fungus) which lives on dead a or decaying tissue.

**Saprophytic.** (Organism) which lives on dead or decaying tissue and plays an essential part in helping to break down plant remains into humus.

**Sarson.** Type of oilseed rape grown in India. A new variety of yellow sarson has been developed at the Division of Genetics, Indian Agricultural Research Institute, New Delhi. This variety matures in 132 days.

**Sarvah.** Intensive subsistence system of rice production found in south and South-east Asia.

**Sativus or Sativa.** Latin word meaning "sown" or "planted", used in the generic names of many plants.
Saturate verb take up or dissolve the maximum amount of something, e.g. to fill a substance so that no more liquid can be absorbed nitrates leach from forest soils, thus showing that the soils are saturated with nitrogen; saturated fat = fat which has the largest amount of hydrogen possible.

**Saturation.** (i) Result of saturating; (ii) Point where air contains 100% humidity. When continuous rainfall occurs for long periods, the soil becomes saturated with water; no more water can enter the soil and it ponds on the surface or runs off down slopes.

**Avanna.** Dry grass-covered plain with few trees (usually referring to South America or Africa); growth is abundant during the rainy season but vegetation dies back during the dry season.

**Sawdust.** Powder produced when sawing wood; sawdust is used both as a mulch for plants and as bedding for animals.

**Saw-toothed Beetle.** Dark brown beetle which lives in stored grain; the eggs are laid in the grain and the larvae feed on the grain, causing mould.

**Scab.** (a) disease of which the scab is a symptom; it affects the skin of animals; sheep scab = serious disease of sheep, caused by a parasitic mite, which results in intense irritation, skin ulcers, loss of wool and emaciation; a notifiable disease. (b) Fungal disease of fruit and vegetables; including potato scab and apple and pear scab.

**Scabies.** Very irritating infection of the skin caused by a mite which lives under the skin.

**Scaly.** Covered in scales; scaly leg = disease of affecting the legs of poultry; caused by a mite which burrows under the legs scales causing considerable itching; large hard scales develop on the unfeathered parts of the legs.

**Scar.** Mark on the skin of animal or fruit, or on the bark of a tree, where a wound has healed.

**Scarifier.** Machine with tines which stirs the soil surface without turning it over.

**Scots Pine.** Pinus sylvestris, common commercially grown European conifer.

**Scottish Blackface.** Very hardy breed of small mountain sheep; the fleece gives a long, coarse springy wool, valued for making carpets. Older ewes are crossed with Border Leicester rams to give rey face hybrids.

**Scottish Half Breed.** Crossbred type of sheep obtained by using a Border Leicester ram on a Cheviot eve; they are used widely in lowland Britain.

**Scraper.** Steel-framed attachment for a tractor; it has a rubber scraping edge, and is used for heavy duty work, clearing slurry from farmyards.

**Scratch Plough.** Ard, plough made of a sharpened piece of wood made of a sharpened piece of wood which is dragged across the surface of the soil; this was the first type of plough to be used for cultivating the land (first used in South-West Asia).

**Screenings.** Grains which are small and pass through the sieve when screening grain.

**Screwworm.** *Cochliomya hominivorax*, a fly similar to the bluebottle, but dark green in colour. It is common in Central and South America; it devastated cattle in the USA in the 1950s, but has now been eradicated there. It is found in North Africa and is a particular threat to cattle in tropical regions. The fly lays its eggs in open wounds, where maggots develop very quickly. It can kill an animal within a few weeks if left untreated.

**Scrub Typhus or Tsutsugamushi Disease.** Severe form of typhus caused by Rickettsia bacteria, passed to humans by mites, found in South East Asia.

**Seakale.** Crambe maritime, plant of the mustard family whose cabbage-like leaves are used as vegetable.

**Season.** (a) One of the four parts into which a year is divided (spring, summer, autumn, and winter) (b) time of year when something happens; growing season =time of year when a certain plant grows; rainy season or wet season = time of year when most rain falls (c) the oestrus period of a female animal.

**Seasonal.** Referring to a season; occurring at a season seasonal changes in temperature; plants grow according to a seasonal pattern.

**Seaweed.** General name for several species of large algae, growing in the ea and usually rooted to a surface; several species of seaweed are used as human food, particularly in the Far East and Wales (where it is called "lavel" and eaten at breakfast); seaweeds are also used as animal feeds, as soil conditioners and fertilizers. Seaweed contains nitrogen, phosphate and potash in addition to salt. The organic matter in seaweed breaks down very quickly. It is also a source of iodine and other trace elements, as well as of vitamins A,B,C and D.

**Secondary.** Secondary substances = chemical substances found in plant leaves, believed to be a form of defence against herbivores; secondary succession = succession that takes place in an area where a natural community existed and was removed; secondary host = some parasites need two hosts; the secondary host is one in which the parasite completes its life cycle.

**Sedentary Agriculture.** Subsistence agriculture practiced in the same place by a settled farmer.

**Seed.** Fertilized ovule which forms a new plant on germination; seed bank = (i) all the seeds existing in the soil; (ii) collection of seeds from plants, kept for research purposes; seed certification = the testing, sealing and labeling of seed sold to farmers; this ensures that the seed is free from disease and from weeds; seed coat = testa, the outer layer which surrounds a seed and protects the embryo; seed corn = cereal grown to give grain which is used as seed; seed dressing = treatment of seeds with a fungicide and/or an insecticide to prevent certain soil and seed-borne diseases; seed leaf =cotyledon, the first thick leaf on a plant as it germinates; seeds mixture = seeds of different plants supplies by seed merchants to farmers to produce a new ley; it will include grasses and legumes; seed onion see Set seed potato = potato tuber which is sown to produce new plants; in the UK, these are grown mainly in Scotland, and produced under a certification scheme.

**Seedbed.** Area of land tilled to produce a fine tilth, firm and level, into which seeds will be sown; some crops such as potatoes, do not need a fine tilth and a rough damp bed is preferable; seedbed wheels = set of wheels bolted onto the front of a tractor which will give even compaction and a uniform sowing depth.

**Seed-borne.** Carried by seeds.

**Seed-brone Disease.** Disease which is carried in the seed of a plant.

**Seedbox.** (a) Box in which seeds can be planted for cultivation in a greenhouse (b) part of the plant head which contains the seeds.

**Seed Drill.** Machine consisting of a hopper carried on wheels with a feed mechanism which delivers grain to seed tubes. Most seed drills are designed to plant seed in prepared seed beds; drills for cereals and grasses sow the seed at random while precision drills, used mainly for sugar beet and vegetable crops, place seed at preset intervals in the rows; these are also called "seeder units". Grain drill feed mechanism maybe internal force feed, external force feed or studded roller. Some drills have a hopper divided into two parts one contains the seed, the other fertilizer; this is the combine drill which drills grain and fertilizer at the same time.

**Seeder.** Machine for sowing seeds; seeder unit = precision drill, a seed drill which sows the seed separately at set intervals in the soil.

**Seedhead.** Top of a stalk with seeds, either in a seedcase or separately attacked to the stem.

**Seed Rate.** Amount of seed sown per hectare sown as kilos per hectare (kg/ha).

**Seed Royalties.** Money paid by seed growers to breeders of seeds.

**Seed Weevil.** Pest affecting brassica seed crops; seeds are destroyed in their pods by the larvae.

**Seed Tree.** Tree left standing when others are cut down, to allow it to seed the cleared land.

**Self-feed.** System where the animal takes feed from a large container as it needs; self-feed silage=feeding system where stock feed from silage, the amount of silage available being limited by a form of control.

**Self-Fertile.** (Plant) which fertilizes itself by male gametes from its own flowers; self-fertilization = action of fertilizing itself; self-pollination = pollination of a plant by pollen from its own flowers; self-purification = ability of water to clean itself of polluting substances; self-raising flour = flour with baking powder added to it; self regulating = (ecosystem) which keeps itself in balance most tropical rainforests are self-regulating environments; self-sown plant = plant which grows from seeds which have been naturally dispersed.

**Separated Milk.** Milk from which the cream has been removed; also called skimmed milk.

**Sessile.** (i) Attached directly to a branch or stem (not by a stalk); (ii) permanently attached to a surface.

**Set.** (a) (i) A seed potato; (ii) a seed onion (b) badger's burrow. (i) To form fruit or seed (ii) To plant (iii) (of skin of a newly dug potato) to harden.

**Sewage.** Waste water and other refuse such as faeces, carried away in sewers; sewage farm = place where sewage is treated chemically to make it safe to be used as fertilizer; sewage farming = using sewage as a fertilizer.

**Sex.** (1) One of two groups (male and female) into which animal sand plants can be divided the relative numbers of the two sexes in the population are not equal, more males being born than females; sex organs = organs which are associated with reproduction and sexual intercourse; sex chromosome = chromosome which determines if an organism is male or female; Sex determination = way in which the sex of an individual organism is determined by the number of chromosomes which make up its cell structure (2) To identity the sex of an animal, egg or carcasses.

In mammals, individuals have either a pair of identical XX chromosomes (and so are female) or have one X and one Y chromosome and are male. Our of the pairs of chromosomes in each animal cell, only two are sex chromosomes. Females have a pair of X chromosomes and males have a pair consisting of one X and one Y chromosome. The sex of the offspring is determined by the father's sperm. While the mother's ovum only carries X chromosomes, the father's sperm can carry either an X or a Y chromosome. If the ovum is fertilized by a sperm carrying an X chromosome; the embryo will contain the XX pair and so be female.

**Sex-linkage.** Existence of characteristics which are transmitted through the X chromosomes.

**Shading.** Action of cutting off the light of the sun parts of the field near tall trees suffer from shading.

**Sharecropper.** Tenant farmer who pays a part of his crop to the landlord as a form of rent.

**Sharecropping.** System of land tenure, whereby tenants pay an agreed share of the crop to the landlord as a form of rent.

**Shea Butter.** Kernel oil from the shea butter-nut tree, found in West Africa.

**Sheen.** Bright shiny appearance of a surface (used of fruit, animals; coats, meat, etc.)

**Sheep.** Ruminant of the genus Ovis, family Bovidae; one of many domesticated varieties, formed for their wool, meat and milk; sheep farming = raising sheep on a farm; most sheep are raised under extensive grazing conditions; sheep pox = highly contagious viral disease; symptoms include fever, loss of appetite, difficulty in breathing and in the final stages scabs and ulcers appear; a notifiable disease; sheep run = extensive area used for sheep grazing (especially in New Zealand and Australia); Sheep scab = serious disease of sheep, caused by a parasitic mite, which results in intense irritation, ulceration of the skin, loss of wool and emaciation; a notifiable disease; sheep's fescue = Festuca ovina, species of grass useful under hill and marginal conditions; sheep ked = sheep tick sheep maggot fly = type of fly that lays its eggs on the wool of sheep; the eggs hatch into maggots that burrow into the flesh causing a condition know as "strike"; sheep's correl = common weed (*Rumex acetosella*) sheep walk = area of land on which sheep are pastured; sheep satation = very large sheep farm in Australia; sheep tick = small wingless dipterous insect, parasitic on sheep. Most sheep in the UK are kept for meat, and milk production is relatively unimportant, Wool is the main product of sheep in some other countries, such as Australia; in the UK, however, it is an important by-product of sheep farming. The total sheep population of the UK is approximately 37 million. Sheep are kept under a wide range of environmental and management conditions, from coastal lowland areas such as Romney Marsh to the upland areas of Wales, Scotland and the North of England. Lambs from the upland areas are moved to lowland farms for fattening. In the UK, a great many breeds of sheep have survived and there are some 50 recognized breeds as well as a variety of local types and many crossbreds. More recently, the introduction of continental breeds has increased the variety. A broad classification into three main categories may be made; the long-woolled breeds which include the Romney, Lincoln and Leicester; the short-woolled breeds including the Southdown Dorset Down and Suffolk, and the mountain, moorland and hill breeds which include the Cheviot, gadnor, Scottish Blackface, swaledle and Welshi Mountain.

**Sheepdog.** Breed of dog trained and used by shepherds in controlling sheep.

**Sheepman.** Shepherd, a farm worker who looks after sheep.

**Sheet Erosion.** During heavy rainfall, the saturation of the soil may result in surface runoff down slopes; water flow is even over the whole surface and does not create channels as in rill erosion, but the soil is eroded over the whole area.

**Shelter.** Protection (from windor sun, etc.); shelter belt = row of trees planted to shelter smaller crops from wind; it may also check soil erosion by wind.

**Shelterwood.** Large trees left standing when others are cut, to act as shelter for seedling trees.

**Shifting Cultivation.** Agricultural practice using the rotation of fields rather than crops, short cropping periods followed by long fallows and the maintenance of fertility by the regeneration of vegetation; see also *Fallow*.

**Short Day Plant.** Plant (such as the chrysanthemum) which flowers only if the daily period of light is les than a particular critical length, as in the autumn.

**Sidewalk Farmer.** US farmer who cultivates land some way away from his house in a town.

**Silk.** (a) Fibre produce by silkworms when preparing a cocoon or a web, used for weaving into high-quality fabric (b) silks = the long thin styles of the female flowers of the maize plant.

**Silopress.** Polythene "sac" into which silage is forced; as the sack fills up, it gradually grows longer and when completely full is sealed. A "sack" may contain up to 80 tonnes of silage.

There are many different types of silo: some are pits dug into the ground; others are forms of surface clamp; built silos are towers which may be either top or bottom-loaded, and are built of wood, concrete or steel.

**Silty Soil.** Soil containing a high proportion of silt; such soils are difficult to work and drainage is a problem.

**Silviculture.** Growing of trees, mainly for timber.

**Six-tooth Sheep.** Sheep between two and three years old.

**Skim Coulter.** Part of a plough which turns a small silice of f the corner of the furrow about to be turned and throws it into the bottom of the one before; it is attached to the beam behind the disc coulters.

**Skin.** Outer layer on an animal, fruit or vegetable; skin spot = potato disease causing pimple-like dark brown spots which can harm the buds in the eyes of seed tubers.

**Slaked Lime.** Calcium hydroxide, mixture of calcium oxide and water, used to improve soil quality; the lime is in powder form, having been treated to break it down from large lumbs.

**Slink Calf.** Calf born early, before the normal period of gestation is complete.

**Slurry.** (a) Liquid waste from animals, stored in tans and treated to be used as fertilizer; it may also be stored in a lagoon, from which it can either be piped to the fields or transferred to tankers and then distributed b) lime slurry = mixture of lime and water added to hard water to make it softer.

**Smooth-stalked Medowgrass.** Poa pratensis, species of grass which can withstand quite dry conditions; a perennial grass with smooth greish-green leaves and green purplish flowers.

**Softwood.** White wood from pine trees and other conifers.

**Soil.** Loose material on the surface of the earth in which plants grow; it consists of distintegrated rock, organic material, water and living organisms;; rich soil =soil with many useful nutrients in which plants grow well; poor soil = soil with few useful nutrients and so less suitable for plants. Soil Atmosphere = Air content of the soil, made up of the gases of the atmosphere but in different amounts, because it is modified by the constituent parts of the soil; aeration is the replacement of stale air in the soil with fresh.

**Soil Association.** Organization whose main aims are to promote organic farming and gardening, and to protect the environment.

**Soil Ball.** The rooting system of a plant, complete with the soil attached to it; as when a plant is lifted from a pot or seedbed.

**Soil Capping.** Hard crust on the surface of the soil which can be caused by heavy rain drops r the passage of heavy farm machinery.

**Soil Compaction.** Firming of the soil into a condensed state, often brought about by the use of heavy machinery; compaction lowers the infiltration rate and increases the likelihood of runoff.

**Soil Conservation.** Maintenance of soil structure, moisture levels and nutrient status, by careful management such as by irrigation, planting and mulching, and preventing it being eroded.

**Soil Creep.** Slow movement of soil material down a slope under the force of gravity.

**Soil Fertility.** Potential capacity of soil to grow plants.

**Soil Flora.** Minute plants (such as fungi and algae) which live in the soil.

**Soil Profile.** The various layers of soil particles, as seen in avertical section obtained by making a pit.

**Soil Sterilization.** Treatment of glasshouse, greenhouse and other horticultural soils in order to kill weed seeds, plant disease organisms and pests.

**Soil Survey.** Mapping of soil types using a soil classification system.

**Soyabean or Soyabean.** Bean fro a soya plant.

**Soyoil.** Oil extracted from the soyabean. Soybans are very rich in protein and, apart from direct human consumption, are used as a livestock feeding stuff and for their oil; after the oil has been extracted, the residue is used as a high protein feeding stuff. Other by-products are sobean milk and soy sauce, both widely used in China and Japan. Soybeans are widely grown in China (where they are the most important food legume) Brazil and in the USA.

**Spading Machine.** Machine which uses rotating digger blades to cultivate compacted topsoil and dig out pans created by other cultivators.

**Spear.** Shoot of a green plant, such as asparagus or broccoli.

**Specimen Tree.** Tree planted in a garden in a position by itself, where it can be seen to advantage.

**Sphagnum.** Type of moss which grows in bogs, noted for its ability when dry to absorb large quantities of water; sphagnum peat = peaty soil made up of dead sphagnum moss.

**Spice.** Pungent or aromatic parts of plants used a flavouring in cooking; spices are obtained from seeds, fruit, flowers, roots, bark or buds plants; the commonest are pepper, mustard, ginger, cloves and nutmeg.

**Spider.** One of a large group of animals, with two parts to their bodies and eight legs.

**Spinner.** Device used for harvesting potatoes; the potatoes are left on the surface of the soil for picking later.

**Spinach Beet.** Beta vularis, plant similar to sugar beet, but grown for its leaves which are cooked in the same way as spinach.

**Spinney.** Small wood with undergrowth.

**Spoilage.** Making food bad and inedible (by rotting, damp, etc.)

**Spread.** To put manure or fertilizer or mulch out over a large area.

**Spring.** (a) Place where water comes naturally out of the ground the first settlers found springs of resh water in the mountains (b) device like a coiled wire, used to support; spring-tined harrow or harrow with spring-loaded tines = cultivator which has tines of spring steel which vibrte in the soil; this gives fast seedbed preparation (c) the first season in the year (around April in the Northern Hemisphere); spring wheat = whet which is sown in the spring and harvested towards the end of the summer (the wheat is softer than winter wheat).

**Squash.** Plants of the Cucurbitaceae family, such as marrows, cucumbers.

**SSLRC.** Soil Survey and Land Research Centre.

**Stabilization Lagoon.** Pond used to purify sewage in warm countries by allowing sunlight to fall on the mixture of sewage and water.

**Standard Man Day (SMD).** Eight hours of work, used as a measure for calculating labour costs on a farm.

**Staphylococcus.** Bacterium which grows in a bunch like a bunch of grapes, and causes boils and food poisoning.

*Staphylococcus aureus* causes mastitis in cows, sheep and pigs.

**Stoneleigh.** Home of the National Agricultural Centre and proposed site for the National Museum of Food and Farming.

**Straight.** Animal foodstuff composed of one type of food; straight fertilizer = inorganic fertilizer containing one essential mineral, as opposed to compound fertilizers which contain more than one mineral; these fertilizers are also simply called "straights'.

**Strain.** Distinct variety of a species, which will breed true, usually referring to cultivated plants they have developed a new strain of virus-resistant rice.

**Straw.** Dry stems and leaves of cereal crops left after the grains have been removed by threshing; usually obtained from cereals, but sometimes from grain legumes; barley straw may be used as a low quality feed for livestock; wheat straw is used as litter.

**Straw Burning.** Cheap method of disposal of straw, which helps to control diseases, but is soon to be banned.

**Straw Chopper.** Device fitted to the back of a combine which chops straw into short lengths and drops it on the stubble; chopped straw is easier to plough in.

**Straw Spreader.** Device attached to the back of a combine when the straw is not wanted; the straw is spread over the ground and then ploughed in.

**Straw Walker.** Part of a combine harvester where straw is carried away from the threshed grain after it has been separated from the stalks.

**Streptococcus.** Genus of bacteria which grows in long chains, and causes fevers. *Streptococcus uberis* (informally "strep uberis") affects the udders of cows and causes mastitis;

streptococci are treated with anitibiotics such as streptomycin.

**Streptomycin.** Antibiotic used against many types of infection, especially when streptococcal.

**Strip.** Long thin piece of land.

**Strip Cropping.** Method of cultivation in which ploughing follows the contours; this is to check soil erosion on slopes.

**Strip Cultivation.** Method of communal farming where each family has a long strip or strips of land to cultivate.

**Strip Farming.** Method of farming where strips of land across the contrours are planted with different crops.

**Strip Grazing.** System of grazing which allows animals access to a small part of the field; the rest of the field is protected by a temporary fence, usually electric. To remove a covering from something spraying with defoliant strips the leaves off all plants; nutrient stripping = removing nutrients from sewage to prevent eutrophication of water in reservoirs.

**Strip Cup.** Container into which the first drops of milk are drawn by hand from the teats of the cow before the milking machine is attached to the udder.

**Stripper-header.** Machine which harvests a crop such as linseed, and strips off the seedheads.

**Strippings.** Last drops of milk from a cow's lasts at the end of milking session.

**Studded Roller Feed Drill.** Type of external force feed seed drill; fluted rollers are replaced by rolls with studs or pegs; it is suitable for drilling most types of seed.

**Stud Farm.** Farm where horses are bred.

**Stump.** Tree stump = short section of the trunk of a tree left in the ground with the roots after a tree has been cut down.

**Stunt.** (1) Plant disease characterized by retarded growth (2) To reduce the growth of something the poor mountain soil supports a few stunted trees.

**Style.** Stalk-like structure at the top of the carpel of a flower, bearing the stigma.

**Subsoil.** Layer of soil under the topsoil, which contains little organic matter and into which leached chemical substances from the topsoil are deposited; subsoil water = water held in the subsoil.

**Subsoiler.** Heavy cultivator consisting of a strong frame with long tines attached to it; it is used to break up compacted soil to allow free passage of air and water, a process called "subsoiling"

**Succession.** Series of stages, one after the other by which a plant community reaches its final stable state (or climax); ecological succession = series of communities of organisms which follow one another in an area until a stable climax community is formed.

**Successional Cropping.** (i) Growing several crops one after the other during the same growing season; (ii) sowing a crop (such as lettuce) over a long period, so that harvesting takes place over a similarly long period.

**Succulent.** (Plant such as a cactus) which has fleshy leaves or stems in which it stores water; succulent foods = feeding stuffs which contain a lot of water; they are palatable and filing, and usually have a laxative effect. Most root crops (for example Swedes and turnips) are succulents.

**Suffruticose.** (Perennial plant) which was a wooden base to its stem and does not die down to ground level in winter.

**Sugar.** Sucrose, sweet substance ($C_{12}H_{22}O_{11}$) obtained from sugar cane or sugar beet.

**Sugar Beet.** Beta vulgaris, specialized type of beet grown for the high sugar content of its roots; it is cultivated in temperated regions, and in Britain is an especially important crop in East Anglia. The crowns and leaves of the crop are used for feeding stuff, as is also the residue after the sugar content has been extracted from the roots.

**Sugar Beet Harvester.** Machine for harvesting sugar beet; it may be trailed or self-propelled; the machine cuts off the beet tops, lifts the root, cleans off the soil and conveys the beet to a hopper which is then emptied by a second elevator onto a striler.

**Sugar Beet Topper.** Attachment to a sugar beet harvester which collects the sugar beet tops; some have choppers and blower units, which chop up the tops and then blow them into a trailer.

**Sugar Cane.** *Saccharum officinarum* a large perennial grass, whose stems contain a sweet sap.
Sugar can is rich in sucrose which is extracted and used for making sugar; rum is a by-product of sugar cane. Cane sugar is now one of the most scientifically produced tropical products, although cutting is still often done by hand. Cane is grown in many tropical and subtropical regions, in particular in the Caribbean. The principal sugar producers are Cuba India. Brazil, China, Puerto Rico and Hawaii for cane sugar, and the USSR, France and Germany for beet sugar.

**Suitcase Farmer.** US farmer who lives some distance from his holding (i.e. more than 30 miles).

**Sulphuric Acid.** Acid formed from suplhur dioxide ($H_2SO_4$) which forms in the atmosphere and is a nutrient for some types of plant (it is used to make chemical fertilizers and also in the plastics industry)

**Summer Feeding.** Feeding of cattle on permanent pastures in the summer months; summer solstice = 21st June, the longest day in the Northern Hemisphere, when the sun is as its furthest point south of the equator.

**Sunflower.** *Helianthus annuus*, an important oilseed crop grown in temperate areas; sunflower oil = oil extracted from sunflower seeds; seeds contain between 25 and 45% of semi-drying oil which is high in unsaturated fats.

**Support Buying.** Intervention buying, a system used under the Common Agricultural Policy, whereby governments or their agents offer to buy surplus agricultural produce at a predetermined price.

**Support Energy.** Total energy expenditure necessary for the production of plant and animal agricultural foodstuffs; support price or intervention price = price at which the EC will buy farm produce which farmers can not sell, in order to store it.

**Surface Drainage.** Removing of surplus water from an area of land by means of ditches and channels.

**Surface Water.** Water (after rain) which lies on the surface of the soil and does not drain into the soil, but flows across the surface as a stream and drinks into rivers.

**Surface Wind.** Wind which blows across the land surface (as opposed to winds higher in he atmosphere)

**Swampland.** Area of land covered with swamp.

**Sward.** Cover of grasses and clovers which makes a pasture; sward height record pad = notebook in which the height of a sward is recorded.

**Swardsman.** Farm worker who looks after or grows pasture.

**Swath.** Row of grass or other plants lying on the ground after being cut; row of potatoes which have been lifted and left lying on the ground.

**Swath Turner.** Haymaking machine used to move individual swaths sideways and turn them over at the same time, so making the drying process faster; also used in wet conditions to scatter a swath to dry it more quickly; finger wheel swath turner = machine used for raking.

**Swedish Red and White.** Dual purpose breed of cattle found in Central and Southern Sweden; the animals are cherry red in colour with white markings.

**Sweeper Bull.** Bull used to serve cows not caught up by Artificial insemination.

**Sweet Corn.** Type of maize in, which the grains contain a large amount of sugar rather than starch; grown for human consumption, and also known as corn-on-the-cob.

**Sweet Potato.** *Ipomoea batatas* a starchy root crop grown in tropical and subtropical regions.

The sweet potato is valuable as famine food in parts of Africa and South America. The main producing countries are Indonesia, Vietnam and Japan. In the Southern USA. The tubers are called "yams". The plant has no connection with the ordinary potato.

**Swill.** Waste food from kitchens used for pig feeding. Swill must, by law, be boiled for at lest an hour before feeding; any excess fat should be skimmed off before use. A license must be obtained for premises where swill is processed and fed. It is illegal to feed kitchen scraps to pigs.

**Sycamore.** Acer *pseudoplatanus*, large hardwood tree of the maple family.

**Symbiosis.** Condition where two or more organisms exist together and help each other to survive.

**Symbiotic.** Referring to symbiosis; living in symbiosis the rainforest has evolved symbiotic mechanisms to recycle minerals.

**Syndicate.** Group of people or companies working together to make money; machinery syndicate = group of farmers who join together to buy very large items of equipment, which they can use in turn.

**Systematic Ploughing.** Ploughing a field by sections, each of which is called a land.

# T

**Tabanids.** Family of horse flies which are often large and fly fast; they have strong antennae. Most females such blood, and attach large mammals such as called with their blade-like jaws.

**Tackroom.** Room for storing harness equipment; the tack should be kept in damp-free conditions.

**Tailbiting.** Biting the tail of another animal, a vice associated with pigs; the cause is not known but could be due to bad housing.

**Tailpiece.** Extension of the mouldboard of a plough which help stop press down the furrow slice.

**Tamworth.** Breed of pig, red-gold in colour which makes the animal almost immune to sunburn. Tamworth are widely exported to the USA and Australia because of their ability to standhoot sunshine; they are hardy and can thrive on the roughest land.

**Tank Mix.** Mixing several herbicides or pesticides into one mixture to be used as a spray.

A variety of mixes are available from manufacturers, and farmers also prepare their own tank mixes. The most dangerous operations are the handling of concentrated pesticides during mixing and dilution. FEPA will make only recommended mixes legal in the UK.

**Tan.** Light brown colour to convert animal skins to leather.

**Tanning.** The process of converting animal skins to leather. Hides are soaked in a mixture of chromium salts and after a certain period of soaking they become leather.

**Tap.** To cut a thin ring round the bark of a rubber tree to let the sap run out.

**Tapper.** Person employed on a rubber plantation to tap trees.

**Tap Root.** Thick main root of a plant which grows straight down into the soil. The tap root system is the primary root system of a plant; it has a main root with smaller roots branching off it, as opposed to a fibrous root system which has no main root.

**Tape Worm.** Parasitic worm with a small head and a long body like a ribbon.

**Tar Oil.** Winter wash used to control aphis and scale insects on fruit trees it also clears moss and lichen.

**Target Price.** Wholesale target price within the EC for certain products, such as wheat, which market management is intended to achieve; it is linked to the intervention price.
Target prices are set in terms of fixed agricultural units of account, which are converted into different national currencies using adjusted exchange rates known as "green rates" (in the UK, the "green pound"). A system of lives on non-EC agricultural imports is used to protect target prices when they are set above the general level of world prices.

**Tea.** Dried leaves of one more shrubs of the Camellia family (the commonest is *Camelia sinensis*) Black tea = tea where the leaves wither and are then allowed to ferment in a dry place before drying and crushing; green tea = tea where the

leaves are heated to prevent fermentation.
Tea is one of the hardiest of all subtropical plants. The plants are pruned to form low bushes and to encourage the production of leave sand help plucking. The principal tea-producing countries are India, Bangladesh, Sri Lanka, china, Indonesia and Japan.

**Teat.** Nipple on an udder (in cattle there are fur quarters to the udder, each drained by a teats); teat cup = part of a milking machine, a tube which fits over the teat of the cow; teat dipping = measure for control of mastitis in cattle; the teats are dipped in a cup containing an iodophor disinfectant.

**Teak.** Tropical hardwood which is resistant to water.

**Teaser Ram.** Vasectomized ram, used to stimulate ewes by 'non-fertile' mating prior to the introduction of fertile rams.

**Teat.** Nipple on an udder (in cattle there are four quarters to the udder, each drained by a teat).

**Teat Cup.** Part of a milling machine, a tube which fits over the tat of the cow.

**Teat Dipping.** Measure for control of mastitis in cattle; the teats are dipped in a cup containing an iodophor disinfectant.

**Tenderize.** To make meat tender (by keeping it for a certain time in cold conditions, by applying substances such as papain, by injecting with enzymes, etc.)

**Tendril.** Part of a climbing plant which holds onto a surface, so allowing the plant to climb; members of the pea family climb by twining their tendrils round convenient supports.

**Testa.** The seed coat, and outer layer surrounding a seed and protecting the embryo inside.

**Tetanus.** Infection caused by *Clostridium tetani* in the soil, which affects the spinal cord and causes spasms which occur first in the jaw (also called jockjaw)

**Tetrachlorodibenzoparadioxin (TCDD).** Dangerous gas made as a by-product of the manufacture of 2,4,5-T (this was the gas which escaped during the Seveso disaster in 1976).

**Taxas Longhorn.** Rare breed of long-honed cattle found in Texas; the animals are mainly red in colour.

**Texel.** Breed of sheep from the North of Holland; used to cross-breed as a flock sire.

**Tharparkar.** Zebu breed of cattle found in Pakistan; the animals are used for draught purposes and also for milk; they are a variety of colours, including blue-grey and red.

**Thinnngs.** Small plants removed to let others grow more strongly.

**Thornless.** (Plant) without thorns he developed a new thronless variety of blackberry.

**Thresh.** To separate grains from stalks and the seedheads of plants; in wheat and rye, the chaff is easily removed from the grain; in barley, only the awns are removed; threashing machine = machine formerly used to thresh cereals, now replaced by the combine harvester.

**Thrifty.** (Animal) which is developing well.

**Tillage.** Husbandry or action of tilling the soil.

**Tillering.** Developing several seed heads in a plant of wheat, barley or oats. Tillering leads to the production of a heavier yield, and can be induced by rolling he young crop in the spring when it begins to grow; tillering is used to compensate for poor establishment. It is also important in grasses.

**Timothy.** Palatable tufted perennial grass (*Phleum pratense*). It grows on a wide range of soils and is winter hardy. It is used in grazing mixtures and as a hay plant in conjunction with ryegrass.

**Tissue Culture.** Method of plant propagation which reproduces clones of the original plant by growing plant material on nutrient media containing plant hormones.

**Toadstool.** General name for a poisonous fungus which looks like a mushroom.

**Tobacco.** Leaves of a plant (*Nicotiana*) which are dried and smoked, either in a pipe or as cigarettes or cigars; tobacco mosalic virus = virus affecting both tobacco plants and tomatoes.
The tobacco plant is a coarse fast-growing plant with a simple cylindrical stem from 1.2 to 2.4 metres in height. Each leaf is broad, often 30 cm in width, and 90cm in length. Tobacco contains nicotine, which is an addictive stimulant. Nocotine is a poisonous alkaloid obtained mainly from tobacco and is used in agriculture as a n insecticide, usually in a 40% solution of nicotine sulphate.

**Tolerant.** Which does not react to something; tolerant variety = variety of crop which has been developed to withstand a disease or attacks by certain pests.

**Tolerate.** To accept or not to react to (something).

**Toleration.** Not reacting to something; toleration level = level at which an organism will tolerate something.

**Tomato.** *Lycopersicon esculentum*, an important, food crop; the ripe fruit are used in salads and many cooked dishes; also pressed to make juice and sauces; large quantities are canned. In Britain, tomatoes are cultivated in heated greenhouses to provide out-of-season crops. In Spain, Italy, and other countries with a Mediteranean climate, tomatoes are cultivated out of doors.

**Top Link Sensor.** The mechanism which most draught controls sense the draught on a tractor implement (it uses the top link of the three-point linkage)

**Top-saving Attachment.** Attachment to a topper unit which collects the tops of sugar beet after they have been cut off.

**Topsoil.** Top layer of soil, often containing organic material, from which chemical substances are leached into the subsoil below. The topsoil is the part of the soil which is cultivated and in which most plant roots are formed; see also *Soil Horizon.*

**Towbar.** Strong bar at the back of a car or tractor, to which another vehicle can be attached to be pulled along.

**Townshend.** Viscount Townshend, (1674-1738) an 18th century Norfolk landowner; nicknamed "Turnip" Townshend, he did much to make the Norfolk four-course rotation system popular.

**Toxic.** Poisonous or harmful; toxic agent = substance which is harmful; toxic substances = substances, such as lead, which are harmful to living organisms; toxic waste = waste which is poisonous.

**Toxicity.** Level to which a substance is poisonous or amount of poisonous material in a substance; acute toxicity = level of concentration of a toxic substance, which makes people seriously ill, or can even cause death; chronic toxicity = exposure to harmful levels of a toxic substance over long period of time.

**Toxicology.** Scientific study of poisons and their effects on the human body.

**Toxoplasmosls.** Infectious disease affecting ewes, which causes pregnant animals to abort.

**Trace Element.** A micronutrient, an element which is essential to organic growth, but only in very small quantities. Plants need traces of iron, manganese, copper, zinc; human beings need the trace elements cobalt, chromium copper, magnestium, manganese, molybdenum, selenium and zinc.

**Tractor.** Heavy vehicle, with large wheels, which provides the main source of power in modern farms; tractor-mounted loader = loader which is mounted on a tractor, and not trailed; tractor vaporizing oil (TVO) = fuel formerly used in many tractors, but now replaced by diesel oil.
By 1920, the tractor was established an alternative to the horse, In its early days, the tractor was used to pull trailed implements and to drive stationary equipment with a belt drive. Today, the general purpose tractor does most of the work on arable and livestock farms and may be either two or four wheel drive. Lighter tractors, usually two-wheel drive models, are used by market gardeners and farmers who grow row crops. More powerful four-wheel drive tractors are needed for ploughing and heavy cultivation. One type has four large wheels, all the same size; another type has smaller front wheels and larger back wheels. The heaviest tractors are tracklayers, or "crawlers", which are used for very heavy work and on heavy soils. Besides pulling tailed implements such as balers, forage harvesters and drills, the tractor's hydraulic system can be used to raise and lower mounted implements and operate lifting and loading equipment.

**Trailer.** Machine used for carrying purposes; trailers are of the two-wheel or four-wheel types, and are used for carrying cereal and root crops, and for general use on the farm.

**Tramline.** Paths left clear for the wheels of tractors to drive over; they are used as guide marks for spraying and when applying fertilizer so that damage to crops is kept to a minimum.

**Translocate.** To move substances through the tissues of a plant; translocated herbicides = herbicides (such as *glyphosate*) which kill a plant after being absorbed through its leaves or through its roots if applied to the soil.

**Transplant.** To take a growing plant from one place and plant it is the soil in another place either to give it more growing space or to check its root growth.

**Transplanter.** Machine for translating seedlings (especially used for planting brassicas).
There are two types of transplanter: the hand-fed machine, where a worker feeds seedlings into the machine as it passes over the field. The other is the automatic transplanter, where seedlings are raised in special containers and placed in the machine before transplanting starts.

**Tree.** Tree ferns = very large ferns founding Australasia, growing like trees with a single large stem; tree surgeon = person who specializes in the treatment of diseased trees, especially by pruning or lopping.

**Tree Preservation Order (TPO).** Official ruling by a local authority forbidding the cutting down of an important tree.

**Trenching.** Method of double digging which loosens the soil to a depth of two feet, twice as deep as in plain digging.

**Trickle.** (of liquid) to flow gently; trickle system = irrigation system where water is brought to the base of each plant and drips slowly into the soil.

**Trimmings.** Small pieces of vegetation which have been cut off a hedge when trimming.

**Triple-purpose Animal.** Breed of animal (usually of cattle) which is used for three purposes (milk, meat and as a draught animal).

**Tropics.** Tropical countries, hot areas of the world between the Tropic of Cancer or Tropic of Capricorn and the equator.

**Topical.** Referring to the tropics.

**Truck Farming.** US term used to describe intensive vegetable cultivation at a considerable distance from the urban markets where the produce is sold.

**Trypanosomiasis.** Sleeping sickness, a serious disease attacking both livestock and humans, spread by the tsetse fly.

**Tsetse Fly.** African insect which passes trypanosomes into the bloodstream of humans and other animals, causing sleeping sickness.

**Tuber.** Fat part of an underground stem or root, which holds nutrients, and which has buds from which shoots develop a potato is the tuber of a potato plant.

**Tuberous.** (i) Like a tuber; (ii) (plant) which grows from a tuber. Potatoes, cassavas and sweet potatoes are all tubers from which new shoots develop.

**Tundra.** Cold treeless arctic and alpine region which may be covered with low shrubs grasses, mosses and lichens.

**Turmeric.** Tropical plant (*Curcuma longa*); its tubers produce and oil which is used in making curry powder; mainly grown in India.

**Turn Out time.** Season, usually in the spring, when animals which have been kept indoors during the winter are let out to grass.

**Tussock Grass.** *Deschampsia caespitosa*, a coarse grass growing in tuffs.

**Two-sward System.** Grazing system where the area being grassed is kept separate from the area being conserved for cutting.

## U

**Udder.** The mammary gland of an animal, which secretes milk; it takes the form of a bag under the body of the animal with teats from which the milk is sucked. In the cow there are four glands, each with a teat. In the ewe there are two glands, each with a teat, and in the sow there are two glands per teat and from 12 to 20 teats.

**UHT Milk.** Milk which has been sterilized at a very high temperature, and which can therefore keep much longer than normal milk.

**Ulster White.** Breed of pig popular for bacon production in Northern Ireland; quite rare today, having been replaced by the Large White.

**Ultra High Temperature (UHT).** Process of sterilization at very high temperatures; UHT sterilization = sterilization of milk at very high temperatures; milk which has been treated in this way may be stored for period of up to one year.

**Ultra Heat Treated Milk.** Milk which has been treated by sterilizing at temperatures above 135°C, and then put aseptically into containers (it has a much longer shelf life than normal milk).

**Umbel.** Flower cluster in which the flowers all rise on stalks from the same point on the plant's stem (for example, the carrot or polyanthus).

**Umbelliferous.** Referring to a plant of the Umbelliferae.

**Unavailable Water.** Water in the soil which is held in the smallest soil pores and so is not available for plants.

**Uncultivated.** (land which is not cultivated.

**Undercoat.** Coat of fine hair under the main coat of some animals.

**Under-drain.** Drain under the surface of the soil, such as a mole drain or pipe drain.

**Undergrowth.** Shrubs and other plants growing under large trees.

**Unenclosed Land.** Area of land without any walls or fences round it.

**Unisexual.** (Plant) which has either male or female flowers, but not both.

**Unpalatable.** Not palatable, feeding stuff which has an unpleasant taste.

**Unpasteurized.** Which has not been pasteurised unpasteurized milk can carry bacilli.

**Unploughed Land.** Land which has not been ploughed.

**Untreated Milk.** Milk which has not been treated and which is sold direct from the farm to the public (in the UK this is called "green top milk" and sales are now banned).

**Urban Fringe.** Area of land use where the urban activities meet the rural (usually a source of conflict between townspeople and farmers).

**Uric Acid.** Chemical compound which is formed form nitrogen in waste products from an animal's body' uric acid is the principal nitrogenous excretory end-product in birds and land reptiles.

**Urticceae.** Family of shrubs and herbs with stinging leaves (such as the common stinging nettle *Urtica dioica*).

**Uterus.** Hollow organ in a female animal linked to the ovaries; the lower end opens into the vagina. When an ovum is fertilized it becomes implanted in the will of the uterus and develops into an embryo inside it.

# V

**Vaccination.** Action of vaccinating mass vaccination of poultry has been carried out against Newcastle disease.

**Vaccine.** Substance which contains the germs of a disease, used to inoculate or vaccinate.

**Vacuum Silage.** Silage placed in large polythene bags, usually by a baler specially adapted for this purpose; air is excluded, so preventing the development of moulds and the green crop is conserved in succulent form.

**Variant.** Specimen of a plant or animal which is different from the normal type.

**Variegaton.** Phenomenion in some plants where two or more colours occur in patches on the leaves or flowers.

**Vasectomy.** Operation to cut the duct which takes sperm from the testicles, so making the animal infertile.

**Vasectomie.** To perform a vasectomy on (an animal).

**Vegeculture.** Type of agriculture based on vegetatively propagated crops.

**Vegetable.** Plant or parts of plants grown for food, not usually sweet (including some fruits, such as tomatoes, and some seeds, such as peas); vegetable oils = oils obtained from plants and their seeds, which are low in saturated fats: vegetable protein = protein obtained from cereals, oilseeds, pulses, green vegetables and roots, which provides for the feeding requirements of both humans and livestock.

**Vegetation.** (i) Plants in genera; (ii) Plants which are found in a particular area.

**Vegetative.** Referring to vegetation; vegetative propagation or vegetative reproduction = reproduction of plants by taking cuttings or by grafting not by seed.

**Ventilation.** Allowing air to circulate; measures necessary to remove polluted air from a building without making too many draughts; good ventilation is of prime importance in housing livestock.

**Verandah.** Type of housing for poultry or pigs with a slatted or wire floor, through which the droppings fall.

**Vermiculite.** Substance which is used in soilless gardening. Vermiculite occurs naturally as a form of silica and is capable of retaining moisture. It is processed into small pieces and used instead of soil in horticulture.

**Vernalization.** Treatment of seeds to make them flower at a set time; seed is made to germinate early by refrigerating it for a time.

**Vertebrate.** Animal with a backbone (all animals raised on farms are vertebrates, with the exception of edible snails).

**Veterinary.** Referring to the care of sick animals; veterinary science = scientific study of diseases of animals and their treatment; veterinary service =branch of the Agricultural Development and Advisory service; veterinary surgeon = person who is qualified in veterinary science.

**Vibrojet.** Jet for irrigation, sending the water out in small sharp pulses (useful to control spray drift).

**Vice.** Bad habit in an animal, such as the habit of biting other animals; tails.

**Vigorous.** Which grows strongly plants put out vigours shoots in warm damp atmosphere.

**Vine.** (a) Grape vine = plant of the genus *Vitis*, yielding grapes, either for eating fresh, for drying or for making into wine (b) vine crops = crops (*Cucurbitaceae*) a such as cucumber, marrow, gourds and melons, which are annuals and produce long trailing shoots and heavy fleshy fruit.

**Virgin Land.** Land which has never been cultivated.

**Virgin Oil.** First pressing of olive oil, which produces oil of the best quality.

**Virus.** *Tinycellformed* largely of genetic material and protein, which can only develop in other cells and often destroys them; all viruses are parasitic; virus pneumonia = disease affecting pigs and calves; the animals suffer from a hard cough and are unthrifty. In calves, shivering, loss of appetite and noise breathing are symptoms; virus yellows = disease of sugar beet and mangolds; the leaves turn yellow and the sugar content is greatly reduced. Crops are most at risk when virus-carrying aphids infest the plants at the two-leaf stage.

**Viral.** Disease, caused by a virus.

Viruses produce disease in man, animals and plants. Many common diseases such as measles or the common cold are caused by viruses; viral diseases cannot be treated with antibiotics (which only destroy bacteria). Viruses can be transmitted from one animal to another, reproducing the same disease. Insects, particularly aphids, transmit certain virus diseases implants.

**Vitamin.** Essential nutrient usually needed by animals in minute quantities for growth and health; Vitamin deficiency = lack of necessary vitamins.

Vitamins are a group of chemical compounds found in a

variety of foodstuffs, which are necessary for the healthy regulation of physical processes in an animal's body. Vitamins are classified by letters: Vitamin A is fat-soluble and is stored in the fat compounds in the body. It protects mucous membranes and is necessary for the growth and good health of the animal. It Is formed in the animal's body from the yellow substance, carotene, which is available to animals in green foods, carrots, maize and milk.

Vitamin B is water-soluble, and is a group of several different substances; riboflavin , thiamine, nicotinic acid, biotin, choline and pantothenic acid. It is necessary for the nervous system and for oxidation processes in the body. It is found in whole grains, grass, milk and yeast. Cattle supply their own needs for Vitamin B in the rumen Vitamin C is ascorbic acid and is found in fruit and vegetables Vitamin D is fat-soluble. It is necessary to young animals as it is important in bone formation. It is formed in the skin of an animal by the action of sunlight Vitamin E is fat-soluble and is important for muscle development and normal reproduction. It is found in green food and cereals Vitamin K is fat-soluble and prevents blood-clotting: it is available in green foodstuffs such as spinach. Vitamin deficiencies in animals can cause serious health problems and once identified, can be cured by the use of mineral supplements either as an individual simple substance or by complex mixtures added to normal rations and supplied according the animals' needs.

**Volatile Oils.** Concentrated oils from a scented plant used in cosmetics or as antiseptics.

**Volunteer (Plant).** Plant that has grown by natural propagation, as opposed to having been planted volunteer cereals are a problem in establishing oilseed rape.

# W

**Wages.** Money paid to an employee for work done; wages fro farm workers are set by the Agricultural Wages Board. The minimum rate of full-time adult workers.

**Wall Barley Grass.** Weed (*Hordeum murinum*) found in grassland.

**Walnut.** Hardwood tree of the genus *Juglans*, with edible nuts; the timber is used in furniture making.

**Warble Fly.** Parasitic fly, whose larvae infest cattle.

**Warbles.** Swellings on the backs of cattle caused by the warble fly.

Eggs of warble flies are laid on the legs or bellies of cattle. On hatching, the maggots burrow into the skin and cause swellings on the back of the animal. When adult, the maggots leave the body through the skin and fall to the ground to pupate. They cause severe irrigation, loss of condition and in young animals may cause death.

**Ware.** Potatoes grown for human consumption, as opposed to those grown for seed; ware growers = farmers who grow potatoes for consumption, not for seed.

**Warping.** Farming paractice which permits a river to flood low-lying land to cover it with silt in which crops will be grown.

**Waste.** (1) Useless or which has no use waste products are dumped in the sea; waste matter is excreted by the body in the faeces or urine; waste lime = lime obtained from industrial concerns after it has been used as a purifying material; waste product = substance which is not needed in a process (2) Unenclosed land used for pasture.

**Water.** (1) Common liquid ($H_2O$) which forms rain, rivers, the sea, etc., and which makes up a large part of the bodies of organisms; water balance = (i) state where the water lost in an area by evaporation or by runoff is replaced by water received in the form of rain; (ii) state where the water lost by the body (in urine or perspiration, etc.) is balanced by water absorbed form food and drink. Water salt balance = state where the water in the soil balances the amount of salts in the soil; water bowl = container for water in a stable or loose-box; Water meadow = grassy field near river, which is subject flooding. (2) To give water to (a plant) plants may need watering two times a day in hot dry weather.

**Watermill.** Mill which is driven by the power of a stream of water which turns large wheel.

**Watershed.** Dividing line between two catchment areas.

**Water-soluble.** Which can dissolve in water some vitamins are water-soluble.

**Waterwheel.** Wheel with containers which catch and hold water as the wheel turns. Waterwheels have two purposes; placed over a moving stream the pressure of the moving current turns the wheel and so drives machinery (as in a watermill); in the second case, the wheel is also placed over a moving stream, but the water collects in the buckets on the wheel, which as it turns, raises the full buckets and tips the water into an irrigation channel.

**Weather.** (1) Daily atmospheric conditions (e.g. sunshine, wind, precipitation) in a certain area, as opposed to climate which is the average weather for the area; weather chart or weather map = map which shows the weather in a certain area at a certain time; weather forecast = description of what the weather will be like for a period in the future, important for the farmer when carrying out certain jobs such as spraying; weather forecasting = scientific study of weather which allows forecasts of the weather to be made (2) To wear down (rock) under the influence of frost or wind or rain, etc.

**Weathering.** Changing the state of soil or rock through the influence of the climate (rainfall, hot sun, frost, etc.) or by chemical pollutants present in the rain or the atmosphere.

**Weed Beet.** Weed affecting sugar beet crops; the weed can harbour rhizomania. It is controlled by limiting bolters and so preventing cross-pollination. The most effective control is by hand-pulling bolters.

**Weed killer.** Substance used to kill weeds; selective weed killer = substance which is meant to kill only certain types of weed.

Although weed killers are widely used in farming and horticulture, they can have serious side-effects. They may blow away from the area where they are being sprayed: excess weed killer enters the soil and is leached away by rain into watercourses, killing water plants.

**Well.** Hole dug in the ground to the level of the water table, from which water can be extracted either by a pump or by a bucket; artesian well = well bored into a confine aquifer.

**West African Dwart.** Breed of goat which is about half the height of other African breeds; it is mainly reared for meat production, and is extremely resistant to trypanosomiasis.

**Wetlands.** Area of land which is often covered by water or which is very marshy there are two important wetland sites in the area.

**Wet Rice.** Cultivation of rice in water for most of the growing period; also called "paddy rice"

**Wheat.** Triticum sp., the most important of the cereals, grown in the temperate regions; hard wheat = wheat with a high protein content, used to make flour for bread; soft wheat = wheat with a lower protein content, used to make flour for cakes; spring what = varieties of wheat which are sown in spring and harvested towards the end of the summer; winter wheat = varieties of wheat sown in the autumn or early winter months and harvested the following summer (these are harder than the spring wheat); wheat belt = the wheat-growing regions of the North American prairies; wheat bulb fly = fly whose larvae feed on the roots of wheat; the central shoot turns yellow and dies.

**Wheatfeed.** See *Wheat Offals*.

**Wheatgerm.** Central part of the wheat seed, which contains valuable nutrients.

**Wheatmeal.** Brown flour with a large amount of bran, but not as much as whole meal.

**Wheelwright.** Person who makes wooden wheels for farm carts.

**Whip.** Short stick with a lash attached, used to control horses; also called a "crop"; whip and tongue cutting = form of graft, where the stock and scion are cut diagonally to form large open surfaces with a small notch in each the surfaces are bound together tightly with twine.

**Whipworm.** Variety of worm affecting pigs, especially weaners.

**White Clover.** Type of perennial clover (*Trifolium repens*). There are several varieties including the large-leaved variety suitable for silage or hay and the small-leaved variety which is quick to establish and keeps out weeds and other grasses.

**Wiltshire Cure.** Special method of mild curing and smoking sides of bacon mover wood fires.

**Windbreak.** Hedge or line of trees, panted to give protection from the wind to land with growing crops.

**Wind Chill Factor.** Way of calculating the risk of exposure in cold weather by adding the speed of the wind to the number of degrees of temperature below zero.

**Windmill.** Building with sails which are turned by the wind, so driving a machine; used originally to mill grain and pump water.

Windmills were originally built to grind corn or to pump water from marshes. Large modern windmills are used to harness the wind to produce electricity.

**Windrower.** Machine which lifts a crop (such as potatoes) and leaves it in a swath on the surface of the soil.

**Winter.** (1) The cold season of the year, when the days are short, when plants do not flower or produce new shoots, and when some animals, hibernate; winter feeding = system of feeding livestock during the winter months, giving them feeds of hay, silage and concentrates; winter greens = hardy and concentrates; winter greens = hardy Brassicas which are grown for used during the winter; winter solstice = 21st December, the shortes today in the Northern Hemisphere, when the sun is furthest north of the equator; winter wash = egg-killing spray applied to fruit trees in the dormant winter period; tar oil is the commonest winter spray; winter wheat = varieties of wheat that are sown in the autumn or early winter and harvested the following summer 92) to spend the winter in a place.

**WOAD.** Welsh Office Agriculture Department.

**Wood.** (a) Hard tissue which forms the main body of a shrub or tree; new wood = growth made during the current year; old wood = growths made during previous years (b) building material that comes form trees; weed alcohol = methanol, alcohol manufactured from waste wood, which can be used as fuel; wood ash = ash from burnt wood, a source of potash.

**Woody.** Plant tissue which is like wood or which is becoming wood.

**Wool.** Soft curly hair, the coat of the domesticated sheep; also produced by goats and rabbits; wool ball = mass of wool found in the first or fourth stomaches of lambs; small amounts of wool swallowed by the lamb collect to form a ball which can increase in size until it blocks the stomach and causes death; wool fat = lanolin, fat which covers the fibres of sheep's wool.

**British Wool Marketing Board (BWMB).** Government body responsible for the buying, grading and marketing of home-produced wool.

The British Wool Marketing Board is responsible for the specifications by which wool is graded. These are based on the length of staple, luster, softness, springiness, strength colour and fineness.

**Workability.** The ability of soil to be cultivated; it is an interaction between climatic conditions and the physical condition of the soil.

**World Food Programme.** Part of the Food and agriculture Organisation of the United Nations; the programme is intended to give international aid in the form of food from countries with food surpluses.

**Wormer.** Substance used to worm cattle.

# X

**X Chromosome.** Sex chromosome.

**Xenobiotics.** Chemical compounds that are foreign to an organism (such as some food additives).

**Xeromorphic.** Plant which can prevent water loss from its stems during hot weather.

**Zerosere.** Succession of communities growing in dry conditions.

**Xylem.** The solid tissue in plants which takes water from the roots to the rest of the plant; the xylem is formed of tubes made from dead cells (as opposed to the phloem, which are formed of living cells), thickened with lignum; they occur both in stems and roots.

# Y

**Yak.** Domesticated animal found in Tibet; a draught animal which also yields milk. The animals are black or brown in colour, with long thick hair and large black curved horns; they can be crossbred with domestic cattle.

**Yam.** (i) Term applied to several tropical root crops; and in the southern USA also applied to sweet potatoes; (ii) in particular, the thick tubers of a tropical plant (*Diosorea sp*) which is mainly grown as a subsistence crop.

**Yard.** Open space in a farm, surrounded on three sides by barns, stables and farm buildings.

**Yard and Parlour.** System of housing dairy cattle in yards and bringing them through a parlour for milking.

**Yarrow.** Common weed (*Archillea millefolium*) which can cause taints in milk; also called "milfoil"

**Y Chromosome.** Male chromosome. The Y chromosome has male characteristics and does not form part of the female genetic structure. A normal male has an XY pair of chromosomes.

**Yeariling.** Animal aged between one and two years.

**Yeast.** Fungus which is used in the fermentation of alcohol and in making bread and is a valuable source of vitamin B.

**Yellow Rust.** *Puccinia strififormis* a fungal disease of cereals, mainly affecting wheat and barley; yellow pustules form on leaves, stems and ears; also called "stripe rust"; yellow dwarf virus = fungal disease affecting barley, and also wheat and grass; the leaves turn red and yellow and yields are reduced; the disease is carried by wingless aphids; the common name for its (BYDV".

**Yellow Rattle.** Annual weed (*Rhinanthus minor*) found in grasslands.

**Yellows.** (a) general term for any plant diseases in which the leaves become yellow (b) jaundice in animals.

Yellow diseases are often caused by viruses, but may also be caused by bacteria and fungi. Yellowing is a common symptom when there is a deficiency of elements which are important to chlorophyll production.

**Yeoman Farming.** System of farming by a class of small freeholders which resulted from the enclosure movement in the Middle ages.

**YFC.** Young Farmers' Club

**Yield.** Quantity of a product produced from a plant or animal or from an area of land the normal yield is two tonnes per hectare; the green revolution increased rice yields in parts of Asia.

**Yoke.** Wooden crosspiece fastened over the necks of two oxen.

**Yolk.** Yellow central part of an egg.

**Yolk Sac.** Membrane which encloses the yolk in embryo fish, reptiles and birds.

**Yorkshire Fog.** Weed grass (Holcus lanatus) able to grow under poor conditions; it is unpalatable and of little value.

**Young Farmers' Club.** Social organisation for young farmers.

# Z

**Zero Grazing.** Practice of harvesting forage crops and taking the green materials to feed housed livestock.

**Zero Tillage.** Technique using herbicides instead of tilling the soil before sowing an arable crop by direct drilling.

**Zigzag Harrow.** Light harrow used for final seedbed work, and also for covering sown seeds; the frames are zigzag in shape, with short tines bolted to them.

**Zinc.** While metallic trace element, essential to biological life.

Zinc deficiency in plants prevents the expansion of leaves and internodes; in animals zinc forms part of certain enzyme systems and is present in crystallized insulin.

**Zoo.** Meaning animals.

**Zoonoses.** Diseases transmitted between farm animals and humans; for example, tuberculosis and disorders caused